DATE DUE

DEC 1 3 1985	
JAN 1 5 1986	
SEP 1 2 1988	

BRODART, INC.

Cat. No. 23-221

TRENDS IN LANGUAGE TEACHING

TRENDS IN LANGUAGE TEACHING

Edited by

ALBERT VALDMAN
Indiana University

McGraw-Hill Book Company

NEW YORK / ST. LOUIS / SAN FRANCISCO
TORONTO / LONDON / SYDNEY

TRENDS IN LANGUAGE TEACHING

FOREWORD

The articles in this book report the search for progress in foreign language education during the exciting years since the passage of the National Defense Education Act in 1958. The list of authors is impressive, their caliber reflecting a growing insistence that the best of university scholarship in all the contributing disciplines be concerned with practical teaching problems at all levels of instruction from kindergarten on. It is fitting that the views of the authors should differ, sometimes violently. For as I have already hinted, the keynote here is *search*, not exposition of alleged panaceas, and to search is to exploit differing assumptions, to ask new questions.

The directions the search has taken are complex. They are complex because language teachers and scholars have accepted the challenge of new goals. In the United States, learning to feel at home in a foreign culture by learning to understand and speak its language has only recently been accepted as a serious goal of foreign language instruction, in addition to the traditional goal of a useful reading knowledge. In a country where powerful motivation to learn languages is hard to maintain, the full implications of accepting these newer objectives are still not widely understood. If the words understanding and speaking a foreign language have any important meaning at all, they must mean participating more than casually in live interactions with representatives of the foreign culture, and in a manner which is neither offensive nor unduly conspicuous. To talk more than casually demands a more than casual acquaintance with the foreign culture and its literature. To talk meaningfully yet neither offensively nor unduly conspicuously, one must somehow have learned to produce acceptably formed and spoken strings of socially appropriate utterances, most of which cannot possibly have been said in just that way before. The intricate modulations of the voice and the interwoven body movements that carry important but different meanings in different cultures must not so violate the expectations of the native speaker that the meaning of the verbal message is unintentionally confused or contradicted. To understand more than casually means to understand the rapid speech that is appropriate in a variety of contexts as the native speaker produces utterances in the manner to which he is accustomed. This book presents the strengths and weaknesses of current theory and practice in foreign language teaching and learning, while stressing the most recent thinking of linguists, psychologists, and teachers of language as they continue to explore how such complex behavior is best acquired in school and college.

The complex directions the search has taken can be frustrating to many language teachers, who are obligated to students in classes that meet with inexorable regularity, regardless of the state of search or research. For simple historical reasons few teachers could have been well trained for the tasks they are now called upon to perform, and even now language teachers cannot be asked to become linguists and psychologists, anthropologists and sociologists. They are nevertheless the catalytic agents in the continuing development of a viable technology of language education, the indispensable link between theory and practice in fostering learning. To play this role effectively on the emerging American educational scene, they must somehow cease to regard "methods" as matters of "belief," while learning to understand and to question the assumptions underlying suggested approaches. Only through such understanding and such questioning can they come to recognize inconsistencies. As they then observe their students' problems in coping with language learning tasks as posed by themselves, their teaching materials, and their presentation devices, they will have a sounder basis for interpreting student difficulties and thus for asking new questions of themselves and others about both the validity of the learning tasks and the way the student is supposed to perform them. This questioning, as students are observed going through the learning process, is a rich potential source of new theory, of new research, and ultimately of even more effective teaching practices. Such questioning is a vital component of the search I have been speaking of. This book invites both practicing foreign language teachers and teachers in training to participate in the excitement of the chase. English teachers, too, should read these articles with care, for there are many implications here for their increasing concern with English as a foreign language and with the school problems of native speakers of nonstandard varieties of English. Administrators, scholars, and teachers in other fields, as well as educated laymen seeking information about current thinking in language matters, will also be able to find much of interest, for most of the articles hold technical language to a necessary minimum. And no one can finish this book without a better understanding of foreign language learning problems and a deeper appreciation of the dedication of the teachers and scholars who help to solve them.

ALFRED S. HAYES
Center for Applied Linguistics

PREFACE

New and promising avenues of inquiry are being opened in the extremely complex phenomenon of human language by the growing interest of anthropologists, psychologists, and sociologists. Since more sophisticated models explaining the process of language learning are being put forward by psychologists, linguists can now return to "cultivating their gardens," to describing with greater accuracy all aspects of linguistic behavior.

Yet responsibility for imparting linguistic competence and inducing linguistic performance still lies with the classroom teacher, whose irreplaceable attribute is precisely his ability to impart knowledge, to induce skills, and to motivate learners of various age groups and socioeconomical levels. To be most effective, the foreign language teacher must, of course, have flawless and fluent command of the target language, familiarity with the culture and institutions of the target language community, and detailed knowledge of the structure of the target language and the relation of that structure to other aspects of behavior. If he is equipped with suitable materials, including prognostic and proficiency tests, and trained to utilize the vast array of electro-mechanical devices available to him, the language teacher can increase his effectiveness. He can focus on the elaboration of a teaching context that will make it possible for him to still offer individualized instruction to the growing and more heterogeneous student masses of today and tomorrow.

Unfortunately, there is a widening gap between current research and incipient trends, on the one hand, and classroom practice, on the other. Effective methods based on the latest research are seldom in evidence even in the foreign language courses of the large universities where the majority of prospective secondary school and college foreign language teachers are trained. And few supervisors of instruction or teachers of methods courses have been trained as serious researchers in any field pertinent to language instruction or as efficient consumers of relevant research. Hence, faced with the exigencies and pressures of the classroom, the foreign language teacher tends to teach as he was taught. At best, he employs New Key methods and materials whose theoretical bases are seriously questioned by linguists and psychologists; at worst, he perpetuates an uninspired and caricatural brand of the grammar-translation approach, as inappropriate to the desiderata of contemporary society as it is contrary to current educational philosophy.

It was for the purpose of instituting mechanisms through which new ideas and techniques could be disseminated rapidly to the foreign language classroom that the Seminar for College Teachers of French, German, and Spanish was organized at Indiana University under the auspices of the Ford Foundation-supported Indiana Language Program and in conjunction with the 1964 Summer Linguistic Institute of the Linguistic Society of America. The seminar, directed by Prof. Archibald T. MacAllister of Princeton University and myself, was attended by thirty-two college instructors entrusted with the training of prospective teachers or the supervision of elementary and intermediate language instruction at their home institutions. The seminar curriculum, like most NDEA summer institutes for primary and secondary school foreign language teachers, comprised formal courses in methods and applied linguistics. Its striking innovations were courses in the psychology of language learning and in the teaching of a foreign literature. In addition, a series of public lectures was offered. Entitled "Current Trends in Foreign Language Teaching," these lectures featured topics not covered specifically by the courses of the seminar: "Teaching Pronunciation," by Pierre Léon; "Teaching Foreign Cultures," by Howard L. Nostrand; "Foreign Language Testing," by Paul Pimsleur; "The Implications of

Bilingualism for Language Teaching and Language Learning," by Joshua A. Fishman; and "The Application of Programmed Instruction to Foreign Language Learning," by myself. As its title indicates, the idea of the present volume was born during the seminar, and it is one of the numerous works, many of an interdisciplinary nature, to have been inspired by the 1965 Linguistic Institute.

In September, 1964, I had the privilege of attending the International Conference on Modern Foreign Language Teaching sponsored by the Pädagogische Arbeitsstelle und Sekretariat, Berlin Pädagogisches Zentrum, and I was able to secure from the conference's director, Prof. Kurt Spangenberg, the kind permission to include in this book "state of the art" presentations given in plenary session by John B. Carroll, S. Pit Corder, and me; H. H. Stern, who served as the conference's rapporteur and who had authored a 1962 UNESCO report on foreign languages in primary education, agreed to contribute a paper summarizing recent developments and current problems in that field. To ensure adequate representation of all areas and trends which bear directly on the way languages will be taught in the immediate future, original and hitherto unpublished papers were solicited. Bela Banathy, Edith Crowell Trager, Carl D. Waddle, and Sol Saporta (linguistics), Roger Buiten and Harlan Lane (programmed instruction), Joseph C. Hutchinson (language laboratory technology), Moshe Anisfeld, who taught the seminar course in the psychology of language learning, and Miguel Enguídanos, whose presentation of the teaching of literature received the warmest praise of critical colleagues, agreed to represent their respective disciplines in these pages.

I should like to acknowledge a debt of gratitude to Melvin Fox of the Ford Foundation, Samuel E. Braden, vice-president and dean of Undergraduate Development, Indiana University, George E. Smith, director of the Indiana Language Program, and Thomas A. Sebeok, director of the 1965 Linguistic Institute, whose foresight and timely support made the Seminar for College Teachers, and hence this volume, possible. The assistance of Anita H. Reynolds and Diana R. Shields in preparing the manuscript for press is gratefully recorded.

ALBERT VALDMAN

CONTENTS

INTRODUCTION

The last two decades have seen profound changes in the foreign language teaching environment. Yet, despite the installation of more than 8,000 language laboratories in the United States alone and the development throughout the world of new materials and the use of a wide variety of teaching aids, it might perhaps be premature to speak of a "revolution" in foreign language instruction. Innovating foreign language teaching techniques and materials employed currently in the United States—and referred to now as the "New Key" —are characterized by (1) emphasis on audiolingual skills, i.e., comprehension and speaking ability; (2) the assimilation of conversational-style target language texts through mimicry and memorization; (3) the presentation of authentic target language samples by the use of live native speakers in class or recordings in the language laboratory; (4) the learning of pronunciation and grammar through pattern drills; and (5) a claimed application of structural (or scientific) linguistics to language teaching problems.

In view of the last-named claim and the fact that it sprang directly from the linguist-dominated Intensive Language Program of the early 1940s, an evaluation of the New Key might more usefully proceed from a critical examination of the fundamental principles held by linguists qua language teachers from the comfortable vantage point of two decades of hindsight.

THE PRIMACY OF SOUND

Linguists associated with the Intensive Language Program were called upon to implement courses designed to train the learner to communicate orally. Common sense, therefore, dictated an exclusive concern with spoken speech patterns. Many of the linguists turned language teachers had extensive experience in the description of languages used by pre-literate communities and were led to postulate the primacy of speech as a language universal. There are indeed numerous instances in which it is useful to consider speech and writing two parallel but distinct codes. When one asks the average educated layman to give the rules for the formation of the regular plural of English nouns, i.e., to relate *cat* and *cats, dog* and *dogs, horse* and *horses,* the answer is invariably a confident: "One adds *-s* or *-es.*" But this type of formulation is not particularly useful to a foreigner who is interested primarily in learning to speak accurately. He would find the following statement more relevant: to form the regular plural of English nouns one adds /ɨz/ if the noun ends with the consonants /s z č ǰ š ž/, for example, *rose/roses, church/churches;* one adds /s/ if the noun ends with a voiceless consonant, with the exclusion of those listed previously, for example, *cat/cats, lip/lips;* and, finally, one adds /z/ elsewhere (voiced consonants except those listed previously, vowels, and semivowels), for example, *dog/dogs, bird/birds, bee/bees, radio/radios.* Writing often does not have machinery to represent many of the phonic features that keep words and phrases apart: in English, for instance, the differences in level of stress that distinguish the *white house* from the *White House.*

But unquestionably in language communities with long-established traditions of literacy the written word often determines the spoken language. For an educated Latin American *sita* ("located") and *cita* ("date") are more than alternative representations of /sita/. While the spelling *sita* will evoke only ['sita], *cita* calls forth in addition the latent response ['Ɵita]. French speakers react to the circumflex accent by producing a vowel which is always longer and sometimes of a different timbre than an unmarked vowel; thus *tache* is always [taš], but *tâche* may also be [ta:š] or [tɑ:š]. Were it not for the influence of the orthography, the contrast [a] versus [a:] or [ɑ:] would probably be lost, as would contrasts like [ø:] versus [œ] (*jeûne/jeune*) and [ɛ:] versus [ɛ] (*bête/bette*), which are maintained in the same way. Most of the structural linguists who have dealt with the question have alleged that French spelling provides an inconsistent representation for the sounds of that language, particularly because it is cluttered with "silent" final consonant letters, and they point to a dozen presumed variant spellings of /ɛ/ as -*ait*, -*ais*, -*aient*, -*et*, etc., or the homophones *sans* ("without"), *cent* ("one hundred"), *il sent* ("he feels"), *sang* ("blood") /sã/. As even first-year students of French know, final consonant letters represent potential liaison consonants realized in phrases or compounds: *sans* contains a /z/ in *sans issue*, *cent* a /t/ in *cent ans* or *centenaire*, and *sang* a /k/ in *qu'un sang impur abreuve nos sillons* or a /g/ in *sanguinaire*. In sum, the spoken language and the writing system do not correspond directly, and their complex relationships will receive the careful scrutiny they deserve only after linguists and language teachers abandon the notion that one is a direct representation of the other.

A corollary of the primacy of speech is the strict separation between audiolingual skills and reading and writing. Many New Key methods require an extensive time gap between initial audiolingual presentation and the introduction of the conventional spelling system, but as John B. Carroll points out in Chapter 6, current learning theories suggest that better learning and retention are achieved by adding the visual sensory modality to support the auditory signal.

INTENSIVENESS

Structural linguists first viewed language as a complex aggregate of sensory and motor habits, and they concluded that nothing short of relentless practice could lead to audiolingual fluency. As Leonard Bloomfield, the leading theoretician of wartime applied linguistics put it: "Language learning is over-learning. Anything else is of no use." On the positive side, this emphasis on the brute mechanical aspect of language impressed upon the educated public the need for intensive contact and active participation in the acquisition of audiolingual skills. But it also firmly established a simplistic model for language learning, appropriately labeled the "sunburn model" by Harlan Lane: the student was to be exposed to target language patterns until he soaked them up. Reliance on a simple model that could be shown to correspond to commonsense notions delayed the consideration by language teachers of the considerable body of research findings in verbal learning described by Carroll and the introduction of programmed instruction techniques. Coupled with a disinterest in the semantic aspect of language, this emphasis on drill resulted in unthinking and mechanical manipulation of linguistic features, which hardly constitutes a use of language and the validity of which as a learning device has never been convincingly demonstrated.

AUTHENTICITY OF MODEL

Linguists carried over into the classroom the anthropologist's concept of the *informant,* the native speaker as sole authority and ultimate source of the language. Only a native speaker could manifest the structure of the language at all levels, and his constant presence in the classroom—live or recorded—was required. This reliance on authentic target language speech led to a healthy reaction against normative statements and adhesion to very formal styles of speech. Contrary to the allegations of many traditionalists, this reaction was not accompanied by a glorification of "incorrect" speech, and where dialect and style variations were extensive —as in the teaching of French, German, and Spanish, for instance— linguists chose the best-educated and socially prestigious speakers available and based materials on standard dialects. But emphasis on authenticity, particularly at the level of pronunciation, further distracted attention from the most important activity of the foreign language classroom, language learning. Sight was lost of the fact that the well-trained and competent traditional foreign language teacher, while he might not imitate perfectly subphonemic and suprasegmental features of the target language, was equipped with a sound knowledge and control of its grammar and, most important, possessed insight on how that knowledge and control might best be imparted to the learner.

INDUCTIVE GRAMMAR

For the structural linguist grammar consisted essentially of the enumeration of the constituents and types of sentences and the listing of forms. Generally grammar was presented inductively through pattern drills. Inductive presentation was followed by sometimes quite technical statements, but it was asserted that only after mastery of a pattern had been acquired would formal explanation be useful. The use of grammatical rules as "predictors" of linguistic behavior was expressly banned: "they [rules] are the description of the student's own performance. *Rules ought to be summaries of behavior.* They function only secondarily as 'predictors.' "

The Linguistic Method of organization of subject matter and instruction followed literally the order of descriptive fieldwork: first, phonemic contrasts; then, assimilation of forms through pattern drills; and last, presentation of syntactic arrangements. Since the phonological and morphophonemic structures of a language can be analyzed in terms of finite sets or lists readily discoverable by the analyst, Linguistic Method techniques led to satisfactory assimilation and control at these two levels. Most pattern drills are of the substitution or correlation variety: the student is provided with a *basic sentence* and *cues* which are to be substituted in specified slots of the basic sentence; in correlation drills the substitution of an item in one slot is accompanied by an obligatory change in another. In effect, these drills do not differ substantially from traditional conjugation and declension except that substitution and variation take place within complete utterances.

The most serious shortcoming of New Key materials is that they constitute a closed system. The student learns a finite stock of basic sentences which he can parrot if the proper circumstances present themselves; at best he can only be expected to vary the sentences by inserting lexical items in the slots of the pattern drills he has manipulated. Recent experiments in language acquisition by children suggest that human beings do not learn their first language by *mim-mem* (mimicry-memorization) but that they construct from their linguistic environment a model which can be projected beyond what has been heard in the past to form and recognize new combinations. It has shown, for instance, that American preschool children and first graders can extend rules for noun plural formation to nonsense words with a high degree of accuracy; on the basis of *dog/dogs, cat/cats, horse/horses* they analogize *wug/wugs, fap/faps, gutch/gutches*. Similarly, on the basis of the productive *-er* verbs French children incorrectly analogize **vous disez* instead of *vous dites,* and on the basis of *ils boivent* they construct **nous boivons*. It is reasonable to posit that adult second language learning consists of more than the storing up of rehearsed utterances and involves the construction of a grammatical model on the basis of which utterances which have never been heard before are "created." The construction of the model might be catalyzed by the artful presentation of material, for instance, contrastive pairs which point up generative processes, or more simply by providing *deductive* rules.

The ultimate objective of a foreign language course is to lead the student to generate all and only grammatically correct and stylistically congruent sentences in the foreign language. This ability presupposes the previous assimilation of a finite set of grammatical patterns and a knowledge of the substitution possibilities within specific structural slots, but some provision must be made for the extension of patterns beyond the limits of drilled substitution possibilities. This suggests a very careful ordering of the subject matter to give priority to patterns characterized by greatest generality. In French, verb forms manifesting the bare stem of one-stem verbs (*donne, donnes, donnent*) would obviously be presented before forms showing endings (*donnez, donnons*) and two-stem verbs (*finis/finissent; vend/vendent*); for the latter, priority would be given to the /is/ verbs since these constitute a marginally productive class whereas the others make up a closed and residual list. Syntactic rules with high predictive potency will have to be discovered and presented to the learner if, for instance in the teaching of English, he is to produce, say, *he tells me to do it* and *he asks me to do it* but not **he says me to do it.*

LINGUISTIC INTERFERENCE

If I have dealt at such length with the basic tenets of the Linguistic Method, it is only to underscore the fact that curiously enough they do not derive from any profound or adequate view of language but rather from a very primitive behavioristic concept of learning. As Sol Saporta observes in Chapter 5, it is paradoxical "that linguists whose central concern is precisely the formulation of accurate grammatical statements are identified with a method in which the value of such statements is limited to 'summaries of behavior.' "

Even after twenty years of direct contact between structural linguistics and language teaching the possibilities of applied linguistics proper remain relatively unexplored. One promising area lies in contrastive analysis but with an emphasis on positive rather than negative transfer from native to target language. Heretofore contrastive analysis has been widely practiced only at the phonological level; problems of grammatical interference are usually identified on the basis of actual classroom experience. Without challenging the validity of such observations, one can only welcome the extension of the prediction of possible positive and negative transfer at all levels of language structure. But contrastive analysis at the grammatical level presents difficulties. In what terms are similarities and differences between two grammatical systems to be stated: grammatical categories, sentence types, transformations that operate on kernel sentences?

TOWARD A NEW APPLIED LINGUISTICS

The classroom teacher and persons involved in the preparation of materials are seriously handicapped by the dearth of pedagogically oriented grammars. For instance, to my knowledge there is no syntactic classification of French verbs that will account for the types of sentences that even beginning and intermediate learners are expected to produce. A pedagogical grammar is more than the simplified version of a scientific description of a language: while a scientific grammar will adhere consistently to a single model of description and will strive for the greatest simplicity and elegance compatible with noncontradictory and rigorous presentation, a pedagogical grammar will use whatever grammatical theory proves most useful for a specific aspect of the structure of the language. Thus, the transformational item-and-process style would be used to relate the masculine and feminine forms of French adjectives occurring following the head noun: masculine = feminine-final pronounced consonant, e.g., /grãd/ → /grã/; /griz/ → /gri/. But the item-and-arrangement model is more suitable to account for the small set of adjectives preceding head nouns. For *grande/grand* the variant forms /grãdə/, /grãd/, /grãt/, /grã/, /grãdz/, /grãz/ would be listed with a statement of the environment in which they occur rather than to provide for rules adding mute -*e* and the plural suffix -*s,* on the one hand, and deleting consonants, on the other.

With the impact of programmed instruction, foreign language teachers are called upon to state with greater precision the terminal behavior which can be guaranteed at the end of a course of study. Needless to say, the state of our knowledge of language structure and the processes of language acquisition makes it difficult to try even to define the steps in foreign language learning. But quite clearly we shall need to depart from the traditional definition of linguistic skills in terms of the number of words (or, more recently, of structures) controlled by the learner.

In Chapter 8, Joshua Fishman tells us that the foreign language teacher in defining desired terminal behavior must ask himself the question: "*About* what topics and *to* what range of social types do I want my pupils to be able to communicate?" And Bela Banathy, Edith Crowell Trager, and Carl D. Waddle point out in Chapter 3 that in addition to selecting linguistic features to be learned, the blueprint for a foreign language course must specify the *type*, as well as the *degree*, of control required. On the whole, New Key as well as direct method language instruction emphasizes active oral control of a limited body of material. But in the use of language in natural communication situations (assuming that this is at least one of the sets of terminal behavior desired) one must be able to adopt the role of "addressee" before one can function as an "addressor."

The first consequence of this observation is that materials developed must establish two inventories, one over which the student must acquire active control and a much more extensive one whose elements he need only recognize and identify.

Second, the clear delineation of active and passive inventories simplifies the establishment of pedagogical norms. One could insist that the student identify slipshod target language utterances, but one would expect him to speak only in a style accepted as prestigious and overcareful by educated native speakers. In French, for example, the student would be trained to realize *il ne veut pas* as /ilnəvø pa/ but in addition, to identify /invø pɑ/ or ivø pɑ/ as variants of that utterance. As a matter of fact, unless the learner has mastered phonological, kinesic, and paralinguistic features perfectly, the use of normal-style and allegro-tempo forms would sound incongruous, if not offensive, to the native ear.

Third, special consideration must be given to listening comprehension. Simon Belasco (Simon Belasco et al., "The Continuum: Listening and Speaking," *Reports of the Working Committees, 1963 Northeast Conference on the Teaching of Foreign Languages,* pp. 3–21) advocates intensive audioidentification practice either preceding differentiation training or supplementary to it in the form of conversations "overheard" by the student and uttered in normal style by native speakers. Alfred Hayes ("New Directions in Foreign Language Teaching," *Modern Language Journal,* 1965, **49**, 281–293) seems to opt for listening practice that follows oral manipulation and analysis:

> Repeated listening to recorded bits of real human interaction . . . should on different occasions permit different relevant parts of the whole (as previously manipulated) to come to the listener's attention according to his momentary perceptual set, and in relation to the strength of the habits he himself has already established. The material he listens to must not extend beyond his depth, a depth established by the scope of his previous memory work and manipulative drill. He must be able to listen again and again to recombinations of that material, as often as he wishes.

Finally, the recognition of a distinct listening phase in language learning and the establishment of techniques designed to induce audioidentification delineate an area of language instruction which can be carried on most economically in the language laboratory and controlled most effectively by programmed materials.

DESCRIBING AND TEACHING THE SOCIOCULTURAL CONTEXT OF A FOREIGN LANGUAGE AND LITERATURE

HOWARD LEE NOSTRAND

Howard Lee Nostrand (1910–   ) is professor of Romance languages and literature at the University of Washington, Seattle, after having served for twenty-five years as chairman of the department. A graduate of Amherst College, he earned the M.A. degree at Harvard and the doctorat de l'université *at Paris. He was cultural attaché in Lima, Peru, from 1944 to 1947 and has been decorated by the governments of Peru and of France. He has served as president of the American Association of Teachers of French and as a member of the Modern Language Association Steering Committee for the Foreign-language Program, the U.S. Office of Education Committee on the Newer Educational Media, and the National Education Association's Commission on Teacher Education and Professional Standards. He is currently engaged in thematic and inventory studies of twentieth-century French literature and culture.*

The following paper summarizes the ideas that are developed, with examples and references to supplementary sources and materials, in Understanding Complex Cultures: A Language Teacher's Handbook *(New York: Blaisdell Publishing Company, 1966). The research embodied in the study was supported by a research contract with the U.S. Office of Education, Department of Health, Education, and Welfare, in 1962–1963.*

Enlightened language teaching today shows gratifying progress in all its component parts except one: the teaching of the foreign cultural context. We can teach the spoken language with increasing efficiency. Our long distinguished tradition for the teaching of literature now has the advantage of students who come prepared to read and discuss it in the original. Even in linguistics, we know relatively well what we are trying to do, and we have made relatively good progress in doing it. The weakest aspect of our whole performance is the teaching of the foreign culture and society. If this criticism is well taken, we language teachers should do something about it because we have the best opportunity in all modern education to give students an understanding of a second culture and because such an understanding is critically important today (Nostrand, 1963b).

To learn just a language narrowly conceived, without an understanding of the people's way of life, is not enough for cooperation between peoples in the modern world. Language, moreover, is not self-dependent: it cannot be wholly understood without reference to the culture of which it is a part and the social relations which it mediates. Literature, likewise, cannot be wholly understood without reference to the culture that produced it, because while to some extent literature is universal and to some extent its words and phrases and sounds draw their meaning from the literary structure in which they participate at the moment, there is also a vast extent to which the elements of literature, both the materials and the structure itself, bring something to the work of art from outside. To understand the cultural and social relations of literature is important for understanding literature itself, even if we had no other objective.

Furthermore, the learner's attitude toward the people that use a language influences his motivation, his capacity to learn the language.

We cannot help giving some impression of a people's way of life as we teach its language and literature. It is important that we give an accurate impression, based on defensible generalizations, for the sake of the students' grasp of reality, for the sake of international relations, and for the sake of a true understanding and enjoyment of a foreign language and literature.

At present, one can hardly take satisfaction either in the international understanding we have brought about or in the rationale, methods, and materials we are using. Any language teacher one asks will probably say he brings in the culture. But that can mean a variety of things, and too often it means a superficial, romanticized local color. Not only do we lack agreement on what it should mean to teach about the foreign culture and society, but when natives to a culture are brought together to make teaching materials or tests bearing on their way of life, they disagree on what is true about apparently important aspects of their culture and social structure, and frequently the research data that would resolve the disagreement do not exist. In this field we are behind even the rate of progress in linguistics despite all the differences of opinion that remain to be ironed out.

The problem before us is more one of describing the foreign way of life than of teaching it. If we could solve the problem of describing, we could then make relatively short work of developing pedagogical methods and materials.

I propose that we think through a sequence of fundamental questions. Since the questions form a sequence and we have to approach the second question with some tentative answer to the first, I will give my tentative answer to each question as we go. But let me first state what the questions are going to be.

The first question is as follows: Precisely what purposes do we want to serve by teaching about a foreign way of life? Perhaps I was too early impressed with the method of Aristotle in the *Nicomachean Ethics,* one of the texts that have most influenced my life, but I very much like that method of starting from the basic question of the purposes we are trying to serve. If we can first answer that question, we can then test our subsequent answers to find out whether we are being consistent and intelligently purposeful.

Second, out of the vast mass of material that makes up a socio-cultural system, how do we select what is essential, or at least what is most important, for the purposes we intend to serve?

The third basic question in the sequence, after we have selected the areas of essential content, is how to define the essential features so as to make them enlightening. In the first place, how do we meet the constantly rising standards of evidence for determining what is true about a people's way of life? Then, what is the most enlightened form for presenting the various kinds of data or generalizations that we arrive at?

Fourth, after defining the units, how do we organize them so that the learner can understand them? In other words, how should we synthesize the areas agreed to be essential for understanding a people's way of life?

Finally, after defining our purposes (selecting, defining, and organizing the essential data), how do we teach the essentials?

The reader would probably prefer to start here, with "How do we teach?" But that beginning would inevitably lead to the question of what we are trying to do. Our arguments would lead backward in an infinite regression, which we can avoid if we begin by formulating the purposes, the reasons for teaching about the foreign culture. These purposes are of importance not only to guide discussions but also to serve as the criteria by which we shall have to judge whether we are succeeding in teaching about the foreign people's way of life. It is by appealing to these purposes as criteria that we can measure what progress we are making and what remains to be done.

I think that we can concentrate upon just two basic purposes in teaching about a foreign way of life: cross-cultural communication and understanding.

DEFINING THE TWO EDUCATIONAL PURPOSES

What do I mean by *cross-cultural communication?* We should try to put our definitions of the purposes into "operational terms," terms which permit us to tell whether we are fulfilling the specifications we have set up. So what should the learner be able to do, under our heading of cross-cultural communication?

I think that the learner should be able, first of all, to understand the spoken and written language, excepting specialized terms but including the common expressions whose meaning is peculiar to the culture. He should be able to express himself in the language on nonspecialized subjects. He should be able to elicit the potential friendliness of the foreign community and avoid causing "culture shock," the shock that comes of encountering a distinctly different way of life and set of assumptions. He ought also to be able to represent the good in his own culture and to avoid being irritated by the differences he finds between his and the new culture. All of these things are not easy to do.

The question of defining cross-cultural communication involves a basic issue on which language teachers disagree. Should one try to be a facsimile of a native—to be really bicultural—or should one try more modestly to be a welcome outsider? I first argued that one should choose the ideal of being a welcome outsider and exclude the objective of being in any way a facsimile of the native. A number of persons disagreed with this view. They thought that it was a counsel of defeat, that it contradicted the idealism of striving to master a language and all its paralinguistic periphery. I have changed my formulation to one that is more diplomatic and reflects more accurately what I mean: the learner should strive to be acceptable as an outsider in certain respects but not in all.

He should keep his selfhood undivided and not try to ape another personality. He should thus seek the advantages of stimulating in the host people a generous attitude, such as persons can have when they are on their good behavior with outsiders. He can expect to get by with minor breaches of formalities by reason of being an outsider. He must learn, however, those proprieties of the host country that have to be complied with. Every society has areas of behavior where one has to conform, where the penalties for nonconformity are very severe. Such behavior, moreover, usually cannot be freely discussed in the society. Other areas of behavior, in contrast, are regarded as simply instrumental matters and can be discussed in some if not all social situations. We should teach these distinctions if we are educating for cross-cultural communication.

The other purpose, *cross-cultural understanding,* is much more complicated on the face of it; but since getting along and communicating successfully with the foreign people require also an understanding of them, cross-cultural communication actually comes to involve all that is essential for this purpose. To define this second objective, we must take into account not only a considerable range of aspects of a culture and society but also the techniques for understanding cultures; moreover, I am persuaded, for my part, that we must bring to bear six levels of the problem of understanding about cultures, of which only the sixth and last comprises descriptive knowledge of a given culture.

On the highest of the six echelons, the one of most general applicability, I should place the psychophysical capacity to be patient and kind and reasonable. That capacity is prerequisite to the carrying out of good intentions. It is one of the things that teachers must consider in educating students to understand and to get along with a foreign people. The reader may think that kindergarten teachers should have developed this psychophysical ability once and for all, but, like all civilized qualities, it is developed gradually. A relaxed atmosphere in a language classroom, together with a spirit of intellectual curiosity, can do much to cultivate and strengthen the basic capacity for taking an intelligent, reasonable, patient view under the stress of cross-cultural contact.

Second only in generality is an echelon of life purposes, including the determination to be patient and reasonable in dealing with things that are hard to understand and hard to tolerate. At this level I should give an important place to the intention which I think was well named, by my Jesuit associates in some discussions of American culture, as "intelligent love," that is, love which seeks the well-being of the loved object rather than simply gratification.

At the third echelon we get down to cross-cultural problems. Here the general determination and capacity to be reasonable and patient and kind are applied to the problems that we strike as cultures come into contact and clash. Three such attitudes are of particular importance, and I think that they are part of what we should be teaching, a part at least as important as descriptive knowledge of any one culture. These attitudes I shall call *cultural relativism, perspectivism,* and *imperturbability.*

By cultural relativism I mean not an absolute relativism where "anything goes" but one which takes into account that each culture or society has to be self-consistent in its regulation of conduct. This idea of cultural relativism bears on the question of what to do about the picturesque. We certainly do not want to present people of a foreign land as though they lived every day in holiday costumes, as if bright shawls were their main distinction. But, on the other hand, actual students even at the college level, and particularly at lower age levels, are not easily induced to feel curious about a foreign social structure. We do need to use, for all it is worth, what is picturesque and artistically interesting about the foreign way of life we are studying. We are not wrong to spice our teaching with its interest-attracting power, provided we do not present the Sunday costumes and leave out the rest of the week. We must make sure that we present the facts that are significant because they are predominant, as well as the details that happen to be interesting for a given group of learners. And we should make clear that we, too, are just as picturesque, applying the principle of cultural relativism so that the learner does not think that ours is the natural way while the ways of others are quaint. Provided we overcome that false perspective on ourselves, we can afford to use the picturesque as far as we need, without trusting it too far. But to put the picturesque in its right place would still mean a great change in most of the teaching of foreign cultures that goes on in American schools and colleges.

A second attitude which I propose we should cultivate is the attitude of perspectivism. I am borrowing the term from Wellek and Warren's *Theory of Literature* (1949; 1963), where the concept is advanced as part of an enlightened approach to history. The proposition we can apply to foreign cultures is that when we go to the literature of an earlier age, we should penetrate it just as far as we can, but beyond that take advantage of having a perspective that the people of the past age did not have on themselves. I suggest that when we try to understand a foreign culture, we should penetrate the foreign mentality just as far as we can, but beyond that take advantage of the fact that we do have an outside perspective which the people cannot have on themselves.

A third attitude for approaching cross-cultural realities is one for which I find no satisfactory name. I shall call it *imperturbability,* meaning the capacity to observe new ways of doing things without saying, "I just *can't understand* how those people. . . ." One can hear this in American colonies all over the world, and not only in American colonies. Imperturbability includes the capacity to understand strange things in oneself, as well as in foreign cultures, in an objective, relaxed spirit rather than suffering from culture shock.

Here I should say what I mean by *culture shock.* It is a somewhat psychotic state that people get into when they are in a cultural situation whose cues are misleading because they have learned either responses that are wrong for the cues or no responses at all. For years advisers of foreign students have generalized that a student abroad goes through three cycles. The first is a "honeymoon" stage: he just loves the new country. That stage may last a couple of weeks or only a few days. Then comes a stage of uncomfortableness when the student feels quite disoriented and out of place. During that stage of culture shock, his attitude toward the foreign culture is likely to be hostile, negative, disparaging; and his attitude toward his own culture is likely, correspondingly, to idealize the home situation far beyond reality. Then, if he lives through that stage and remains sane, there comes a stage of adjustment in some way or another to the foreign society. The attitude I am arguing for is one of imperturbability even during the more or less psychotic stage of culture shock.

Let me interrupt theorizing about echelons of cross-cultural understanding to answer the practical question of whether culture shock should be used in the classroom. I suggest that we give little doses of culture shock, though not by dragging in shocking materials for effect. I was testifying not long ago at a school board hearing for a teacher who had been dismissed. I gave testimony on one point: Is it necessary to teach about the foreign culture and, if so, to bring in jarring details that one could avoid if one did (as some school board members, I think, wanted this teacher to do) just teach the language? The teacher had explained, for example, about dating practices and how they differ in Mexico from practices in the United States. This is an area of behavior rightly of interest to high school and college students, and one where there is good reason to teach about the foreign culture, overcoming the notion that our way is the only civilized possible way and warning that we cannot expect our behavior to be acceptable or even safe in all countries. A great deal of grief would have been saved in intercultural contacts, not only where foreign languages are concerned but in the case of American GIs in Britain, if dating practices had been discussed before the travelers came into contact with the foreign culture. I am suggesting, then, that we should give little doses of culture shock in the classroom, but I go on to suggest that we calculate what we are trying to accomplish and ask whether "this trip is necessary." One must not indulge any tendency to take such an attitude as: "Gee whiz, if you students only knew all I know about the world outside your little sheltered haven!" This is a form of status seeking and of ego satisfaction that is not intelligent love of the learner but simply self-gratification.

Now let us recapitulate the first three echelons of considerations that I think important for enlightened understanding across cultures: first of all, the psychophysical capacity to be magnanimous toward strange ways; second, the life purposes that include such magnanimity; and, third, attitudes specifically applying these general good intentions to cross-cultural phenomena.

On a fourth echelon I would put the general ideas about the nature of cultures and societies, for example, the idea that they are highly patterned realities. Such general ideas do need to be included and constantly referred to in our teaching of descriptive information about any one culture.

A fifth echelon, still above the level of descriptive knowledge, belongs to the principles for analyzing and organizing data about cultures and societies. These principles I shall deal with later when we come to the subject of how to describe and organize the data. The point here is that enlightened principles of analysis, definition, and organization are as important as the descriptive data of a specific culture and society.

One part of the problem I shall mention here: the fascinating question of what we should accept as "explanation." Students are always asking you to explain a pattern of language or culture. If I may borrow Susanne Langer's way of putting the question, "What sort of answer *ought* to bring inquiry to an end with satisfaction?" We need to be sophisticated on this subject, even if at the moment we are dealing not with children but with college students, most of whom have learned to keep their questions within the bounds that are customary in our culture.

We certainly should be satisfied with causal explanations, insofar as we can give them. They are the kind of explanation that enables man to predict what will happen and thus to gain some control over his environment. The main problem here is to recognize that when we give a causal explanation of a complex phenomenon—such as why the Spanish use *usted,* a third-person form—our explanation probably does not cover very much of the pattern of causes that converged to produce the present situation. It therefore does not permit us to predict anything. We should try to use causal explanation; yet we should recognize that in most cases we just do not know why. We could not set up a pattern of causes so complete that it would produce the specific etymological change or whatever else actually came about.

One form of explanation that we may rightly use is to say that the case in point is an example of a regularity. "Why did they wash their hands in that peculiar way?" The answer: "They regularly do." There is an "explanation" that is valid, but the trouble is that in most cases we do not know what generalization would be true to fact. I shall claim later that whenever we say some phenomenon is prevalent in a population, we are making essentially a quantitative generalization; and we have to use quantitative techniques, which are the province of social scientists, to establish the generalization that we are making. If we say, "This is the way they do things in that country," we are raising the question of what social groups and in what regions. We need to make quantitative generalizations and to make them very carefully.

Another kind of explanation that I think we should accept is to show that a given style of doing a thing is consistent with a whole pattern of themes and ways of doing things: an explanation by means of putting the detail that we are trying to explain into a factual configuration which is not a set of causal relationships but a pattern which makes sense as a self-consistent whole. There are other kinds of explanation in use which do not seem to me sufficient. Just the fact that one phenomenon covaries, correlates, with another phenomenon, for example, does not go far toward explaining it. I suggest that in dealing with principles for analyzing and organizing, we constantly give attention to the basic question: What should make inquiry come to an end with satisfaction?

The sixth echelon, lastly, is the one at which we try to understand a specific sociocultural system. Let us note that this system is still not a concrete entity but an abstraction. We are abstracting a description of a people's way of life from concrete data. Indeed, if we make generalizations about a whole people, we are a long way up into the successive levels of abstraction, of generality, a long way from the concrete data we are generalizing about. What the student should learn to do with the descriptive knowledge of a culture is different from, but closely related to, what he should learn to do in order to communicate across cultures.

To summarize the operational definition attempted in the study noted at the beginning of this article, the student should be able, first of all, to observe a concrete event in terms of the regularities that make its details significant of the culture. By "regularities," I mean recurrent behavior patterns. The person who has learned to understand a culture would be able, for example, to recognize in a filmed dialogue the nuances and expressive motions which to a native of the culture indicate an attitude or adumbrate a response to be expected. Then, one needs to be able to sense empathically why a given symbolic act in society or in art arouses intense feelings in a bearer of the culture. Further, one must be able to "think" the evolving values, beliefs, and customs that make up the way of life. One must have some categories in which to think these phenomena. And, finally, one needs to be able to keep rectifying one's conception of the whole foreign structure that is being described as new knowledge arises from future research. This implies that, in teaching about any aspect of a culture or a society, it is important that one carefully restrict the generalization one is making so that when other generalizations are added, they need not contradict the first one but will subsume and illuminate it as a special case.

SELECTING THE ESSENTIALS

If the reader is willing to accept my tentative answer to the question of the purposes we are trying to serve, we can proceed to the second in the sequence of basic questions. How do we go about selecting the essentials, for our two educational purposes, out of that vast panorama of a people's way of life with its varied geographical regions, social classes, and all the types and interests of individual persons?

It seems best to use concomitantly two different approaches toward selecting the essentials. One I shall call a *schematic approach*. We schematize the foreign way of life into categories in which, presumptively, there are going to be important aspects of the way the foreign people live, whether it be like ours or different from ours.

For the purpose of this schematic approach I am going to suggest, first of all, that we distinguish between a concept of culture and a concept of society. Now, I have talked with some anthropologists who say that this distinction between culture and society is not worth the powder to blow it up, and they are right in a way. But if we conceive the culture and society as all one, calling the whole a people's culture or some other one thing, then we get into the difficulty I was in when I first went to France as a doctoral candidate. I knew many things about French literary history; I was fluent in French, so that I had the advantage of getting along well with my hosts; I enjoyed discussing ideas; but my understanding of the social structure of France was so weak that I missed a great deal which would have been fascinating, enlightening, and useful to my students after my return home. If I had been prepared to under-stand France not just as a culture, with the society as part, obliquely seen, of the culture; if I could have focused directly at one time on French culture, at another time on French society, I would have been much better prepared to understand the French people. I happened to have teachers who were humanists, largely in Latin and Greek, who thought that the social scientists still had a lot to do before they could be useful to modern understanding, and so I was steered away from the social sciences. That was unfortunate, and I feel that we humanists are still in danger of leading our students to be interested in some aspects of a sociocultural system to the exclusion of others that are also important.

There is good reason, then, for distinguishing between the abstractions of culture and society, even though I admit that if we define society as "the relations among people" (and I prefer to define it that way) instead of as "a population," then culture and society are both abstractions drawn from exactly the same universe of data.

Apart from the practical purpose, I find half a dozen differences between the two foci of attention which may justify making the distinction. One difference you can see in the Hispanic countries. They have essentially the same basic culture, and yet they have separate societies: separate sociopolitical structures and separate systems of relations among people, somewhat different from one another.

If we look below the human level, we find that the primates and the social insects, the ants and the bees, have highly developed societies but only a rudimentary culture. I would have said a year ago no culture at all, but for the primates apparently there is something corresponding to what I am going to define in a moment as a culture.

A third distinction is that a human society, its social relations, can remain stable while the culture changes. In the American Midwest the culture has been changing. Look at the change in taste indicated in the Sears Roebuck catalog over the past thirty years or so. Yet the social structure in the Midwest has been decidedly stable. In contrast, the culture, for example, of the Amish—the beliefs, the objectives of life, and all—can remain very stable while the young people may be moving away from the Amish community, so that the human relations have changed, along with the activities of those left as the community is somewhat depopulated.

A fourth difference appears in the present status of past ways of life. It is perfectly true to say that Greek and Roman cultures have persisted as a live force. The Greek and Latin languages are active as the embodiment of values and beliefs and the expressive forms of literature. Yet one would have to admit that the actual human relations, including the linguistic interchange, among the people in Greek and Roman communities of the ancient world are extinct.

Another difference is illustrated by the status of the Amish in the United States as contrasted with the status of many Negroes. The Amish can be integrated into the society, yet not assimilated into the culture that surrounds them, while the Negroes are assimilated into the culture but not integrated into the society.

I shall cite just one more distinction between culture and society. Some of the goals in life that are shared by a whole population are not accessible to disadvantaged groups through socially approved means, and this is one of the causes of deviant behavior on the part of the under-privileged. A group which shares the cultural objectives, the aspirations, but does not have an equal opportunity for realizing those aspirations, resorts to deviant behavior simply because it cannot use the social means open to others in the population.

We may use the distinction between culture and society immediately to clarify what it means to strive for acceptance as an outsider to a foreign culture: the ideal I propose is to be socially integrated in the host country, just as far as is feasible, but not to be assimilated culturally.

The several contrasts give considerable justification for distinguishing between the concepts of culture and society. After passing them in review, the reader is on his way toward understanding what I mean by the two terms.

I shall borrow, with minor changes, the enumerative definitions of culture and of society proposed by Talcott Parsons, a distinguished sociologist at Harvard. In a study by Parsons, Shils, Neagle, and Pitts (1961, vol. II, pp. 982–984), he differentiates between culture and society by attributing to each a separate set of component parts. Parsons relates them to each other as the top two levels of four progressively more complex levels of human "action" or conduct. To the bottom level he assigns the biological behavior of the human organism. The next level is occupied by the conscious action of the individual personality. The third level, society, is one of human *inter*action, for it comprises interpersonal and intergroup relations. The top level, culture, embraces a still more comprehensive and complex system of human interaction.

Professor Parsons' enumerative definitions of culture and society, as I would adapt them to the present purpose, may be summarized thus:

The value system of a culture is a first component area where one can expect to find important aspects of the people's way of life. I mean values to include both the avowed values, or value concepts, and the purposes implicit in behavior, unconscious as well as conscious.

A second component consists of the unverifiable assumptions made, consciously or unconsciously, about the nature of man and the world, as, for example, whether each individual is a discrete entity or an organic part of some larger whole. The ensemble of such presuppositions together with the basic values is often called the culture's *ground of meaning,* since it determines what ideas will be found meaningful within the culture.

Third is the empirical or verifiable sort of knowledge. Differences in empirical knowledge are a serious problem of mutual understanding between bearers of remotely different cultures. Among Western cultures we strike no difficulties beyond differences of emphasis, except in such cases as Trofim Lysenko's view of genetics, unaccepted west of the Iron Curtain.

A fourth component of a culture is made up of its literature and the oral tradition of art forms, the graphic and plastic arts, music, the dance, and so on (including humor).

The language occupies an interesting place both in a culture and in society. It embodies the culture's ground-of-meaning assumptions in its basic structures, and it also plays an essential part in human relations, which means that it functions again at the level of society.

The schematic approach calls also for an enumerative definition of society, similar to the one just outlined for culture. As the constituent parts of society we may simply take the usual institutions—familial, religious, judicial, educational, intellectual-aesthetic, and recreational. These categories drawn from folk tradition neglect some areas of human relations, such as international attitudes, and they chop up some major social concerns, such as the ecology of the population. The lacks can be made up by additions and by attention to the interrelations and border areas between the "institutions." The categories also overlap (e.g., family and economic, economic and political), a fault which probably will cause them to be replaced in time by radically improved ones. Talcott Parsons (Parsons, Shils, Neagle, and Pitts, 1961, vol. I, pp. 30–79, especially p. 61) proposes, for example, a set of four "functional imperatives" that confront all societies.

The other way of selecting the essentials of the society and culture is an *empirical approach:* it uses the experience of persons in the learner's culture who have had contact with the foreign people to discover precisely what will be easy or hard to understand, congenial or hard to get along with, for learners with a given background. A questionnaire has been worked out, for example, to explore American reactions to the French; and the responses in pretests show that the actual reactions and problem points are markedly different from those imagined by Americans at home.

Just one example will show how such information can be used. Suppose a major conflict point proves to be that Americans are somewhat resentful at not being invited into French homes as French visitors are invited into American homes. I think that if we teach something about what the inviolable privacy of the French family means to the psychology of a French person, the American can then take quite a different view of why he is not promptly accepted into a French family. Once we can pinpoint the things we need to explain, we can apply our sophisticated notion as to what kind of explanation is valid; and we shall be closer to teaching usefully about the foreign way of life.

DEFINING THE ESSENTIALS

The next question in the sequence is how to define the elements identified as essential in the foreign culture or social system. This breaks down into two problems: standards of evidence and the form of definition we should choose. Language teachers who are not engaged in research still need, I think, the ideas I want to present, for we must be sophisticated consumers of others' research in order to select for our students those of the emerging conclusions that seem valid.

As a first principle for defining parts of a sociocultural whole, I suggest that we distinguish between the situational context in which an event happens (*event* in the most general sense) and the schematic context in which we place the event to understand it. By *schematic context* I mean the conception of a sociocultural whole, including the values aspect of the event, the ground-of-meaning aspect of the event, its verifiable-knowledge aspect, and the aspects pertaining to the various social institutions. What we should do about the situational context is simply to observe it and, if possible, record it, for the best of researchers is likely to find, years later, aspects of an event he observed which turn out to be important but which he did not notice at the time. If we can, we should record the event we are going to analyze, either on film or in a notebook, in its situational context. Field anthropologists may abstract card notes from the integral record to arrange them under the headings of a schematic context, but they preserve the original context.

We are always in danger of misapprehending a foreign culture by reason of imposing our categories on it. Even the categories of basic human needs, which seem to us elemental, in some cultures falsify our observation of events as conceived by the culture bearers. This is another reason for recording and keeping in mind the situational context.

Despite the danger involved in classifying data into categories, there are several distinctions to be made which are basic for grasping the situational context. First, we should distinguish between professed and actual norms of conduct. Second, we should try to distinguish between conscious and unconscious behavior. Third, we should observe in the situational context what is usual (recurrent) and what is unusual. It is one of the limitations upon Culture with a capital *C,* as represented by artistic monuments, literary classics, and other achievements, that whatever is outstanding is unusual and atypical to the extent that it is outstanding.

When we go beyond the situational context to devise a schematic context for the events we observe, one more distinction must be made, between the descriptive account and what we add by way of interpretation or explanation. The description will be much more stable than the interpretation, which we can predict will change from one generation of scholars to another, if not sooner.

Since we cannot avoid the bias of our own culture in analyzing a foreign culture, it becomes important to neutralize the bias, and the best device for the purpose appears to be the multicultural team of observer-analysts. This device is almost prohibitively inconvenient and expensive. The only way I can suggest to make multicultural teams practicable is, as far as we can, to select and limit what they will need to observe. If we can shape beforehand our purposes and criteria for selecting essentials, we can employ expensive teams to examine and interpret those points which have been identified as likeliest to be important.

The schematic context must be developed, refined, and yet kept as simple as can be serviceable. I hope it will prove possible to simplify the long list of aspects of culture and of society that I offered in the preceding section.

The defining of what is usual in a people's way of life—the regularities of the sociocultural system—poses two basic problems of theory: the standards of evidence to be demanded and the form in which the generalizations should be stated. To begin, I think it is a point of agreement among humanists as well as social scientists that we should demand the verifiable sort of generalization wherever the nature of the data permits. A verifiable statement about a small part of a foreign population, such as that people of the middle class within given regions, at a given period of time, behave thus and so, is far more valuable than the unverifiable, sweeping generalizations one usually hears. It is necessary therefore to recognize regional and socioeconomic subcultures and also age levels and religious or ethnic groups within a culture. These we need to keep in mind in order not to overgeneralize.

Then, we must recognize that all generalizations as to what is usual are by nature quantitative generalizations. Usual to what extent? Usual in what subculture? If we are to make such generalizations with responsibility to fact, they must be based upon quantitative research, which involves not only a sufficiently large sample of the population for statistical validity but also a representative sample. The famous failure of the pollsters to predict that Harry S Truman would retain the Presidency in the election of 1948 was due to careless sampling. As a matter of fact, a topographically randomized poll taken by a research laboratory at the University of Washington, which could not be published before the election because it might have had political influence, came within 2 percent of the actual vote of the population sampled. Unless the sample is somehow a scale model of the universe we purport to generalize about, size will not assure its accuracy.

Where there is ample evidence for the existence of a pattern, there remains the danger of inferring from it other patterns for which it is not sufficient evidence. We must be cautious, for example, in generalizing from a language pattern to a cultural trait. I once heard a teacher of English in a foreign country say, "In English they have an expression, 'Why! that man must be worth half a million dollars, or must be worth a million dollars!' This shows how materialistic the people are." Apart from the fact that the expression is going out of date, one simply cannot find out whether a people is materialistic and in what sense materialistic by examining dead metaphors. The same caution applies even to instances in which we can learn something from the language about the culture, as we can from the pronouns of power and solidarity *tu* and *vos* (pronouns which express a difference in social status if one person says *tu* downward and the other says *vos* upward and which show solidarity or remoteness if both say *tu* or both say *vos*). One must look further into the society to find out whether any greater social structuring really is implied and maintained by this linguistic device than in English by the device of calling a person "Mister" as against calling him "Bill."

A language may or may not alert one to a trait of national character. We Americans have toward "out" groups a characteristic attitude of wanting to be friends with them. On a store's reader board in Seattle I saw, one weekend, the motto "A stranger is a friend you haven't met." Any culture could provide similar words, but few would have that sentiment. It is not the Spaniard's conception of a stranger, for example. When a Spaniard says to you, after you and he have got acquainted and have warmed up together, *"un amigo más,"* that means a great deal more than it would if every stranger were simply a friend he had not yet met. It means that you are now of the "in" group and not of an "out" group, which is distrusted. The attitudes of peoples toward in and out groups differ, as does also the width of the inner circles of the family, intimate friends, and acquaintances. All of this is important for understanding a people and one's own place among them, and interesting just because human beings are interesting. But such things cannot be inferred from the language.

We need to be cautious, too, in generalizing from literature. Many Russians of today have formed their idea of the American businessman and of Wall Street partly from American novels such as *Babbitt* which reflect a hostile attitude on the part of one subculture in the United States, the writers, toward another subculture, the businessmen (Nostrand, 1963a).

The problem of standards of evidence involves the interesting and important question of the true relationship between the scientific and the humanistic contributions toward understanding a culture. It has been said that the humanistic view and the social science view of a culture are like the two sides of a coin. That analogy makes me uncomfortable, because it implies that we cannot see both sides at once. My idea of combining the two is that we should try, precisely, to see both at once. I suggest that we should scientifically establish little islands of verifiable generalization wherever possible; then we should fill in among those islands as best we can, to build larger syntheses, which can be only partly based on verifiable conclusions. All of us as humanists, including the scientists as humanists acting outside their own sciences, need not only the understanding we can acquire within those little areas of data amenable to verifiable conclusions; we need also a more comprehensive synthesis as the basis for action. This broader understanding, which we could call *wisdom,* involves all the values of the culture's value system, while scientific activity concentrates upon the single value of truth seeking. The sciences, like the humanities, seek a certain understanding, but they have no responsibility to produce a basis for action, while the humanities do have that responsibility. We should look to the social sciences, then, for an understanding of those aspects of a sociocultural whole that permit verifiable description, including all quantitative generalizations. For all else, at all the six echelons I have sketched out, we must look to the humane disciplines.

The form of generalization we should demand is as interesting as the constantly rising standards of evidence. I shall say here just two things about it.

A modal statement is preferable to a point statement. Instead of "The French are all this way," it is a far superior form of generalization to say that on a total range of possible behavior—for example, children's attitudes of submissiveness or recalcitrance toward the father—the French occupy a certain band while other cultures occupy overlapping bands. The behavior of any population in any respect is going to be distributed somewhat, and the modal distribution, that is, the main concentration of cases, is what we should be dealing with. The other requirement for adequate statement that I am singling out for mention is so to delimit each generalization that it can later be subsumed under a larger generalization, instead of seeming to compete with it and contradict it.

Before I go on to the problem of synthesizing a view of a foreign culture, let me bring together several features of the present idea of describing its essentials which seem to me major advances since the first half of the twentieth century, a period when excellent scholars talked about "national traits" in a way that now seems far from sufficiently rigorous. One of these features is the standard of evidence for quantitative generalizations. A second is the standard for the form of statements. A third is the range of the aspects of a sociocultural system that we try to describe, the range in which we search for behavior patterns. The range has extended down into society, from what I am calling *culture,* and it has extended from the conscious down into the out-of-awareness levels of behavior.

A fourth advance that has been made is in the application of generalizations to individuals. Social scientists used to regard a culture as something that a population conformed to. Now, in treating the subject of culture and personality, they are more inclined to look at culture as something that the individuals use for their own diverse purposes, exploiting its patterns quite as much as they conform to them. This point of view brings social science and the humanities much closer together, because it takes the human person to be not a creature determined by the patterns under which he has grown up but rather a somewhat free individual, as humanists have been representing him.

A fifth advance takes us to the topic of synthesizing, of organizing the available generalizations. Instead of talking about separate national traits, an enlightened approach today requires trying to see a context of interrelations influencing each trait and forming a structural whole that has come to be called a *national character*.

ORGANIZING THE ESSENTIALS

From an earlier opinion that we could rely wholly on a thematic description of a culture and society, I have come to the view that we may best include this description as one among half a dozen approaches to be used concomitantly toward the organizing of the essential generalizations.

The first of these approaches is to collect the most promising of the freewheeling generalizations that have been made about a people, to juxtapose these *aperçus,* letting them embarrass one another, and to use the consolidated result as hypotheses to be tested against the evidence. Personal insights are extremely important precisely because they are the antithesis of the methodical approach that characterizes all the other five ways of organizing descriptive generalizations. This collecting of hypotheses is our one chance to use free intuition as a kind of check on the plodding, methodical way of synthesizing.

It proves useful to collect and group hypotheses about a people under the headings of two of the organizing plans that are to follow, one an inventory and the other a thematic plan. Each of these plans surrounds a hypothesis with a set of ideas, and both enhance its suggestiveness.

An inventory arranges the elements of a culture and society in the form of a list. It has the great advantage that it allows us to store and retrieve information; but it has the disadvantage that it ignores real relationships among the parts of a culture and society, for these are not the additive relationships of items in a list but rather the dynamic relationships of interacting parts. The inventory I have found the best is the *Outline of Cultural Materials,* or *OCM,* produced at Yale University under the program of the Human Relations Area Files (Murdock et al.,

1961). It is the best, despite numerous unsatisfactory categories, partly because it permits one to compare the culture one is describing with some 200 cultures that have been analyzed into the Human Relations Area Files, which are available in twenty copies spread over the United States, with one in Paris. A further advantage of the *OCM* is that specialists in different disciplines are gradually elaborating and improving the subdivisions of the categories they work with.

The third form of synthesis, after the hypotheses and inventories, consists of structural-functional models. These overcome the fault of the inventories by describing the interaction of the parts. We can make structural-functional models for a value system. Charles Morris (1956) has done this for American values by drawing a billiard-ball model and spacing the values from each other according to calculated correlations. But only limited parts of a culture can as yet be represented in this way, and meanwhile the physicists are abandoning as an oversimplification the kind of model that social scientists have borrowed from physics for their complex data. Decidedly, we need to continue using inventories as we experiment skeptically with models. The schematic enumeration offered above has the good feature of being an inventory on its way toward becoming a model as structural-functional systems are worked out within it.

The fourth approach is the thematic one. Themes are taken to mean not motifs, which are symbolizing devices, but the ideas or orientations, explicit or implicit in the culture, which the symbols convey. Each theme centers in a value, a purpose, with attendant beliefs, intellectual methods, social norms, and so on. Prof. Morris Opler, the anthropologist at Cornell who has done the most to develop "themal" analysis, finds a tendency of cultural systems, as they evolve, to keep the number of themes down around a dozen or less. His interpretation of this trend is that since each theme contains a value people feel strongly about, the addition of a new theme multiplies conflicts of value, which are painful, so that subconsciously a population tends to simplify its value system.

To analyze a culture thematically, one begins by collecting little theme expressions, which are symbolizing devices, such as images in literature or expressive gestures in conduct. These are organized by putting like with like. From groups of theme expressions one can abstract subthemes, which can be grouped together to form larger themes. The check on this essentially subjective process lies in comparing the findings of different investigators and in comparing the results of the whole thematic analysis and synthesis with those obtained by using inventories and models.

Themes are a main hope of achieving and of conveying an understanding of a foreign people. They are the way of formulating a "life-style" of a people.

The historical approach, the fifth of these approaches, needs no introduction except a reminder that it poses the familiar dilemma of whether to emphasize the past of our present concerns or to emphasize the concerns that were uppermost at each past moment. In reconciling these two emphases, history can utilize the collecting of hypotheses, the inventory, the models, and the thematic synthesis already mentioned. The historical dimension is inescapable even in drawing a synchronic tableau, for at any moment a society and a culture contain stresses and forces in a state of momentum which cannot be described in static terms.

The sixth and last is the contrastive approach. A definitive contrast of one culture with another must await the full description of both; but from the very start we can use a contrastive method, in the empirical way of selecting essentials by finding out how groups in one society react to another. Contrastive analysis can build upon all contrasts of historical developments.

TEACHING THE ESSENTIALS OF A FOREIGN WAY OF LIFE

The basic problem of teaching is to transform the organization of the materials from the structure of the subject matter to the structure of the learner's personality: to make the essentials that we have determined from a descriptive point of view assimilable into the understanding and the conduct of the learner. I am assuming that the stream of thought we have followed here is now being met by another stream of thought about human growth and development and about the process of internalizing patterns of behavior.

One way of trying to make education an influence in the learner's life is to give thought to his motivation. Presumably, the learner will be interested in his age mates in the other culture; but there are some surprises, for he is readily interested in some other things about the other culture. The schematic approach helps us to find things that may presumably be of value; but the empirical approach pays off beautifully as a device for pinpointing precisely the aspects of family life, of the educational system, and so on, which our American college and high school students would really be spontaneously interested in if they should have any contact with the foreign way of life. It is more useful to know this than to know what they *think* will interest them, if they have misguided notions of the reality, as appears to be the case; the most educational experience for them will be based on their reactions to the real thing.

Besides meeting the interests of the group of learners to be taught, one can go further and find the interests of individual students, talking with them separately out of class and then personifying each topic of a course ("Mr. Brown is interested in this, Miss Smith is doing something about that"), so that each becomes the representative to the others of foreign people, of linguistics, and the like.

The student who just has no reason for wanting to learn a foreign language can sometimes be interested first in the foreign way of life. Almost every recalcitrant student has some personal concerns. They may be family problems. Then perhaps he can be interested to read or, if he is not that literate, to spend fifteen minutes with a teacher talking about how family problems of that sort are handled in the foreign culture. Perhaps a minority problem, a sociological problem, is contributing toward making him a less relaxed and serene learner. Then maybe he can be interested in how the foreign people handle that sort of problem. Such "deeper teaching" could be more widespread if we had better materials, both in English and in the foreign languages, in the form of brief readings about aspects of the foreign culture and society.

Another device that can be more fully exploited is cooperation in the teaching of the social sciences, of English, and of foreign languages.

The essential contributions of enlightened attitudes toward intercultural realities and understanding of the nature of cultures and societies should be taught more and more by representatives of sociology, anthropology, and social psychology, as should the methods of analyzing and synthesizing data about a way of life and, indeed, what to expect of one's own psychology when one is in contact with another people, the expectation of some degree of culture shock and what to do about it, and above all, perhaps, a more coherent understanding of our own sociocultural system.

The analysis of literature is being better taught each year in many departments of English; but in the analysis of language, the more enlightened the teaching of foreign languages becomes, the more conflict there has been between such teaching and what most composition courses are still presenting as language analysis.

The unique contribution of language teachers lies of course in developing the concepts descriptive of the foreign culture, by enabling the learner to combine "experience of" and "knowledge about" into an understanding of one way of life alien to his own. If this is one objective of language teaching, and according to my thesis it is an important objective, then the teaching materials will have to be chosen by a more exacting standard than is current. I suggest adding to the best criteria published thus far (Mead, 1962) the considerations which follow:

Criteria for Judging the Sociocultural Aspect of Instructional Materials and Course Plans

1. Are the natural opportunities utilized for presenting generalizations about the culture and social structure of the people? (Comprehensive coverage is appropriate for a sequence of courses rather than for one segment of the sequence.)
2. Do the generalizations that are made deal with significant topics?
    a. Do they treat a logical part of an inventory, a model, or a thematic description?
    b. In an elementary course, are the situations those that the beginner needs most to know?
3. Are the generalizations accurate?
    a. Are romantic sentimentality and glamorizing avoided?
    b. Have the best research conclusions available been used?
    c. Is the momentary tableau presented as a situation in process of change?
4. Are the generalizations well presented?
    a. Are the sources and dates indicated (for the benefit of the teacher, in the case of elementary school materials)?
    b. Are "dated" words avoided, e.g., *today?*
    c. Are generalizations made in such a way that subsequent larger generalizations will subsume rather than contradict them? (Is their scope explicit?)
    d. Are statistics generalized over a significant span of time?
    e. Does the documentation enable the user to update the generalizations made?
5. Are the generalizations supported and made vivid by "experience of" what they seek to describe?
6. Are the generalizations and interacting experience adapted to the grade level of the intended learners?

Let me make a few suggestions about teaching materials for the college level. A main kind of cultural material for college beginners in a foreign language consists of situational dialogues, and we already have good ones in a few textbooks. The innovation I suggest is that the models be available not just in print and on tape but on film. Experimentation with filmed recitations of French poetry has confirmed my conviction that an audiovisual model leads to more intense attention on the part of the learner and to better retention. Our greatest weakness, however, is a failure to combine concrete experience of the foreign way of life, such as dialogues give, with knowledge about what is significant in it. If we give experience of some situation in a foreign culture but leave the learner to draw his own inferences about what is going on, he will draw wrong inferences from his own culture rather than the truer inferences we can give him. I suggest, therefore, that in presenting dialogues we help the learner first to observe the situational context and then to understand the schematic context in which a person who knows the culture would see the illustration. Until students can discuss such things in the language, this should be done in English, very briefly, or by arousing their curiosity to consult a written source. This procedure will pay off because it will make the learner more wary about misunderstanding the culture and more expert in looking for the clues to what is really meant.

Apart from situational dialogues, I suggest using filmed recitations of literary works: small, simple works, but good literature, and recited by a professional. These works can serve three purposes. First, they teach the language, complete with its intonations and its paralinguistic and kinesic aspects. The experimentation with French poems recited by Pierre Viala led not only youngsters but adults to say, "The way he said that haunted me, just as a musical tune goes 'round and round' in your head." Second, they arouse an expectation of enjoying literature in the language. And, third, they give experience of patterns in the culture, to be put with relevant knowledge, such as has been embodied in a booklet of cultural commentary we have written for use with the film.

For the second-year course, I would suggest, first of all, audiolingual presentations, such as interviews of persons representing social types in the foreign culture about their ideals, ambitions, fears, their personal philosophy, their political attitudes, their social role, their attitudes toward their own role and toward other roles in the society, and such general questions as what they consider to be social injustices in modern Western society. Another possibility is a good compendium of useful, interesting information about the society and culture, the values, the social structure, the economic life, and so on. A book such as *Guide France* (Paris: Librairie Hachette, 1964) could be used in conversation courses, for example, and later in an area study course.

I would suggest also for the second-year level small works of literature recited on film by good actors, with the cultural commentary now in the target language. The commentary can be used in guided class discussion, spoken on tape for the students to absorb by hearing it, or presented in writing. When the students are getting the cultural and social commentary in the foreign language, I suggest trying to keep present in it the upper echelons that I described above, so that the students are not just dealing with descriptive knowledge of one foreign culture but are relating it to other cultures and to a general context in which they try to understand the nature of cultures and societies and learn the ways of describing them and forming a usable synthesis of the whole. One way of keeping the upper echelons present is to introduce a third culture, so as to avoid the narrow understanding which results in the polarization "They do that; we do this."

At the third-year level it becomes possible to use the historical approach and to place the history of literature in a framework that embraces the history of ideas and of science, the history of sentiments and tastes, and the history of movements and themes. Literature thus proves to illustrate movements more significant than they would be if they were discoverable only within literary history. For historical courses the thematic organization, among the six that I listed, is particularly promising. The problem, then, is to trace the changing conception of each major theme and its changing importance. The themes of the classic moment in our Western cultures, for example, were submerged for the period of the Romantic explosion and then reemerged into a new and larger synthesis.

Whether or not there should be an area study course is a local question. In any case, I recommend a checklist of the essentials to be taught, as one means of flexibility and resourcefulness.

I suggest, for either a historical or a topical sequence, a plan of organization that historians have developed for survey courses. They began with a "block-and-gap" organization and subsequently refined the plan to that of the "block and bridged gap": the intervening topics are briefly bridged over so that the whole becomes more coherent in the students' mind. After all, we seek understanding as well as communication, and incoherent understanding is a contradiction in terms.

It is time to rest the case I have endeavored to make. In sum, if cross-cultural communication and understanding are given an important place among the aims of education, as I believe should be done in American education today, then those two purposes generate the activities of deliberately selecting, defining, organizing, and teaching certain essentials of every sociocultural system whose language we teach, so that every member of our national society who has the ability may learn to understand, in some depth, the way of life of one of the peoples with whom we share this shrinking planet.

REFERENCES

Mead, Robert G., Jr. In Mary J. Ollman (Ed.), *MLA selective list of materials*. New York: Modern Language Association of America, 1962, p. 145.

Morris, Charles. *Varieties of human value.* Chicago: The University of Chicago Press, 1956.

Murdock, George P., et al. *Outline of cultural materials.* (4th rev. ed.) New Haven, Conn.: Human Relations Area Files, 1961.

Nostrand, Howard L. Toward agreement on cultural essentials. *Journal of General Education,* 1958, **11,** 7–27.

Nostrand, Howard L. Literature in the describing of a literate culture. *French Review,* 1963, **37,** 145–157. (a)

Nostrand, Howard L. A second culture: New imperative for American education. *Curricular change in the foreign languages.* Princeton, N.J.: College Entrance Examination Board, 1963. (b)

Parsons, Talcott, Edward Shils, Kaspar D. Neagle, and Jesse R. Pitts. (Eds.) *Theories of society: Foundations of modern sociological theory.* New York: The Free Press of Glencoe, 1961. 2 vols.

Wellek, René, and Austin Warren. *Theory of literature.* New York: Harcourt, Brace & World, Inc., 1949. 3d ed., 1963. Pp. 42–43.

2

THE INTRODUCTION
OF HISPANIC
LITERATURE TO
AMERICANS

MIGUEL ENGUÍDANOS

Miguel Enguídanos (1924–   ) was born in Spain. He did under-graduate work at the University of Valencia and took his doctorate at the University of Madrid, where he taught from 1947 to 1950. He has taught Spanish and Spanish-American literature and civilization at the University of Puerto Rico, Long Island University, the University of Houston, the University of Texas, and the University of Wisconsin. He is currently professor of Spanish and Portuguese at Indiana University. He is coeditor of Image of Spain *and author of* La poesía de Luis Palés Matos *and of numerous articles in the field of literary criticism and Hispanic literature published in the leading literary reviews and scholarly periodicals.*
The following paper was originally written in Spanish; it has been translated by Joseph Schraibman, Princeton University, a participant in the Indiana University Seminar for College Teachers of French, German, and Spanish.

THE PROBLEM

Rather than offer a series of new ideas on the teaching of Hispanic literature at the beginning levels in college, I should like to present a résumé of my commentaries during the summer of 1964 before a group of colleagues who worked with me in the first Seminar for College Teachers of French, German, and Spanish at Indiana University (MacAllister & Valdman, 1964). I should like to communicate here, above all, the spirit of inquiry and reexamination which we achieved during the meetings of the seminar, once a certain initial reserve had been overcome. This reserve stemmed in almost all of us from the pressure of academic routine and, indeed, from a commonplace belief within our universities that insists upon the untouchable, sacrosanct nature of programs, methods, and texts used in the teaching of Spanish and Hispanic-American literature, thus serving to excuse their imperfection.

Why subject to revision that part of our programs which, for better or for worse, has served and continues to serve to prepare good Hispanists in the United States? Why not concentrate our efforts on solving the problems of language teaching which linguists consider so urgent? I would venture to answer these questions in the simplest manner: that the mere opportunity of discussing our doubts and problems was enough to make us, a select group of professional teachers, realize that in the teaching of literature we too were faced with new difficulties, new problems, which we had to solve with urgency.

But such a simple answer, "My dear colleagues, come together and speak about the obstacles you encounter daily in your teaching, and you will see that something happens to the manner in which you teach a foreign literature," would scarcely justify these pages. Actually I must resort to that which I can affirm with some certainty, that is, my personal experience, which was precisely what led me to undertake the task of leading the seminar. This experience has resulted in some ideas which I shall present here without wishing to seem dogmatic and without claiming to have discovered new ways to meet our common objectives. If I do assign them a certain value, it is as reasonable starting points from which to review the postulates and the methods of our teaching. In other words, I am offering a number of suggestions rather than firm conclusions. And these suggestions ought to be taken for what they really are: possibilities of improvement which should be tried in the classroom. There is an illness, actually only a chronic complaint, in the best Spanish departments, against what in reality is a serious threat to our whole educational system, namely, mass education. Rather than attempt to prescribe practical remedies for the illness or to paint a rosy future for the profession, I feel it would be wiser to ask the profession to take stock of itself and propose its own remedies.

THE NATURE OF LITERATURE

The first matter professors of literature ought to consider is the dual nature of their subject: (1) literature as an aesthetic human experience, which not only gives pleasure but also teaches life in varying degrees of intensity (one *re-creates* what has been created by the writer); and (2) literature as the object of our study, or of our intellectual curiosity. One might well ask the professor of literature whether in his teaching, and even in his research, he recognizes the inseparable nature of these two aspects of literature. Might we not be running the risk of falsifying, or hiding, the true nature of literature by overlooking in our classes or seminars the first of these aspects? Should we neglect the reader so that the scholar may function more efficiently? Are there still professors of literature who ignore this initial and inescapable problem or who fail to make use of the excellent works on literary theory that are so readily available (Wellek & Warren, 1949)?

Whatever the answers to my initial question, one cannot fail to recognize that the professor who is up to date in the trends of modern criticism and tries to relate them to the pedagogical problems of introducing literature—Hispanic literature, in this case—cannot fail to consider seriously the view of literature as life, an approach increasingly predominant these days. Literature can no longer be considered merely an adventitious or decorative object in life or in culture; it must be seen rather as one of the deepest expressions of the ethos of a nation. Professors of literature cannot ignore this reality: literature *is* life, readily available to the reader and full of humanizing tension.

Having clarified this initial matter and supposing that we accept the premise of literature as life, then we ought to concentrate all our teaching efforts in this direction. If literature is a transcendental aesthetic experience which not only is *present* in the "then" and "there" of the text and the feelings of the author but can also *be moving toward* the "here" and "now" of the reader, then the student of literature ought to be considered first of all as a *reader*. And in order to help him be a real reader— the best possible reader—we have to make him see that being such a reader comes very near to being a writer: a writer or a poet in the widest meaning of the word, but in a passive sense one who re-creates in his reading what was felt and intuited by the original, active author or poet. How can we prepare a student to develop such creativity from his very first contact with literature? How help him avoid the two attitudes that would hinder his task: the attitude of the superscholar, withdrawn from and not concerned with the exercise of re-creating literature; and the attitude of the snob, dilettantish and superficial, not only in art and literature but also in life?

We might propose as a starting point that all literary study, even on the most elementary levels, aim at the following three points:

1.   To stress the uniqueness of the literary-aesthetic experience, an

act of poetry per se; and to recognize that to fail to enter into the imaginative play of "writer-reader" may be whatever else you wish but most certainly is not to come to grips with the essence of literature. To abstain from this aesthetic experience of being a "participant" is, in the final analysis, not to study literature.

2.   To give the student such scholarly assistance (historical, philosophical, sociological, and philological contexts, etc.) as may be necessary to illustrate and help him understand and place the literary text in the then and there in which it was conceived. But all effort along these lines ought to be subordinate to the first one, the aesthetic purpose.

3.   To orient the student in the search for ethical implications (absent or present, implied or readily seen) which all works pose. The moral responsibility (or irresponsibility) of an author is inseparable from his aesthetic vision. In this way the student would examine the value of the literary text in a double perspective—one ethical, the other aesthetic— and new dimensions would be added to the traditional historical-literary analysis.

HISPANIC LITERATURE

Having established the three premises listed above, we ought to examine next the difficulties inherent in beginning not just the study of literature in general but, in this case, Hispanic literature in particular. I know that, when facing the issue of crossing linguistic and cultural frontiers, the teacher feels himself assailed by doubts, by as yet unanswered questions, but, despite this, we can enumerate some considerations, even if these be tentative. They should be taken as provisional answers to the problems that confront us:

1.   An adequate knowledge and use of the Spanish language, spoken and written, ought to be an indispensable condition for beginning the introduction to Hispanic culture. Without a thorough apprenticeship in the real language, the non-Spanish speaker would be initiated into literature as a "translator" and not as an "inhabitant" or "experiencer" of the foreign culture. Translation, even at its highest possible literary quality, is nothing but a falsification or, at best, an approximate re-creation of the original work. It stands to reason that to require this preparation from the student is tantamount to requiring, too, that the professor give his introductory course to Hispanic literature in Spanish; the reasons seem obvious to me.

2.   The study of Hispanic culture ought to be inseparable from the study of its language. It would be ideal to be able to undertake the study

of culture in a real situation, e.g., to live and study in a Spanish-speaking country. Additional courses in the curriculum would present Hispanic culture not as a repertory of facts, names, dates, and works but rather as a series of findings of lasting value and would constitute a desirable and fruitful alternative to foreign study. One reservation might, however, be made; namely, that it is very difficult to determine whether the introduction to the study of culture ought to precede or follow the introduction to one of its most intimate manifestations: literature. One might even suggest that if the introductory course in literature is taught with aesthetic and vitalistic criteria, this would be the best way of penetrating the very essence of the culture. Perhaps through literature one might reach an understanding of the mechanism of outward choice and of inner thought and be able to appreciate better the value system of the culture in question, in this case, Hispanic culture. To study literature in this way as a deeply rooted manifestation of life would lead to a better understanding of the customs, the social institutions, and the individual historical events, as well as its general lines. Literature would also provide an approach to the visual arts, whose deeper meanings often escape the eye of the foreign observer because of his tendency either to isolate cultural phenomena from their context in order to describe them with supposed and misleading intellectual objectivity or to judge them in the context of his own culture where these phenomena may have little or no meaning or a totally mistaken one.

3. One ought to select as texts for introduction to Hispanic literature courses those books which are closest to the American student's own experience. One might even conceive of giving a masterpieces course in inverse chronological order. Going from the immediate present to the remote past, the student could perhaps pass more efficaciously, first, from his familiar context to the transcendental aesthetic experience and, second, from the experience of his own culture to that of the foreign one.

4. One ought never to falsify the cultural reality (life, art, literature) which is the goal of the student's study. One would thus have to oppose all sorts of simplified, or supposedly simplified, literary texts and stress instead the methods which will achieve the best possible access to *real* Hispanic life, language, and literature. I cannot say to what extent one can accept the supposedly pedagogical reasons used to justify the widespread simplifications or mutilations of the numerous texts currently on the academic market. I am of the opinion that in such a vast literature as that of the Hispanic world there would be no great problem in finding texts of varied and gradual linguistic difficulty to correspond to the age and level of experience of the student. On the other hand, I think it dangerous and misleading to give the student texts which have been

abridged or cut according to the editor's caprice. The task of choosing, or highlighting, significant portions in each work ought to be reserved for the professor so that he may do so according to the level and aims of different courses. I find totally unacceptable many widely used textbooks in which the editor, generally a person not particularly preoccupied with culture or literary values, *rewrites* novels, short stories, and even epics, with supposedly grammatical and pedagogical criteria!

5.   One ought to consider Hispanic literature as a unified body of material, abandoning the established practice of dividing its study into Spanish and Latin-American literature. Some American universities have been making progress in this direction for quite some time now; unfortunately they are definitely in the minority. A separation generally results in the undermining of one or the other of the two branches which comprise the great literature written in the Spanish language. To recognize in a practical way the unity of Hispanic literature (common language, a shared history for centuries, and, above all, the survival of a system of fundamental values) does not mean that one must forget the rich and fecund variety inherent in the geographic, ethnic, sociological, and historical diversity of the Spanish-speaking peoples.

6.   Finally, when faced with the concrete and practical problem of organizing an introductory course in which one would keep in mind the ideas and reservations presented above, one might consider a course entitled "Introduction to the Masterpieces of Hispanic Literature" as the most viable for experimenting in the future. In such a course one would study from six to eight key works representing the various literary genres. These would be complete works, not abridged, simplified, or presented piecemeal, and would be chosen first and foremost for their literary quality. One would try also, though always remaining faithful to this criterion, to present adequately the variety of Hispanic literature in space and time. Survey courses as they are usually taught in many universities, with the corresponding array of anthologies and manuals, may well not be the best kind of course to introduce a student to Hispanic literature. This, of course, does not deny the fact that such courses might be useful later on to present the students with a composite view of the general literary currents or tendencies in various epochs. But, as introductory courses, "surveys" of literature lead to superficial, shallow, and all too rapid views which are, in sum, not at all conducive toward awakening in the student an interest for and an understanding of the new literature. There is, on the other hand, nothing to prevent the professor from supplementing the reading of masterpieces with background lectures and assignments in works of history and literary criticism.

CONCLUSION

All the observations I have made above are not directed at the discovery of any method or pedagogical panacea. I present them in complete modesty because I believe that, in the final analysis, what matters is not the method but the professor. May they serve then, at best, as a starting point for that self-examination which, I assume, many of us undergo year after year when we begin a new introductory literature course and gaze upon the hopeful faces of young people who, for whatever reasons, have come to the threshold of Hispanism. Since the teaching of the art of literature is, or ought to be, itself an art—and one to which we are deeply committed—I venture to address my colleagues in the profession with the hope that they will not only give serious consideration to my doubts and perplexities but also strive to suggest better solutions than those I have here proposed. It is obvious, of course, that nothing I have said will appeal to those who do not view their teaching effort as a creative task. To them I can say little, except to express my regret at the number of potential Hispanists who turn toward other literatures or toward other disciplines because they have failed to find in their introductory course in Hispanic literature that spark which fate, or instinct, had led them to expect in it.

REFERENCES

MacAllister, Archibald T., and Albert Valdman. (Eds.) *Report of the Seminar for College Teachers of French, German, and Spanish.* Bloomington, Ind.: Indiana University, 1964 (mimeograph).

Wellek, René, and Austin Warren. *Theory of literature.* New York: Harcourt, Brace & World, Inc., 1949.

3

THE USE OF CONTRASTIVE DATA IN FOREIGN LANGUAGE COURSE DEVELOPMENT

BELA BANATHY
EDITH CROWELL TRAGER
CARL D. WADDLE

Bela Banathy (1919–   ) did undergraduate and graduate work in his native Hungary. He completed graduate studies at San Jose State College and is working for his doctorate at the University of California, Berkeley. Since 1951 he has been with the Defense Language Institute, West Coast, where he is director of the East Europe–Middle East Language Division. He is the author of several language texts, the Common Concept Foreign Language Test (CTB), and articles and studies in the field of foreign language education.

Edith Crowell Trager (1924–   ) received degrees in linguistics from the University of Pennsylvania and Hunter College and is now teaching linguistics and English structure at San Jose State College. She has collaborated with Alan Lomax on articles on folk-song phonotactics, and with Paul Garvin on the orthographic conversion of speechwriter output, and has written other articles on Amerind languages. She has coauthored a book widely used by teachers of English as a second language and has taught, at both university and secondary school levels, French, Spanish, and Russian.

Carl D. Waddle (1938–   ) received his B.A. degree from San Jose State College in 1964. He is at present completing his M.A. work at San Jose State and has served for two years as a teaching assistant in the English for Foreign Students program. His special interest is in applied linguistics and contrastive studies.

35

The opinions and conclusions presented herein are those of the authors and do not necessarily represent the views of the Defense Language Institute, with which Mr. Banathy is affiliated, nor those of any other governmental agency.

The application of scientific findings to human affairs has become a significant phenomenon in recent times. The teaching of foreign languages is a human endeavor which has at its disposal several disciplines offering scientific discoveries for application. The linguist established the relevance of his discipline to language teaching some time ago. It was only recently, however, and especially during World War II and the postwar years, that this relevance was brought clearly into focus (Moulton, 1963). In addition to linguistics, other fields which have significant offerings to make to language teaching are cultural anthropology, psychology, sociology, and educational technology.

The interest of the scientist in language teaching has been reciprocated, if not surpassed, by the interest of the language teacher in pertinent scientific data. The language teaching profession has expressed an increasing desire to avail itself of relevant findings and their applications. As a result, language teaching is becoming an interdisciplinary field of endeavor. With the cooperation of the language teacher, the linguist, the psychologist, and representatives of other related disciplines, new approaches to it have evolved. New materials and aids have been developed, and new learning environments created. The application of scientific findings has truly revolutionized language teaching, and the final outcome of these revolutionary changes is not yet in sight.

In the field of foreign language education many questions have not been answered; in fact, there are many questions which are yet to be asked. It is suggested that the inquiry which has attracted the most attention is related to the "how" of language teaching. The application of the linguists' understanding of the nature of language has helped to identify the audiolingual approach as a way to learn languages (Brooks, 1960; Carroll, 1961; Lado, 1964; Moulton, 1963). A preoccupation with "how" may be the reason why the question of "what" has not received the attention it deserves. It should be noted, however, that the recent development of programmed instruction in foreign languages has generated considerable interest in the latter question. An examination of many of the presently used foreign language textbooks reveals some serious discrepancies between the linguistically oriented approach to foreign language teaching and its application in the development of foreign language text materials. Perhaps dissatisfaction with student achievement, in spite of the conscientious use of the audiolingual method, may be due to this gap between "how" and "what."

The purpose of this article is to discuss an approach which would apply up-to-date linguistic principles to the development of foreign language text materials. Our initial assumption is that learning means changing behavior. Learning a foreign language, thus, means changing one's native language behavior to that of speakers of the target language. Acquiring this different communication behavior means, first, changing one's listening habits to the point at which the incoming auditory data of the target language will be automatically decoded in terms of its linguistic structure and referential system. Second, it means learning the production of the sound sequences of the target language so that its native speakers can comprehend them immediately and identify them as acceptable. This change of communication behavior also involves differences to be learned on the videographemic band of communication, as well as differences in kinesics, paralinguistic features, and cultural behavior.

A summary statement of this line of reasoning will establish the fundamental assumption of this study: the change that has to take place in the language behavior of a foreign language student can be equated with the differences between the structure of the student's native language and culture and that of the target language and culture. The task of the linguist, the cultural anthropologist, and the sociologist is to identify these differences. The task of the writer of a foreign language teaching program is to develop materials which will be based on a statement of these differences; the task of the foreign language teacher is to be aware of these differences and to be prepared to teach them; the task of the student is to learn them.

CONTRASTIVE ANALYSIS

Differences between two languages can be established by contrastive linguistic analysis. Lado (1957) wrote an informative discussion of the principles and practices of such analysis.

Prerequisite to the preparation of a contrastive linguistic analysis are adequate linguistic descriptions (Gleason, 1961, chap. 21) of the native language of the student and of the target language. A careful comparison of the two systems will furnish the data for the contrastive analysis. (Sources which have been little used as yet for such information are the computer programs for machine translation which have been developed at various machine translation centers in the United States.) The data thus accrued constitute the most significant information the linguist can offer to language teaching since they identify the target elements of a language course. Again, what the student has to learn equals the sum of the differences established by the contrastive analysis.

TABLE I Spanish and English in California

OUTLINE GUIDE TO CONTRASTIVE PHONOLOGY

I. Consonants
   A. Phonemic differences
      1. + Spanish, − English: /ñ/, /x/, /R/
      2. − Spanish, + English: /v, Θ, š, ž, ǰ, ŋ, ð, w, h/
      3. Distributional: − Spanish: final /p, b, t, d, k, g, j, z, m/ and final
         C clusters /C+t, d/, /C+s, z/, /r+C/, /l+C/ and
         their combinations
         + Spanish, + English: initial /C+l, r/
         + English: initial /s + C+(l, r)/
         + Spanish: initial /e/ + /s+C+(l, r)/
   B. Phonetic differences
      1. /p, t, d/ Spanish unaspirated, English aspirated before stressed V
         except after /s/
      2. /t, d, s, n/ Spanish dental, English alveolar
      3. /b, d, g/ Spanish [b̦, d̦, g̦] fricatives intervocalically, [b, d, g] stops
         elsewhere
      4. /s/ Spanish *s, z* voiced before voiced C
      5. /r/ Spanish tap, English retroflex, etc., /rr/ Spanish trill

CONTRASTIVE ARRAY OF PHONEMIC AND GROSS PHONETIC DIFFERENCES BETWEEN
CALIFORNIA SPANISH AND ENGLISH

Spanish array (columns 1 2 3 4):

1	2	3	4
p b[b̦, b̦]	t d[d̦, d̦]	č —	k g[g̦, g̦]
f	s[s, z]	—	x
m (Nasals)	n	ñ	—
— (Others)	l r R	y	—

Obstruents / Nasals / Others

English array (columns 1 2 3 4):

1	2	3	4
p b	t d	č ǰ	k g
f v	Θ, s ð, z	š ž	—
m (Nasals)	n	—	ŋ
w (Others)	l, r	y	h

II. Vowels
   A. Phonemic differences
      1. + Spanish: /i, e, a, u, o/, /ai, ei, oi/, /au, eu/
      2. + English: /i, e, æ, a, u/, /iy, ey, ay, oy/, /uw, ow, aw/, V + r/

TABLE I *Continued*

3. Spanish *V*'s occur in all positions, English short stressed *V*'s never final

B. Phonetic differences

Spanish *V*'s are short, tense, and "pure"; stress does not affect quality

English *V*'s are short and lax or diphthongal; quality varies with stress

($V+/r/$ not included here)

SPANISH

High	i	u
Mid	e	o
Low		a

ENGLISH

SIMPLE VOWELS				ENGLISH	SPANISH		KEY
	FRONT	CENTRAL	BACK	/i/	no equivalent		pit
				/æ/	"	"	pat
High	/i/		/u/	/e/	"	"	pet
Mid	/e/	/ə/		/ə/	"	"	putt
Low	/æ/	/a/		/a/	"	"	pot
				/u/	"	"	put

COMPLEX VOWELS							
	WITH /Y/-GLIDE			/iy/	i +		see
/i/				/ey/	ei, ey		say
/e/			/o/	/ay/	ai, ay		sigh
		/a/		/oy	oi, oy		soy
	WITH /W/-GLIDE						
			/u/	/uw/	u +		boot
			/o/	/ow/	ou		boat
		/a/		/aw/	au		bout

The Center for Applied Linguistics has undertaken the development of contrastive analyses of English with each of five other languages. In this Contrastive Structure Series, two English-German studies have already been published: Moulton (1962) and Kufner (1962). Among some earlier studies, the Belasco series (Cárdenas, 1961; Hall, 1961; Magner, 1961; Marchand, 1961; Valdman, 1961) and Politzer's work (1961) are mentioned here. To meet the total requirements of a foreign language program, however, in addition to contrastive studies of linguistic structures, similar studies comparing the lexicons and cultural systems of the two languages in question should be made.

As an example of a contrastive linguistic analysis, an outline guide to the contrastive phonology of California English and California Spanish is shown in Table I. It would, of course, need much elaboration to be a complete contrastive statement, but it includes a statement about the segmentals of the two languages, first the phonemic differences and then the phonetic differences. In both categories, statements are made about the presence, absence, and distribution of each element in both languages.

An all-inclusive contrastive analysis of two languages and cultures produces an almost infinite list of differences. The developer of a foreign language course, however, will be satisfied with less than a list of all possible differences. The collection of target elements of a language course will constitute a selective listing of contrastive findings. The kind and number of items selected will be determined by the expected terminal behavior of the student and influenced by the available learning time. Once target elements have been collected, they should be arranged according to certain categories. A systematically arranged list of target elements can be conceptualized as an inventory of target elements of a language course (see Table II, page 43).

A specific instance of a plausible list of target elements might be useful here. Utilizing the work of Noam Chomsky and his followers on generative grammar and transformations, along with some of the more valid traditional notions, a textbook writer of a course in English as a foreign language might decide that the first items to be taught would be kernel sentences, derived by phrase structure and obligatory transformations only. That is, the student would learn that a simple declarative sentence consists of a subject (NP) and a predicate (VP) and that there are three main types of VP: (1) intransitive verb, (2) linking verb followed by a subject complement which may be either noun or adjective, and (3) transitive verb followed by a noun as direct object. He would also have to learn that nouns may be singular or plural, with or without determiners; he must know that a verb has two present-tense forms and a past-tense form and that it may be expanded to an auxiliary plus verb, with the auxiliary manifesting the tense marker. He must learn early which pronouns constitute NP in which position and that two-part verbs (or verb + particle) frequently constitute the formal equivalent of one-word verb forms. It is not yet clear whether other verb states (progressives, perfects, emphatics, passives, and modal forms) should be called transformations or simply regarded as tagmeme variants that fit in the same slot. In any case, they certainly must be dealt with early in any sensible program for teaching English structure. It seems logical to say that then, and only then, should the optional transformations be taught.

Negative sentences and both types of questions would be a logical possibility for the next step. Another valid possibility is to introduce the optional negative and interrogative transformations along with each of the verb states. Compound NP, VP, and S are simply taught, and the lesson which concerns them might serve as a review of the material, i.e., phrase structure and obligatory transformations. Complex sentences involving dependent clauses, the more complicated of the optional transformations, should be introduced thereafter. Of course, adjective and adverb structures and prepositional phrases are part of phrase structure. Although the prepositional phrases have been little explored as yet, they would have to be taught throughout the text. As indicated above, one area of linguistic investigation in which very little contrastive work has been done is the field of transformational grammar. Since so much of importance in the description of the syntax of English and the grammar which underlies the syntactical structures has been done by such men as Chomsky and many others, it would seem that contrastive studies in the kernel sentences and transformation rules of source and target languages would yield extensive data in precisely that area of language in which the structuralists have obtained the fewest results: the structure of the whole sentence. For example, in English a derivation of the construction "the feared situation" is as follows:

$$\underset{NP_1}{\text{All}} + \underset{VP}{\text{feared}} + \underset{NP_2}{\text{the situation}}$$

is transformed by means of the passive transformation to:

$$\underset{NP_2}{\text{The situation}} + \underset{BE}{\text{was}} + \underset{V}{\text{feared}} + \underset{(by + NP_1)}{\text{(by all)}}$$

The deletion transformation [-Rel(tense + BE)] yields:

$$\underset{NP_3}{\underbrace{\underset{NP_2}{\text{The situation}} + \underset{V}{\text{feared}} + \underset{Part}{} + \underset{(by + NP_1)}{\text{(by all)}}}}$$

which is a noun phrase that may occur in any NP position open to the NP *the situation*. If, however, the optional $(by + NP_1)$ had not been included in the passive transformation, the passive sentence would have been:

$$\underset{NP_2}{\text{The situation}} + \underset{BE}{\text{was}} + \underset{V}{\text{feared}} + \text{Part}$$

which would yield:

$$\text{The} \quad \text{situation} \quad \text{that} \quad \text{was} \quad \text{feared}$$

Then the deletion transformation would yield:

$$\text{The} \quad \text{situation} \quad \text{feared}$$

which could not be used as an NP in another sentence. A further transformation, which Paul Roberts calls the transformation-noun modifier (T-NM) is necessary, as follows:

$$\text{The} \quad \text{situation} \quad \text{feared} \quad \Rightarrow \quad \text{The} \quad \text{feared} \quad \text{situation}$$

which may now be substituted for NP in any NP position open to *situation*.
Again,

$$\underset{NP_1}{\underline{All}} + \underset{VP}{\underline{feared}} + \underset{NP_2}{\underline{the\ situation}}$$

$$\underset{NP_2}{\underline{The\ situation}} + \underline{BE} + \underline{V} + \underline{Part} + \underset{(by + NP_1)}{\underline{(by\ all)}}$$

$$\underset{NP_2}{\underline{The\ situation}} + \underline{Rel} + \underline{BE} + \underline{V} + Part$$ *or*

$$\underset{NP_2}{\underline{The\ situation}} + \underline{Rel} + \underline{BE} + \underline{VP} + \underset{(by + NP_1)}{\underline{(by\quad all)}}$$

$$\underset{NP_2}{\underline{The\ situation}} + V + Part \quad or\ \underset{NP_2}{\underline{The\ situation}} + V + Part + (by + NP_1)$$

$$\underset{V}{\underline{The}} + \underset{Part}{\underline{feared}} + \underset{NP_2}{\underline{situation}}$$

SOURCE SENTENCE	$\underset{NP}{\underline{All}}$	$\underset{VP}{\underline{feared}}$	$\underset{NP}{\underline{the\quad situation}}$

$$\emptyset + N + V + Past + Det + N$$

T-PASSIVE $\underset{Det}{\underline{The}} + \underset{N}{\underline{situation}} + Past + BE + \underset{Part}{\underline{was}} + \underset{V}{\underline{feared}}\ (by + \emptyset + N)\ \underset{}{\underline{(by\ all)}}$

T-DELETE $\underset{Det}{\underline{The}} + \underset{N}{\underline{situation}} + \underset{Part}{\underline{feared}} + V + \underset{(by + \emptyset + N)}{\underline{(by\qquad all)}}$

$$NP$$

or

T-DELETE $\underset{Det}{\underline{The}} + \underset{N}{\underline{situation}} + \underset{Part}{\underline{feared}} + V$

T-NM $\underset{Det}{\underline{The}} + Part + \underset{V}{\underline{feared}} + \underset{N}{\underline{situation}}$

$\left.\right\} = NP$

In Spanish a similar transformation occurs:

$$\underset{NP_1}{\underline{Todos}} + \underset{VP}{\underline{temían}} + \underset{NP_2}{\underline{la\ situación}}$$

$$\underset{NP_2}{\underline{La\ situación}} + SER + \underset{V}{\underline{fue}} + \underset{Part}{\underline{temida}} \quad \underset{(+ por + NP_1)}{\underline{(por\ todos)}}$$

$$\underset{NP_2}{\underline{La\ situación}} + Rel + SER + \underset{V}{\underline{fue}} + \underset{Part}{\underline{temida}} \quad \underset{(+ por + NP_1)}{\underline{(por\ todos)}}$$

$$\underset{NP_2}{\underline{La\ situación}} + V + \underset{Part}{\underline{temida}} \quad \underset{(+ por + NP_1)}{\underline{(por\ todos)}}$$

It can be seen from this contrastive presentation that although the
mechanism of this transformation is very similar in the two languages,
one important difference is the absence of the T-NM obligatory rule
in Spanish.

ENGLISH	SPANISH
The situation feared by all	La situación temida por todos
or	*or*
The feared situation	La situación temida

The inventory of target elements forms the raw data for a language course. To be functional for developmental purposes, however, each target element is to be identified by several qualifiers.

The first qualifier is the description of the differences supplied by the contrastive analysis. For example, in English the function word *will* plus the basic form of the verb indicates future; in Spanish a different medium is used, namely, inflection: a set of six person-and-number endings which are added to the infinitive used as future stem. The referential meaning of the grammatical device of future is similar in these two languages, but the device used to signal this meaning is different.

The second qualifier, inferred to some extent from the first, *is a description of the nature of the difficulty which the item presents for the learner.* For example, an English-speaking student learning to listen to the *p* sounds in the Korean way has the problem of learning to assign phonemic status to two phonetic entities which are allophones, not phonemes, in English. In Korean aspiration makes a phonemic difference

TABLE II *Inventory of Target Elements of a Foreign Language Course*

TYPE OF LEARNING	CATEGORIES OF TARGET ELEMENTS	LIST OF ELEMENTS
Acquisition of skills*	Phonology, graphemics, grammatical system, lexical stock, paralanguage, kinesics, culturally conditioned behavior	Phonemics, phonetics, writing system, morphology, syntax, vocabulary; tones of voice, gesture, etc.; eating habits, etiquette, etc.
Acquisition of information	Learning elements related to cultural information (literature, art, music, etc.), area information (political structure, economy, social structure, history, geography, etc.), culture patterns, information specific to the terminal behavior	Kinships, religion, work patterns, child rearing, marriage, age, status, groups, etc.
Acquisition of attitudes	Attitudes that speakers of the target language usually have toward their culture, social institutions, and values; attitudes expected from foreigners	Elements of these attitudes to be specified in each instance

* Here more complex skills, such as competence in translation and interpreting, may also be included.

which does not occur in English. As the English-speaking student does not have the habit of paying attention to aspiration as a signaling device, the task of learning to react to Korean /pʰ/ and /p/ as a phonemic opposition between aspiration and nonaspiration becomes a listening hurdle. Thus it must be treated first as a discrimination problem.

The third qualifier is the significance of the item. Significance is determined by such factors as frequency and usefulness. The frequency of the item in relationship to the other items may be already available as statistical data; if not, it should be estimated. The second factor of significance is related to usefulness. Although we shall usually select items which are of high frequency, we may at times choose a less frequent item because it is needed for a certain purpose. For example, in teaching students to discriminate between the short /ö/ and the long /ö:/ in Hungarian, we may use items in the discrimination drill which are of low frequency in order to "make the point" and then discard them after the student has learned to discriminate.

The fourth qualifier is the nature of control. An item may be selected for recognition control only or for production control as well. To use an example from Fries (1954, p. 33), the "genitive inflection of nouns" may become, for a learner of English, a recognition goal only, as it has a less than 5 percent occurrence; the use of the function word *of,* however, should be a production goal. The nature of control should also include a description of the condition or conditions under which the learner is expected to exhibit the desired control. Variables of conditions may include such aspects as normal live conversation, comprehension of speech delivered through mechanical media with different degrees of channel noises, functioning under stress, etc.

The fifth and last qualifier is the degree of control. It refers to phonological accuracy and automaticity. Based on contrastive understanding, the text developer has to make a decision, for instance, as to how far to go in requiring phonetic accuracy. Such decisions then should be reflected in the text, which should have sufficient amounts of teaching material to enable the student to acquire a desired competence. In teaching Spanish to an English-speaking student, e.g., the question of accepting an alveolar *t* instead of the dental is a question of degree of control. If such subphonemic accuracy is desired, then materials should be developed for the teaching of this feature.

In summary, the writer of a foreign language text must consider these things about each structure point he wants to teach: (1) description of the difference between the structure points of language X and language Y, (2) difficulty for the Y speaker in learning the particular structure point of X, (3) frequency and usefulness of the illustrations of the particular structure point of X, and (4) nature and (5) degree of control of the structure point of X for the Y speaker.

A reexamination of the application of the qualifiers discussed above will bring into focus again the significance of contrastive data. Qualifiers of differences and difficulties cannot be made without such data. The significance of the item directly relates to linguistic factors, and the nature and degree of control cannot be established without a precise understanding of linguistic description and difficulty factors.

BLUEPRINT FOR A FOREIGN LANGUAGE PROGRAM

Having considered the qualifiers of difference, difficulty, significance, and nature and degree of control, the developer of a foreign language course will be able to determine the position of each target element in a linear sequence. The arrangement of all the target elements in a linear sequence would furnish the *blueprint* for a foreign language program. This blueprint, however, is not a one-track projection. It is to be conceptualized as a multitrack complex of several strings, namely, those of the phonological, morphological, and syntactical elements, lexical items, situational elements, cultural patterns, paralanguage features, kinesics, etc. In the possession of such a blueprint, the writer of a course will proceed to segment the entire sequence into lesson units.

In most instances it will be desirable to equalize completion time for each lesson unit. If each of the units is to be completed in the same amount of time, the segmentation of the linear sequence of target elements into units should be guided by three main criteria. It appears to us that these criteria for a good blueprint merit detailed discussion which would go beyond the scope of this study. Therefore, they will be identified here only in a general way.

The first criterion is equal difficulty of the material to be learned in each lesson. This implies, of course, that some structure points will require more numerous lessons than others. Said in another way, this means that the sum of learning problems presented in each lesson should be just about the same. The second criterion is the feasibility of having the students achieve an automatic and authentic use of the target elements of the unit, within the context of the previously learned elements. Corollary to the second is the third criterion, that of digestibility. Only such an amount of learning material as the student can readily digest or internalize within the time allowed for the unit should be programmed into a lesson.

The criteria of equal difficulty, feasibility of automatic use, and digestibility will govern the text developer in the selection and program-

TABLE III *Blueprint for Lesson No. 1, Hungarian Course*

PART ONE: INVENTORY OF TARGET ELEMENTS

LINGUISTIC FEATURES*

SOUND SYSTEM

SEGMENTALS

VOWELS: Of the fourteen vowels in Hungarian, five will be introduced:
/i/, /i:/, /e:/, /ɛ/, and /ɔ/.

CONSONANTS: Of the twenty-five consonants, eight will be introduced:
/b/, /m/, /l/, /n/, /t/, /s/, /z/, and /k/.

SUPRASEGMENTALS

STRESS: Stress in Hungarian is a syntactical device only. Each word
has a potential position for stress, which is the first syllable. Secondary
stress, if used, falls on the third, fifth, etc., syllable or on the first syllable
of the second component of a compound word. In the utterances introduced, there is no secondary stress.

PITCH: Like stress, pitch is also a syntactical device. There are three
pitch levels in Hungarian; all three will be introduced.

RHYTHM: In Hungarian, rhythm is syllable-timed.

GRAMMATICAL SYSTEM

FORM: Only free forms will be introduced.

ARRANGEMENT: Four sentence patterns will be introduced. Of the declarative, the normal order (fragmentary) and the negative order will be introduced. In both, only the falling-intonation patterns will be used. The
interrogative will have two patterns of intonation: the falling and the
rising.

LEXICAL ITEMS (VOCABULARY):   Three function words and four content words
will be introduced.

SITUATIONAL SETTING: Classroom.

CULTURAL FEATURES: Behavior in a classroom environment.

PART TWO: LEARNING PROBLEMS

LINGUISTIC FEATURES

SOUND SYSTEM

SEGMENTALS

VOWELS: Vowels /ɛ/ and /ɔ/ in Hungarian are phonetically similar
to their English vowel counterparts; vowels /i/, /i:/, and /e:/, however,
are phonetically different. The Hungarian /i:/ in /i:r/ and /i/ in /igɛn/
are phonetically different from the English /iy/ in /biyt/ *beat* and English /i/ in /bit/ *bit*. In Hungarian there are a long /i:/ phoneme and
a short /i/ phoneme. These are phonetically identical except for length.
The position of the tongue in the articulation of these two vowel sounds
is the same as in the English /iy/ in /biyt/ *beat*. Unlike the situation
in English, however, in Hungarian there is no tendency to diphthongize
the long /i:/.

/e:/ in /se:k/ is phonetically different from its English counterpart
/beyt/ *bait*, as Hungarian, unlike English, does not have the tendency
to diphthongize long vowels.

CONSONANTS: All the consonants introduced in this lesson have a
phoneme counterpart in English. There is a difference, however, in

TABLE III *Continued*

the phonetic shapes of /t/, /n/, and /l/, as these are dental rather than alveolar in Hungarian.

SUPRASEGMENTALS

STRESS: In English, stress is used to signal meaning within a word as well as in a sentence. In Hungarian, it is only a syntactical device. Primary stress in English may occur in different syllabic positions; in Hungarian it can fall only on the first syllable of a word. In English there are four stress levels; in Hungarian, only three. These differences create learning problems.

PITCH: Three pitch levels are recognized in Hungarian, and four in English.

The intonation patterns in the lesson will not present special difficulties.

RHYTHM: English has a phrase-timed rhythm; Hungarian is syllable-timed. The phrase-timed rhythm, coupled with the stress features of English and neutralization of vowel quality in unstressed syllable, is in sharp contrast to the situation in Hungarian. For the English speaker to learn syllable timing and the production of long vowels in unstressed position is a major hurdle.

GRAMMATICAL SYSTEM: For the English-speaking student a significant problem is to learn to use a noun as a predicate in the sentence (in third-person position for *to be* only).

EXAMPLE:

This   is   a   chair.
/ɛz/   /se:k/

CULTURAL FEATURES: In the physical sense, a Hungarian classroom is similar to the American, except for the black color of the chalkboard and the probability of having the teacher's desk on an elevated podium. The windows are usually constructed with a vertical opening slit in the center of the frame. In the psychological sense, the discipline in a Hungarian class is likely to be more strict (authoritarian) than in an American class.

---

* Tompa, 1962.

ming of target elements for a lesson unit. What should be pointed out again is that the basic information needed to apply these criteria consists of the data accrued from the contrastive analyses.

Selected target elements for a lesson unit, arranged according to appropriate categories as in Table II, provide the inventory of target elements for a lesson. Taking each target element and qualifying it as to the degree and nature of difficulty result in a definition of learning problems. It is suggested that the inventory of target elements and description of learning problems may serve as a blueprint for a lesson unit. It is only if such a blueprint is available that one has a clear definition of the terminal objective of the lesson and of the learning goal that the student should attain by the end of a particular unit. It is this

TABLE IV *Blueprint for an Early Lesson of a Hungarian Course*

PART ONE: INVENTORY OF TARGET ELEMENTS

CUMULATIVE: Those elements previously introduced.

NEW ELEMENTS

LINGUISTIC FEATURES*

SOUND SYSTEM

VOWELS: /o/ will be introduced in addition to the vowels already programmed.

GRAMMATICAL SYSTEM

FORM: The grammatical signal of plural will be introduced. The plural is formed through affixation by the bound morpheme /-k/. There are numerous allomorphs of this morpheme. Their use is determined by both specific and more generalized aspects of morphophonemics. (1) Of the specific aspects, two will be introduced: (*a*) root ending with a consonant + linking vowel + /-k/ and (*b*) root ending with a vowel + /-k/. (2) The more generalized types have a commonality, namely, noncontiguous vowel assimilation. Also called *vowel harmony*, this means that vowels of successive syllables must be similar in some way. Of this kind, two will be introduced: (*a*) root with consonant ending having a front vowel in its vowel nucleus + front vowel linking-vowel + /-k/, e.g., /se:k-ɛ-k/ ("chairs"); and (*b*) root with consonant ending having a back vowel in its vowel nucleus + back vowel linking-vowel + /-k/, e.g., /ɔblɔk-o-k/ ("windows").

ARRANGEMENT: Added to the features previously learned will be (1) nonfragmentary, normal-order (subject and predicate) use of the declarative arrangement and (2) a new intonation pattern called falling-level (suspensive) intonation. This type of intonation indicates that a further clause is to follow in the same sentence:

    3   2   2   3   2   1
    /nɛm   se:kɛk   ɔstɔlok/
    (These are not chairs but tables.)

(3) The interrogative clause will also have another intonation pattern:

    1   2   3   1
    /se:kɛk   ɛzɛk/
    (Are these chairs?)

PART TWO: LEARNING PROBLEMS

GRAMMATICAL SYSTEM

FORM: In comparing the grammatical systems of two languages, the criterion of comparison will include similarities or differences in meaning, medium, item, structure (allomorphic), and distribution. In comparing the grammatical devices of plural used in English and Hungarian, the following statements can be made:

1.   Meaning is similar. In the referential systems of both languages, as interpreted in grammar, only singular and plural categories exist.
2.   Medium is similar to some extent in the most frequent occurrences (suffix).
3.   Item, structure, and distribution are different.

TABLE IV *Continued*

Difficulties in this particular lesson will be kept to a minimum by design. These difficulties will relate to differences between the way the two languages select item, structure, and distribution. Allomorphs introduced will be:

1. Vowel harmony (front vowels): /ɛz-ɛ-k/ ("these")
2. Vowel harmony (back vowels): /ɔz-o-k/ ("those")
3. Correlation of forms: /mi-k ɛz-ɛ-k/ ("what are these?")
4. Root — linking vowel — ending: /ɛz-ɛ-k/ ("these")
5. Root — ending: /mi-k/ (the plural form of "what")

Items 1 and 2 are learning hurdles. To overcome them will require the development of a new habit of selecting the particular variant of the plural form which matches the pattern of vowel harmony.

Item 3 is another hurdle for the English speaker. Although the question word *who* does have a plural form in English, the *what* does not in normal usage. Therefore, to "pluralize" the question word /mi/, which corresponds to the English *what*, is a problem.

Items 4 and 5 contrast two different patterns. The plural morpheme /-k/ must be preceded by a vowel. If the root does not have a vowel ending, a linking vowel corresponding to the pattern of the vowel harmony must be added to it. This problem is judged to be of lesser difficulty than the previous ones, as some similarity exists in English, although not segmented according to the same line of pattern function (e.g., one of the allomorphs of the English plural is /ɨz/).

ARRANGEMENT: No particular difficulty is expected with the learning of the normal-order declarative patterns and with the falling-level intonation. The interrogative intonation pattern introduced here, however, is not used in English as an interrogative device. This pattern, therefore, requires special attention.

* Tompa, 1962.

blueprint which the developer will take as a base and from it devise materials which will help the learner to overcome the identified learning problems and achieve the desired competence.

The remainder of this study will be devoted to the presentation of sample lesson blueprints and a discussion of the use of blueprints in the development of teaching materials. In the samples, it is assumed that Hungarian and Spanish are the target languages and that English is the native language of the student. The blueprints for the Hungarian material are for very early lessons of the beginning phase of a course; the Spanish blueprints (outlines) cover a wider scope of a beginning program. The blueprint presented first is a design for the first lesson of a Hungarian course (see Table III).

The kind of data presented as examples in Table III furnish the raw

TABLE V *A Linguistic Outline for a Lesson in Spanish Intonation*

In this lesson, in addition to the /211 ↓ / intonation pattern for declarative sentences and the /311 ↓ / question word pattern, which have been programmed in a previous lesson, the pattern /233 ↑ / will be introduced. This pattern indicates that further information is to follow in the same sentence:

```
2        3 3      2    1 1
/no son Rubies ↑    sino perlas ↓ /
```

The interrogative pattern for sentences without question words, /322 ↑ /, will also be introduced:

```
3      2 2
/son Rubies ↑ /
```

NOTE: The notation system for Spanish is taken from Cárdenas (1961); for English, the Trager-Smith system as used in Cárdenas is employed, with 1 for low pitch, 3 for high pitch, and /→ ↑ ↓ / for / | ‖ # / to indicate terminal junctures.

LEARNING PROBLEMS: As noted in previous lessons, the pattern in English corresponding to Spanish /211 ↓ / is /231 ↓ /, and the use of the English pattern in Spanish results in an unintended signaling either of emphasis or of courteous interrogation. The intonation patterns introduced in this lesson also differ from the corresponding patterns in English.

Spanish /233 ↑ / corresponds to English /232→/:

```
2        3 3      2   1
/no son Rub*i*es ↑    sino p*e*rlas ↓ /
2        3    2       2   3
/ðer nat r*uw*biyz→|    ðer p*ə*rlz ↓ /
```

Spanish /322 ↑ / corresponds to English /233 ↑ /:

```
3   2 2         2    3   3
/son Rub*i*es ↑ /    /ar ðey r*u*biyz ↑ /
```

The substitution of the English /233 ↑ / for Spanish /322 ↑ / results in undue emphasis or even impolite insistence on an answer. The fact that /233 ↑ / occurs in both languages but with different meanings (English, question; Spanish, more to come) represents a special problem. The above-listed difficulties represent learning problems.

CONTROL DESIRED

KIND: Recognition and production.
DEGREE: Exact production of Spanish pitch sequences and understanding of their significance.

material and the frame of reference within which the developer of a foreign language text will prepare materials aimed to assist the learner to hurdle his learning problems. An example of how to prepare materials will be discussed here briefly within the framework of the blueprint previously described.

The developer's first problem is to solve a discrimination hurdle. A discrimination drill on learning to differentiate between the long /i:/ and the short /i/ should be developed for this purpose. Next, short model sentences which incorporate the selected linguistic elements will be constructed. A collection of these sentences is considered to be the closed repertory of a lesson. If the closed repertory meets the appropriate criteria, it can be called a dialogue. Utterances extracted from the closed repertory will be arranged into optimal learning steps as listening exercises. As an utterance was treated for listening purposes, appropriate drill materials will be developed to teach authentic sound production. The identified learning problems will be the base for preparing sound production drills. The development of these drills will constitute the major portion of developmental efforts.

In the sample blueprint, the production problems of major significance are the syllable-timed rhythm and the phenomenon of nonreduction of unstressed vowels. On the subphonemic level it was decided to make it a goal to help the student overcome his tendency to diphthongize the two long vowels /i:/ and /e:/. It was also decided that alveolars /l/, /n/, and /t/ will be accepted and tolerated as alveolar sounds and no particular effort will be made to achieve a dental production.

The task of the developer, therefore, is to prepare a sufficient amount of sound production drills for the items identified above which will help the student to attain the desired change in his language behavior. The Hungarian pattern of not using a verb corresponding to the English *is* in the present singular third person, although disturbing to the student, is a production problem only in a negative sense. As it would go beyond the scope of this article, the issue of how to prepare materials will not be discussed here.

It should be pointed out again that the information contained in the blueprint is a language teaching–oriented interpretation of contrastive linguistic data, and the use of this information is predicated upon the text developer's ability to apply the contrastive data to the development of teaching materials.

As a second example, the blueprint of an early lesson teaching a Hungarian grammatical pattern is presented next (see Table IV).

The solution of the learning problems presented in Table IV is based on the following considerations: Learning the use of a grammatical pattern involves, first, the perception of the pattern as a grammatical device signaling a certain change in the referential system. Second, it involves the habituation of the pattern through practice until authentic and automatic response capability has been achieved. The developer of a structural lesson unit will base the preparation of materials on the identi-

TABLE VI *A Linguistic Outline for a Lesson in Spanish Morphology* *

In this lesson the grammatical signal of plural will be introduced. It is formed by the bound morpheme -(*e*)*s*. There are two regular allomorphs of this morpheme, and the distribution is determined by specific aspects of morphophonemics. The distribution is (1) root ending in a consonant, /í/ or /ú/ + /es/; and (2) root ending with other vowel + /s/.

LEARNING PROBLEMS

FORM: In a comparison of the devices used for the formation of the "regular" plural, the following statements can be made:

1. Meaning is similar.
2. Medium is similar. The most frequent allomorphs in both languages are suffixes.
3. Item is similar. Both languages use -(*e*)*s* as the graphemic representation of the plural morpheme.
4. Allomorphic structure is different:

> ENGLISH: $<$-(*e*)*s*$>$ has allomorphs /s/   /z/   /ɨz/.
> SPANISH: $<$-(*e*)*s*$>$ has allomorphs /s/   /es/.

5. Distribution is different:

> ENGLISH: /iz/ after sibilants.
> /s/ after other voiceless consonants.
> /z/ after other voiced consonants and vowels.
> SPANISH: /es/ after consonants and /ú/ and /í/.
> /s/ after other vowels.

The learning difficulties in this particular lesson will concern the way the two languages select the structure and distribution of the allomorphs. Examples introduced in this lesson will be:

1. After sibilant /lápis/   /lápises/. (English would be /ɨz/.)
2. After voiceless consonant /Relóx/   /Relóxes/. (English would be /s/.)
3. After voiced consonant /árbol/   /árboles/. (English would be /z/.)
4. After /í/ /Rubí/   /Rubíes/. (English would be /z/.)
5. After vowel /pérla/   /pérlas/. (English would be /z/.)

The major difficulties for the English speaker would be these:

1. The presence of a vowel after all consonants, not only sibilants.
2. The /e/ rather than /ɨ/ in the $<$-(*e*)*s*$>$ allomorph.
3. The use of /s/ rather than /z/ after vowels.

CONTROL DESIRED

KIND: Recognition and production.

DEGREE: Native use of the two allomorphs as indicated above.

NOTE: In Table VI the phonemic representation of the English plural allomorph that occurs after sibilants, here used to mean /s, z, š, ž/ and /č, ǰ/ [tš, dž], is sometimes /əz/ and sometimes /ɨz/ in the literature. We have arbitrarily chosen /ɨz/, although there are theoretical reasons not to do so.

TABLE VI *Continued*

There are of course many "irregular" plural morphs in English, such as vowel change, zero, and -a, which are not included in this statement. According to the Spanish Academy (*Gramática de la lengua española*, Madrid: Espasa-Calpa S.Z., 1931), the only irregular plural morph in Spanish is zero. It occurs with certain compound nouns, for example, *el rascacielos* ("the skyscraper"), *los rascacielos* ("the skyscrapers"); with nouns ending in <*s*> after an unstressed vowel, for example, *el lunes* ("Monday"), *los lunes* ("Mondays"); and with names, for example, *los Pérez* ("the Perezes").

The /-es/ allomorph also occurs after some accented final vowels other than /i/ and /u/, e.g., after the names of the letters. Aside from a few isolated words, that statement is exhaustive.

Angle brackets, e.g., <*-(e)s*>, are used to indicate graphemic representation of both the English and Spanish morphemes.

* Saporta, 1959.

fication of learning problems presented in the blueprint. He will prepare perception and pattern drills which will aid the student to overcome the learning hurdles and achieve the desired competence. The sample blueprint programs the learning of five variants of the Hungarian plural. The first developmental step is the preparation of model sentences containing the target patterns. The collection of these sentences, preferably in the form of a dialogue, will constitute the closed repertory. By extracting appropriate model utterances from the repertory, variants will be introduced one by one in the form of perception drills. If applicable, a new item should be contrasted with one already perceived; e.g., items 1 and 2 in the blueprint present two different vowel harmony patterns. After the front vowel pattern has first been introduced through appropriate drills, the back vowel pattern can be well contrasted with it. Item 3, correlation of forms, suggests a noncontrastive approach, while item 5 can be contrasted with item 4, once that item has been well perceived. The series of perception-drill blocks will be followed by the development of extensive pattern-drill materials. Starting out with controlled variational materials, drills reflecting a gradual progression toward free variational use will be evolved.

Statements in Tables V, VI, and VII introduce samples of linguistic outlines for lessons of a Spanish course. These are not complete blueprints but present only the primary linguistic problem of the lesson; thus, they may be looked upon as blueprint nuclei. The statements are based on contrastive analysis for lessons on the phonological level (intonation patterns), the morphological level (plural allomorphs), and the syntactic level (sentence patterns with indirect objects).

TABLE VII *A Linguistic Outline for a Lesson in Spanish Syntax*

In this lesson the sentence patterns in Spanish corresponding to the subject + verb + indirect object + direct object construction in English will be introduced. The structures are as follows (Ns = subject noun, Vt = transitive verb, Ndo = direct object noun, Nio = indirect object noun, Pndo = direct object personal pronoun, and Pnio = indirect object personal pronoun):

1. (Ns)   Vt Ndo $\left\{ \begin{array}{c} a \\ para \end{array} \right\}$ Nio   El hombre dió un regalo a su hijo.

2. (Ns)   Pnio Vt Ndo   El hombre le dió un regalo.

3. (Ns)   Pnio Pndo Vt $\left\{ \begin{array}{c} a \\ para \end{array} \right\}$ Nio   El hombre se lo dió.

LEARNING PROBLEMS: The English pattern Ns Vt Nio Ndo has no equivalent syntactic structure in Spanish. English has, however, at least two regular patterns expressing the direct object + indirect object relationship. These are (*A*) Ns Vt Nio Ndo and (*B*) Ns Vt Ndo $\left\{ \begin{array}{c} to \\ for \end{array} \right\}$ Nio. For the purposes of this lesson, the following five different sentences in English will be used in contrast with the regular patterns in Spanish. Sentences 1 and 2 are English pattern *A*; sentences 1a, 2a, and 3 are English pattern *B*, which includes the preposition.

1.   Ns Vt Nio Ndo   The man gave his son a gift.

1a. Ns Vt Ndo $\left\{ \begin{array}{c} to \\ for \end{array} \right\}$ Nio   The man gave a gift to his son.

2.   Ns Vt Pnio Ndo   The man gave him a gift.

2a. Ns Vt Ndo $\left\{ \begin{array}{c} to \\ for \end{array} \right\}$ Pnio   The man gave a gift to him.

3.   Ns Vt Pndo $\left\{ \begin{array}{c} to \\ for \end{array} \right\}$ Pnio   The man gave it to him.

Word order is the important consideration in constructing an idiomatic English sentence, especially in pattern *A*. Any other order "sounds wrong" unless other material is added to the sentence.

In Spanish, word order is not so important, and the prepositional phrase containing the indirect object noun may be placed unambiguously almost anywhere in the sentence. Word order is a factor in Spanish, however, particularly when the indirect object is a personal pronoun without a preposition. The three regular Spanish patterns may be contrasted with the corresponding English patterns in the following way:

1. (Ns)   Vt Ndo $\left\{ \begin{array}{c} a \\ para \end{array} \right\}$ Nio   El hombre dió un regalo a su hijo.

2. (Ns)   Pnio Vt Ndo   El hombre le dió un regalo.

3. (Ns)   Pnio Pndo Vt $\left\{ \begin{array}{c} a \\ para \end{array} \right\}$ Nio   El hombre se lo dió (a su hijo).

Spanish sentence 1 corresponds to English sentences 1 and 1a above; Spanish sentence 2, to English sentences 2 and 2a; and Spanish sentence 3, to English sentence 3.

The above-listed differences create learning problems.

TABLE VII *Continued*

CONTROL DESIRED

KIND: Recognition and production.

DEGREE: As for all syntactic patterns, only perfect control is acceptable.

NOTE: In Table VII the subject noun in the Spanish sentence patterns is parenthesized, since well-formed sentences occur without expressed noun or pronoun subjects.

In both the Spanish and English sentence patterns, the particular preposition (*to* or *for*, *a* or *para*) that will occur in a given sentence depends principally on the verb.

CONCLUSION

In the introductory statement it was pointed out that a gap is apparent between the linguistically oriented approach in foreign language teaching and the interpretation and application of this approach in the development of foreign language text materials. The purpose of this study was to present an approach which applies linguistic principles in the development of foreign language teaching materials.

The first step in developing a foreign language course is making a contrastive statement about the two languages and cultures involved. Such a comparison will furnish the target elements of a language course. Then qualification of individual target elements as to difference, difficulty, significance, and degree of control must be made. The selection of target elements for a particular lesson must be identified, and recommendations made for attacking such problems.

In conclusion it is suggested that the gap between linguistics and foreign language teaching can be bridged only if developers of foreign language materials will avail themselves of contrastive data and use these data effectively in the preparation of teaching materials.

REFERENCES

Brooks, Nelson. *Language and language learning: Theory and practice.* New York: Harcourt, Brace & World, Inc., 1960.

Cárdenas, Daniel N. *Applied linguistics—Spanish.* (Ed. S. Belasco) Boston: D. C. Heath and Company, 1961.

Carroll, John B. *Research on teaching foreign languages.* Publication of the Language Laboratory. Ann Arbor, Mich.: The University of Michigan Press, 1961.

Fries, Charles C. *Teaching and learning English as a foreign language.* Ann Arbor, Mich.: The University of Michigan Press, 1954.

Gleason, H. A., Jr. *An introduction to descriptive linguistics.* New York: Holt, Rinehart and Winston, Inc., 1961.

Hall, Robert A. *Applied linguistics—Italian*. (Ed. S. Belasco) Boston: D. C. Heath and Company, 1961.

Kufner, Herbert L. *The grammatical structure of English and German*. Chicago: The University of Chicago Press, 1962.

Lado, Robert L. *Linguistics across cultures*. Ann Arbor, Mich.: The University of Michigan Press, 1957.

Lado, Robert L. *Language teaching: A scientific approach*. New York: McGraw-Hill Book Company, 1964.

Magner, Thomas. *Applied linguistics—Russian*. (Ed. S. Belasco) Boston: D. C. Heath and Company, 1961.

Marchand, James W. *Applied linguistics—German*. (Ed. S. Belasco) Boston: D. C. Heath and Company, 1961.

Moulton, William G. *The sounds of English and German*. Chicago: The University of Chicago Press, 1962.

Moulton, William G. Linguistics and language teaching in the United States 1940–1960. *International Review of Applied Linguistics*, 1963, **1** (1), 21–41.

Politzer, Robert L., and Charles N. Staubach. *Teaching Spanish: A linguistic orientation*. Boston: Ginn and Company, 1961.

Saporta, Sol. Morpheme alternants in Spanish. In Henry Kahane (Ed.), *Structural studies on Spanish themes*. Urbana, Ill.: The University of Illinois Press, 1959.

Tompa, Jozsef. *A mai magyar nyelv rendszere*. Budapest: Akademiai Kiado, 1962.

Valdman, Albert. *Applied linguistics—French: A guide for teachers*. (Ed. S. Belasco) Boston: D. C. Heath and Company, 1961.

4

TEACHING PRONUNCIATION

PIERRE LÉON

Pierre Léon (1926–   ) was born in France. He received degrees from the University of Paris and the University of Besançon. He has taught at the Institut de Phonétique in Paris, at the Faculté des Lettres at the Centre de Linguistique Appliquée in Besançon, and at Ohio State University and has lectured in several European and North American universities. He is now professor at University College, University of Toronto, where he teaches French phonology and stylistics. He has written several books and articles in these fields.

FROM ATOMISTIC TO FUNCTIONAL PHONETICS

Teaching pronunciation has long been considered by some teachers a trivial activity, consisting of having students repeating such tongue twisters as *she sells sea shells by the seashore,* which, although sometimes funny, are rarely useful. For others, pronunciation has been confused with phonetics, which has meant physics, physiology, and linguistics mixed together in order to frighten both teachers and students; and in spite of a large number of good articles in readily accessible publications it is still hard to convince the average teacher that pronunciation can be taught without tears. If the teaching of this important skill has been so greatly discredited, the reason is that the subject has been either ignored or treated in a scientific way rather than in a practical one. As a result, in the latter case, students have become capable of dealing with phonetic principles without being able to utilize them. Teachers who have been aware of the problems involved have been provided either with methods shunning completely the audiolingual approach or with pronunciation manuals full of overly detailed scientific descriptions. The main preoccupation of methodologists regarding the teaching of pronunciation can be found in almost all handbooks which have appeared up to now. They generally have in common the following points:

1. Detailed physiological description of sounds
2. Precise acoustic description of the phonetic realization of sounds
3. Graphic symbolization of sounds
4. Large numbers of orthoepic rules and exceptions about the use of sounds
5. Some ingenious correction techniques

The first phonetic studies (for example, see Ripman, 1889) described with great care physiological features of sounds. More recent examples can be found everywhere. Thus let us consider the following description of the French [i] (Grammont, 1934, p. 45, translated into English) :

> The French *i* is closed. To produce it the mouth assumes approximately the position for closed *é*; but the jaws are drawn closer together (1 millimeter between the front teeth, 3 millimeters between the lips), the tongue is pressed more tightly against the lower front teeth and the upper molars, and it is bunched against the hard palate, but still leaving a very narrow channel. The corners of the lips are drawn back, and the muscles are very tense.

According to Grammont, [o] must be pronounced with a mouth opening of 3 millimeters; [a], with an opening of 7 millimeters; [ɑ], 8; [ɔ], 10; [ɛ], 5; [e], 3; [i], 1, etc. Such a detailed physiological description is praiseworthy from a scientific point of view but perfectly useless from a practical standpoint. (Besides, no two persons have exactly the same mouth configuration.) Of course these instructions must be interpreted merely as general guidelines, and some description of the articulation of speech sounds is often necessary. It would be useful to show American-English learners of Spanish, for example, the difference between the stop and the fricative articulation of *b*. By the same token, it would be helpful when teaching French or German *R* to show the concave tongue shape in these languages as opposed to the English convex one. In fact, consonant articulations are much more precise than vowel articulations:

they are produced with either a complete closure or at least a constriction, and their point of articulation is easy to locate. But an overly precise articulatory description would lead the teacher as well as the student to think that articulations of the tongue and lips are mechanically adjustable and hence that articulatory descriptions are the key to the correction of pronunciation problems.

We now know that the articulation of a given sound depends on many linguistics habits. Thus [d] as in d*ay* and [ð] as in th*ey* both occur in Spanish d*ado* [daðo], but [d] occurs only at the beginning of words or after nasal consonants and never between vowels as in *nada*. This is why Spanish learners of English tend to say "a they" for "a day" and "de man" for "the man." Only a linguistic analysis will make the teacher aware of such facts, and articulatory exercise alone will not solve the problem.

Phonetic habits cannot be mastered solely through articulatory drill. It is quite possible to produce a German or a French [y] with retracted lips as well as with protruded ones, without any significant difference in the sound output, since articulatory compensations intervene at the laryngeal level. To quote Meyer-Eppler (1963, translated into English) :

> One of the fundamental principles of classical phonetics postulated 1 to 1 correspondences between processes underlying articulatory motion and their psychoacoustic effect. We know today that such correspondences cannot obtain, primarily because the number of distinctive articulatory choices is greater than the number of distinctive psychoacoustic choices.

The control of sound production is probably much more auditory than articulatory. Who has not witnessed the classical pronunciation lesson in which the student is given articulatory advice for uttering a perfect [y] but still goes on pronouncing [u] instead? As long as the sound has not been heard correctly, it cannot be reproduced correctly except by chance (P. Léon, 1962). This does not mean that a correct representation of the "ideal" articulation will not help, but it is not sufficient in itself.

Auditory considerations are found everywhere in classical handbooks of pronunciation, but they are not utilized from a pedagogical point of view. On the contrary, they are generally approached scientifically, using the same procedure as phoneticians did when noting all possible realizations of sounds in dialectal studies. As a result, Jones (1937) gives for English a system of twenty-one vowels and diphthongs; and Navarro Tomás (1932) proposes for Spanish a twenty-vowel system, including four *i,* three *e,* five *a,* three *o,* four *u,* and one nasal *a.* (Indeed he could also have added other nasal vowels like [õ] in *corazón,* etc.) Fouché (1952, p. 77) quotes R. de Souza as finding five different colors for the French *E:* acute *e* in *poupée,* grave *e* in *péril,* middle *e* in *pélerin,* acute open *e* in *belle,* and open grave *e* in *père.* All these variations are indeed attested, but they are determined by the phonetic environment. Thus before *r* a vowel is likely to be more open than before *k,* in French *père,* as in Spanish *pero* or in German *gern.* These variations may also be individual or regional. Going further in more precise phonetic description would lead us to posit about fifty vowels for French, whereas from a functional point of view French dialects show a basic system of ten vowels expanded to a larger system of fifteen in standard speech. The Spanish vowel system consists of five rather than of twenty units. When we *speak,* our organs of articulation produce a wide variety of speech sounds; but when we *listen* to people from different regions or special milieus, our ear interprets these variations in terms of a grid with a restricted number of units. The smallest phonic system in any language is the system of sounds abstracted by the *listener* and not the one realized by the *speaker.* Pronouncing [e] rather than [ɛ] in a Spanish word like *perro* will not affect auditory comprehension. These sounds are *allophones* of a single phoneme /E/ which must be distinguished from other vowel phonemes /a/, /o/, etc. Thus a phoneme may be defined here as a sound whose articulatory precision is limited only by the auditory comprehension of the listener.

The notion of the phoneme is not new. It appeared when early phoneticians saw the danger of a phonetic description which might be too precise when teaching a foreign language. As early as 1870, Baudoin de Courtenay, Henry Sweet, and Paul Edouard Passy (see Passy, 1906) pointed out the necessity of distinguishing between significant and non-significant sounds. The International Phonetic Alphabet (IPA), which they established, was the first means of abstracting sounds. It can even be said that the IPA was an oversimplification. As Malmberg (1963a, p. 110) states the problem: "This fact perhaps explains in part why, in traditional academic phonetics, vowels and consonants have always occupied more place than prosodic facts." The IPA, which was very useful, has unfortunately been employed too often as the main tool in the teaching of pronunciation. In fact, the ability to use it properly never proved mastery of good speech habits. Knowing that German /e/ is closed in *Schnee* and open in *Felt* will not guarantee the correct tense pronunciation [e] instead of glided [eɪ] on the part of an American student. Too many teachers have taught orthoepic rules and phonetic transcription instead of pronunciation, particularly when the so-called "reading methodology," whereby pronunciation exercises were based essentially on written literary texts, was in vogue in the United States.

Needless to say, reading aloud literary texts does not present the same problems as imitating everyday speech. Most languages, at least the so-called "languages of culture," are spoken in several levels of style.

This raises the thorny problem of the selection of a suitable model for student imitation: the uninhibited pronunciation of the man in the street or that of the overcareful diction teacher? The final objective would probably be the former for audiocomprehension and the latter for sound production. In French a group of words like *je ne sais pas* would have to be taught for audiocomprehension as:

1. žən se pɑ
2. š   se pɑ
3.   se pɑ
4.   pɑ

but only the first form would be taught for the students' oral use. Even now, however, too many phonograph records present slow, emphatic models instead of natural speech.

For teachers who were interested in remedial work, experimental phonetics proposed a whole set of *orthophonic instruments,* ranging from the tongue depressor to the indicator of tongue and lips movements. One of these gadgets transmitted the aspiration of *p, t,* and *k* through a tube to a small hammer which rang a bell; students of French had to pronounce *papa a une pipe* without making the bell ring. These tools were very ingenious but not always efficient. They reflected the preoccupation with physiological detail that characterized the period of classical corrective phonetics. The language was approached from an atomistic view. Correcting one sound after the other, starting from *i* which traditionally was the first vowel of the list of phonemes, and ending with the last consonant of the list, was like performing speech therapy in the learner's native tongue, as in correcting an English-speaking subject's lisped *s.* But in this instance, once the defective pronunciation has been corrected, the subject has no other problems because his whole phonic system is not involved. For a foreigner, however, a mispronounced sound is seldom an isolated pathological case but an individual manifestation of general linguistic habits organized in a specific phonic structure. And it is with a clear notion of this structure that phonetic correction must start.

A final criticism of classical conceptions of corrective phonetics concerns the technological aspects of the question. We are now very fortunate to have at our disposal the language laboratory (P. Léon, 1962). Instead of wasting time in repeating the same drills hundreds of times we may concentrate on more valuable and difficult work, such as explaining, verifying, correcting, and testing. Previously students could only repeat a few sentences during each class period while teachers exhausted themselves in playing the part of a tape recorder.

Let us sum up this first glance at the problem of corrective phonetics by saying that the methodology of this first period was characterized as follows: it perfected some excellent correcting devices, but it produced a much greater number of ingenious techniques for detailed work than methods in the real sense of the term. It did not isolate the important facts from the secondary ones. This will be the task of structural linguistics, which will allow a more systematic and efficient organization of the phonic substance from the double point of view of phonemics and phonetics.

THE PHONEMIC LEVEL

As early as the end of the nineteenth century a new linguistic approach had appeared. The essential facts brought to the teachers' attention were:

1. A language is a system of oral sounds.
2. From a functional point of view any language has a limited number of sounds.
3. The sounds of any language are organized in a system of general patterns, according to typical linguistic and phonetic habits.

That seems nowadays very evident. This notion was first developed by the Swiss linguist Ferdinand de Saussure at the beginning of this century and later by the American Edward Sapir. But the linguistic theories of this period had no impact on teaching.

In his *Outline Guide for the Practical Study of Foreign Languages* (1942), Bloomfield specified as terminal objectives of a foreign language course: "a command of the spoken forms of the language. This command includes the ability to speak the language fluently, accurately, and with an acceptable approximation to a native pronunciation." Dealing with formerly unknown languages (without any written grammar) led to the same conclusion: the necessity of teaching the *oral* system of the language. With the decision to learn such languages as French, German, and Spanish by listening rather than by reading came a realization of the importance of oral cues. Consider, for instance, the following French sentences:

Le gentil petit garçon arrive.
Les gentils petits garçons arrivent.

They are very well differentiated in their written form by five plural markers (one for each word), but we observe that the five written differences are reduced to only *one* in the oral form: the opposition /lə/ versus /le/ (or even /l/ versus /le/ represented by *le/les*. From an oral point of view the plural of French nouns does not involve the addition of an *s* but a vowel change in an unaccented prefixed marker. In the teaching of French verbs, it has become evident that verbs like *chanter* and *courir,* which have been classified in different groups, belong to the same morphophonemic category since they share endings as well as stem behavior:

je chạnte			je cours	
tu chantes			tu cours	
il chante			il court	
elle chante	/šãt/		elle court	/kur/
ils chantent			ils courent	
elles chantent			elles courent	
nous, on chante			nous, on court	
vous chantez	/šãt-e/		vous courez	/kur-e/

Such facts have been clearly demonstrated by Valdman (1961) and others, but a few years ago teaching phonetics as an integral part of language was almost completely ignored.

Consequently the ideal handbook of phonetics should start by teaching sounds as functional grammatical units. When teaching French, instead of correcting the aspiration of *p, t, k,* for instance, which is useful but of secondary importance, it would be better to start with such oral oppositions as /i/-/e/ in *il-elle:*

> *il* part/ *elle* part
> *il* sort/ *elle* sort
> *il* arrive/ *elle* arrive

or /ə/-/e/ in *le-les:*

> *le* garçon arrive/ *les* garçons arrivent
> *le* chat mange/ *les* chats mangent

In this way, students would practice the opposition of useful sounds—of phonemes. Phonemes could be practiced in such lexical units as:

SPANISH:	mal*o*/mal*a*
GERMAN:	T*o*r/T*ür*
FRENCH:	b*eau*/b*on*

and in such grammatical units as:

> la/la*s*
> ein/ein*e*
> l*e*/l*es*

When such words of similar oral structure differing only by one significant sound are opposed, they are called *minimal pairs;* these (see Delattre,

1960) are very useful for showing students how a language works on the paradigmatic level. The new *Patterns of Spanish Pronunciation* (Bowen & Stockwell, 1960), *Drillbook of French Pronunciation* (Valdman et al., 1964), and *Exercises systématiques de prononciation française* (M. Léon, 1964) are probably (after Charles C. Fries's and Robert L. Lado's work in English) the first books to apply this linguistic principle to the teaching of pronunciation by systematically contrasting phonemic patterns of language.

The concept of the phoneme as a functional unit not only permits the teaching of language in its spoken form but also makes it possible to start with the most important facts. At this point, however, a distinction must be made between the kinds of sounds which are to be given as a *model* and the expected student response. When asked to repeat an utterance such as *la rue,* an American-English student may answer:

1. Something interpretable as *la roue*
2. *la rue,* with a glide in [y]
3. *la rue,* with an [æ] instead of [a] in *la*

Comparing these errors, we see that the first one is phonemic since it changes the meaning of the utterance, the second is phonetic since it does not cause any error of interpretation but only denotes a foreign accent, and the third could be heard as dialectal French (*faubourien de Paris*). At the beginning of language instruction phonetic mistakes can be tolerated, but this does not mean, of course, that the teacher might as well offer utterances 2 and 3 as good models. The phonemic concept, which tolerates phonetic variations, primarily works for the *listener* rather than for the speaker. The phonemic level consists of sounds which are sufficient for audiocomprehension. It shows us, according to Politzer (1954), "what has to be learned for understanding the language and what may be postponed and dismissed as unessential." Trager and Smith (1951) have underlined the fact that, even by neglecting a lot of details, ". . . a phonemic description is more precise. This is particularly true when dealing with prosodic features. Speaking of 4 levels of intonation is more precise than talking about melodic variations."

Structural linguistics made its most important contribution to the teaching of languages by setting forth the theory that areas of difficulty can be predicted in advance by point-by-point comparison of the structure of the native and target languages. A first comparison will enable us to predict (1) which are the new sounds to be learned and (2) which sounds are different according to their distribution in the new systems.

The first step is an easy one. For instance, a comparison of Spanish and English makes it clear that it is necessary for an American-English student to learn how to pronounce the double *r* of *perro* ("dog") as opposed to the single *r* of *pero* ("but"). But learning to produce *ll* /ɬ/ as in the Spanish word lla*ma* would not be a very pressing problem even though that sound does not occur in English. It is likely to be replaced in American-English speech by the first sound of *yes,* but this mistake can be tolerated since it is not really a phonemic one. There are no Spanish minimal pairs like. lla*ma*/*yama, and these two sounds vary freely in Spanish dialects, as noted by Cárdenas (1961). In the same way, when learning German consonants, a speaker of English is likely to pronounce /š/ as in sh*ut* instead of /ç/ in German *ich.* But, here again, this mistake will not affect aural comprehension in German, for there are no contrast-ing pairs /iç/ versus /iš/.

Such an exhaustive comparison of English and Spanish, French, and German would bring us to the conclusion that very few obstacles confront the English learner in the acquisition of the isolated sounds of the phonemic systems of each of these languages. But up to now the adoption of the notion of phonemic level would have resulted only in a simplifica-tion of some traditionally well-known problems. Much more important is the notion of distributional analysis.

The distinctive sounds of a language occur in characteristic sequences. For instance, in English, the sound /ž/ as in *measure* never occurs at the beginning of words. Thus the elementary student of French will probably pronounce *j'ai* as [dže] instead of [že]. As in the case of the sounds themselves, the sound sequences are very limited in number for each language. To quote Fries (1947):

> Of the more than a hundred consonant clusters in English, only /st/, /sp/, and /sk/ occur in both initial and final positions. The facts have practical significance. It's easy for me to pronounce sounds in characteristic sequences in which they occur in my language; it's difficult for me to pronounce them in sequences which do not occur in the pattern of my language.

These distributional problems may involve consonant, vowel, and stress order. Among characteristic examples is the problem of initial clusters like *ps, pn,* which do not exist in word initial position in English but are found in French in words like p*sychologie* and pn*eumatique.*

A still more typical case is that of the distribution of American-English unvoiced stops *p, t, k.* The distribution of *t* is particularly inter-esting. In most American-English dialects, it is represented as follows:

INITIAL	MEDIAL				FINAL
aspirated [t']	voiced flap [ḍ]	aspirated [t']	nonaspirated [t]		unreleased [t-]
t + vowel	accented vowel	*t* + accented	*s* + *t*		-*t*
*t*ool	+ *t* + vowel	vowel	s*t*ool		se*t*
	wà*t*er	a*tt*ention			

The phoneme /t/ has here several different phonetic variants (allophones), each occurring in a characteristic and generally predictable position. It is highly probable that in speaking a foreign language, an American-English student will transfer such habits to the target language. Some of them will result only in phonetic mistakes, like the aspiration of *t* in French or Spanish, but others, like the nonrelease of *t* in final position, will result in a sound that is hard for a Frenchman to perceive since in French final stop-consonants are strongly released in that position. The voicing of [t] (i.e., the use of [d̆]) will lead to dangerous mistakes if transferred to German, Spanish, or French. For these languages, in cases similar to *water,* there are phonemic oppositions between /t/ and /d/:

> leiter/leider
> bota/boda
> bateau/badaut

American-English speakers who consistently distinguish between such minimal pairs as *latter* and *ladder* by opposing an unvoiced flap [t̆] to a voiced flap [d] would still risk confusing the German, Spanish, and French pairs since speakers of these languages do not have flaps and would hear both [t̆] and [d̆] as the same sound.

The sounds [s] and [z] occur in English as well as in French, German, or Spanish. But in Spanish [z] is only an allophone of /s/ occurring before voiced consonants, as in *mismo* [mizmo]. [s] and [z] contrast in German in pairs like *lassen* versus *lasen,* and two phonemes /s/ and /z/ must be posited; but in initial position only [z] occurs (e.g., *sein*), and in final position only [s] occurs (e.g., *wass*). In many American-English dialects [s] and [z] alternate in words like *greasy* and *citizen,* and /s/ followed by /j/ is frequently heard as [š] in sequences like *this year*. Hence sequences like /sj/ and /šj/ which are contrasted in French (*c'est le sien* /sj/ versus *c'est le chien* /šj/) are likely to be confused by American-English speakers. The same confusion will occur with /zj/, a sequence which does not exist in English and which is likely to be pronounced /ž/ as in *vision*.

A typical case showing the importance of distributional facts is that of a vowel preceded by a nasal consonant in American English. Such a vowel tends to be nasalized particularly when followed by a nasal consonant, e.g., *ham, dim,* and *song.* To hear this nasalization more clearly let us contrast, for instance, pairs like *hat/ham* or *dip/dim.* Nasal vowels have no linguistic function in English, for they are generally predictable. Transferred to French, this American-English habit will be very dangerous since in a lot of cases it will obliterate contrasts like *Jeanne/Jean* or *Cannes/Caen;* but transferred to German and, particularly, to Spanish it will not affect oral comprehension. In fact, the same phenomenon occurs very often in Spanish words like *corazón.*

Another effect of distribution can be observed with variations in vowel duration. After a strong consonant, such as the unvoiced stop /p t k/, vowels tend to become shorter in English as well as in Spanish, French, and German. These variations in duration are phonetic and must not be confused with distinctive phonemic length, which is found in English and German vowels but not in Spanish or French (except for a very few words). In German, vowel duration is fully integrated with the system of vowel color. All short vowels are open, and all long vowels are closed in such oppositions as *bitte/biete*. A parallel organization exists in English in such oppositions as *bit/beat*, but as noted by Delattre (1962), in English distinctive duration is much less fully integrated in the system.

Thus far we have considered only the first rank of units of the phonic substance, the phonemes and their distribution according to habits particular to each individual language. The second rank in the hierarchy of the phonic substance is that of the syllable. The syllable has no functional value in itself, except in rather exceptional cases in German and in English where syllable boundaries may have such value. It is a question of different junctures, as in the well-known examples *night + rate/Nye + trait/nitrate* and *a + nice man/an + iceman*. In rapid speech these oppositions tend to disappear.

The third rank of units that we find in the hierarchy of the phonic substance is that of word groups. Word groups are delimited by *accents* which have, according to Martinet's definition (1964), a culminative function: they allow us to recognize larger units of meaning in the succession of syllables. As stated by Martinet, "The accent serves to denote the presence in the utterance of a certain number of articulations and thus facilitates the analysis of the message." Thus, in the English sentence *the dóctor is a súrgeon,* our ear becomes capable of identifying two essential peaks which help us to decode the entire message. We find that in most languages accent has a delimitative value; but if we look closer, we shall discover that from one language to another the value of the accent may vary a great deal according to its position, distribution, and occurrence. There are few languages, as is the case with French, in which the position of accent is unvariable and consequently has no phonemic value. On the contrary, in English pres*ent* (noun) is opposed to *pr*esent (verb), in Spanish término ("terminal point") is opposed to *termino* ("I finish") and to *terminó* ("he finished"), and in German unt*erhalten* ("to hold under") is opposed to unt*er*halt*en* ("to keep up").

The second problem concerning accents results from their distribution and nature as elements of rhythm. From recent studies, it appears that energy and breath tend to be distributed in equal amounts. They are called *quanta* and may correspond to a universal pattern of the human physiological system. Catford (1963) made a very clear demonstration of their distribution in English and French, by stating that the two languages have the same rhythmic regularity but differ from each other in respect to the rank of unit in which this regularity is shown. In French, the syllable is the unit which carries the rhythmic regularity. In English, on the contrary, syllables carry duration and demand a highly variable output of energy. Rhythmic regularity in English is represented at a rank superior to that of the syllable, i.e., at the rank of the rhythmical group.

Fries (1947), following Pike (1947), gives a good example of this phenomenon in using the sentences:

The doctor is a surgeon.
The doctor is a good surgeon.
The doctor is a very good surgeon.

It is claimed that the total length and energy stay the same in all three sentences. (In fact, there is no perfect isochronism from one group of words to another: they only tend to be equal.) The same could probably be said of German, but in Spanish and French the rhythm is provided by syllabic regularity. English and German are stress-timed, staccato languages, and French, like Spanish, Japanese, Hindi, and others, is a syllable-timed language.

But even in the case of German, there is still a problem: English and German words do not always have the same rhythmic pattern. Thus, for an Anglo-American student of French, Spanish, or German, the problem is the same in the long run. If the accent is not in the right position and if, as in English, unaccented vowels are more or less dropped, total misunderstanding will result. An American-English student will tend to pronounce foreign words of three syllables with the English rhythmic pattern of a word such as *excellent* (——— • —). This linguistic transfer would create such errors as *semna instead of semana in Spanish, *abtur instead of Abitur in German, and resté instead of réciter in French.

The fourth rank of units in the organization of the phonic substance is that of sentence intonation. At this rank, and provided that the segmental elements are not distorted, there does not seem to be any dangerous phonemic interference from English in any of the three other languages, French, Spanish, and German. A question will always be understood as such in English as well as in German, French, or Spanish. The same holds true for sentences expressing a statement, an order, and so on. The intonation of the group, however, can be falling in American English even if continuation is indicated. On the contrary, in German, French, and Spanish, the continuity pattern is always rising, and this difference may lead to miscomprehension.

A language must be conceived as a system of oral sounds, and learning grammar consists of mastering the functional value of sounds. The phonemic concept thus provides students with motivation for pronunciation drill and helps teachers to establish a list of priorities among phonetic problems. But the phonemic level must be understood only as a first linguistic approach to pronunciation habits. These habits need to be perfected at a more advanced level, that of phonetic detail. It is useless to say that no occasion for perfecting our students' accents should be neglected. But we cannot hope to correct everything at once, and the distinction between phonemics and phonetics enables us better to evaluate student progress, avoiding at the same time the separation of the grammatical and the sound systems of the language.

PHONETIC PROBLEMS AND TECHNIQUES OF CORRECTION

After problems of the phonemic level have been mastered, phonetic difficulties must be carefully studied. In this area, techniques of correction and learning methods have been improved. Classical remedial phonetics used to study sound in isolation, but a new approach, originated primarily by Pierre Delattre (1946), showed the advantage of studying *general features* of the phonic substance. Thus it would not be logical to correct a diphthongized *o* in an American-English pronunciation of the French word *eau* without starting at the same time to form a general habit of muscular tension which would apply to all similar cases. Here, as at the phonemic level, areas of interference can be predicted by comparing the mother tongue and the target language.

For pedagogical purposes general features can be classified in a few categories (P. Léon & M. Léon, 1964): articulation, syllabification, accentuation, rhythm, and intonation habits. Delattre (1962) established a detailed systematic comparison of the general phonetic features of English, Spanish, German, and French. Our purpose will be only to give some characteristic examples, along with different correction techniques which are essentially articulatory, auditory, and linguistic.

ARTICULATORY HABITS AND METHODS OF CORRECTION One of the most striking features of English pronunciation is its tendency to diphthongize vowels. Hence, special exercises can be established to prevent interference in the target language. What is, then, the best procedure for forming a nondiphthongizing habit? In response to this question, Delattre (1962) gives the following advice:

1.   Take the articulatory position of the vowel before starting it.

2.   Tense the muscles of the articulatory organs (lips, tongue, etc.).

3.   Keep the organs of speech immobile in the open position of the vowel until the vowel has been articulated.

4.   Begin the vowel progressively, not abruptly as in English, with the minimum required effort, and try to increase the effort, the tension, and the loudness to the end of the vowel.

He finally adds: "Test each one of those four methods in turn and determine the ones which give the best result to you. The last one is the most important, the most difficult to apply." We have here an excellent example of what we might call an articulatory technique of correction. We can also advise the student to look at his jaw in the mirror while articulating a sound such as /e/. He will see the movement of the jaw in English as compared with the relative lack of motion in French, Spanish, or German. Except in a few cases, the articulatory technique, of course, does not always work immediately. Even with no visible movement at all, the sound uttered by an American student may always be diphthongized if *he is not given help in hearing the difference between the glided English sound and the pure one to be acquired in the target language.* The most important control is probably auditory. Many agree with the fact, noted by Pimsleur (1959), that hearing a sound is certainly the first step in learning to imitate it. But learning to hear foreign sounds correctly is a difficult task. We hear what we are accustomed to hear in our own language. From this point of view the human ear has often been compared to a filter which blocks out all unknown sounds. To teach the student to hear a foreign language sound the way the native speaker of the language perceives it, it would be helpful to use the following auditory technique: all new sounds are contrasted first with the closest equivalent sound of the mother tongue. Then the new sound is contrasted with another, already-known sound of the target language.

The first type of contrast, for instance, might oppose American English [ei] of *day* to the French [e] of *des,* the Spanish [e] of *pide,* or the German [e] of *Schnade.* The second type of contrast would oppose in French, for example, *les, le,* and *l'eau;* not only do these words belong to the same acoustic series (same first formant) but they also have an important differentiating function.

The first part of this technique has been developed by Varney-Pleasants in her *Phonetic French Dictionary* (1959). The second part has been used extensively by the authors of the Belasco *Manual and Anthology of Applied Linguistics* (1960). It must be noted that the technique of contrasting approximately identical utterances of two different languages is not reliable for testing students' ability to discriminate. For example, Valdman et al. (1964) contrast:

FRENCH	ENGLISH
sonne	sun
code	cud
mode	mud
note	nut
bonne	bun
cotte	cut

The student not only has one vowel to compare with another but also many other acoustic cues which will enable him quickly to recognize the English word, even if he is perfectly unable to analyze the differences between the two vowels. The procedure constitutes an excellent teaching device but is a poor testing technique.

The third corrective technique, which we call *linguistic,* is based on the use of all allophonic or sporadic variants of the mother tongue phonemes which will be transferred intentionally to the target language. For instance, teaching the sound sequence [ɛr] in the French word *serre* or in the Spanish word *ser* to English learners will be better achieved if it is first presented as [sɛ] and if [R] and [r] are added as a kind of second syllable. Otherwise, the /e/ will tend to be diphthongized as in *bear.* Another example of this technique may be given by showing how to correct the substitution of French final /ɑj/ and /ɛj/ in words like *paille* and *soleil* by American-English [aɪ] and [eɪ]. The [j] sound occurs in English but only in initial position. Once shown that this [j] is the same as the first sound of *yes* and that he needs only to learn to produce it in a new position, the American learner should have little difficulty. To guide him to the production of final [j] (as in *paille*) the student should be made to repeat /a/ in the first syllable followed immediately by *yes* [a/jəs]. By eliminating [s] he would get [ajə] and then, by reducing the final [jə] to a small release, French /j/. The linguistic technique of correction is based on the principle that languages belonging to the same family have many points of phonic substance in common. The division of this substance and its distribution may not be the same and the phonetic manifestation may be slightly different, but it is very often a question of small articulatory and auditory adjustments.

Among other general features of articulation which characterize American English is the abrupt onset of vowels, e.g., *at eight.* This phonic habit, called *glottalization,* is caused by an abrupt contraction of the vocal cords, as when one is about to cough. It has to be corrected if it is transferred to French and Spanish, whose vowels start gradually. This correction can easily be achieved by means of the articulation technique if we ask American students to begin vowels with a slight breath, since *aspiration* is the laryngeal articulation most directly opposed to the glottal stop; conversely, when correcting the aspiration of consonants, we may use in its place the glottal stop as an excellent correction device. Aspiration can be eliminated from the French /t/ of *athée,* for instance, by requiring the student to pronounce the /e/ with a preceding glottal stop, as in English *at eight.* Here the linguistic remedial approach should also be used. It can be shown that after *s,* in words like *spike, stool, school,* /p/, /t/, and /k/ are not aspirated. This can be contrasted in words like *pike/spike, tool/stool, cool/school.* Naturally, the auditory technique must always be used in conjunction with the others. In the same manner, interference from other typical articulatory habits of English speakers, such as the absence of release after final consonants and the centralization of vowels, could be checked.

Syllabification habits have to be corrected early. We know that, as in German, about 60 percent of English syllables end in a consonant. In contrast, more than 70 percent of French and Spanish syllables end in a vowel. A consequence of closed syllabification is the nasalization of vowels that are followed by a final nasal consonant. An American student will tend to transfer this habit to the target language. We have seen that this transfer will have little undesirable effect in Spanish or German, which do not oppose oral and nasal vowels, but in French the mistake must be avoided. A good technique is to contrast oral and nasal vowels in pairs like *hat/ham* or *sit/sin.* Then contrasts will have to be drilled in French minimal pairs like *fade/fane.* We may write these words on the blackboard as follows:

Then we ask the students to think of *fade* and to utter a very long /a/ and pronounce the /d/ only when we point to it. From time to time we change direction rapidly and point to the /n/ so that a nonnasalized /a/ is retained despite the presence of final /n/ in *fane.* But sometimes the nasalization habit is so strongly embedded that the mere fact of thinking of the nasal consonant will affect the pronunciation of the oral vowel. Such mistakes are attributable to orthographic factors, but most of the time they are purely a matter of linguistic transfer: for an American-English listener nasal vowels occur in the immediate vicinity of a nasal consonant.

From the point of view of rhythm, English, as we have seen, is characterized by an almost unpredictable alternation of long and short syllables. Rhythm is closely related to stress in English and in German. Unaccented vowels may disappear almost completely, as, for example, in English *geography* or *excellent* and German *guten* or *gegen*. In Spanish and French, rhythm will have to be learned at the syllabic level. An American student can easily be given the sense of syllabic rhythm by showing him that such a rhythm does exist in English when the group is reduced to the syllabic unit, for example, when saying the alphabet, A B C D . . . . , or when counting digits of one syllable, 1 2 3 4 5 6, and so on. These rhythmic patterns are then associated with corresponding patterns in French and Spanish. For instance,

> 1 2 3/ j'ai fini
> 1 2 3/ j'ai mangé
> 1 2 3/ j'ai couru
> 1 2 3/ no lo se
> 1 2 3/ te le doy

Concerning intonation, we know that in English and German accented vowels are longer, louder, and higher than other vowels of the same word, whereas loudness is much less important in Spanish and in French accentuation. One of the most striking features of American English is its intonation contour after the accented vowel. As English words are almost never accented on the last syllable, English intonation contains the general form of a falling wave. This acoustic impression is reinforced by the fact that words tend to be said on an unstable diphthongized note. Neither German, Spanish, nor French exhibits this intonation contour. In these languages the syllabic intonation is stable: each syllable is uttered on the same equal note, and the final group contour depends much more heavily on its function than in English. For instance, continuation is always marked by rising intonation; this is rather unusual in English, in which finality and continuity intonation patterns are nearly identical. In contrast, as shown by Delattre (1962), these two intonation patterns differ markedly in German, Spanish, and French. In the correction of intonation errors, it is evident that the auditory technique is the best one. Visual representation of pitch contours, however, is generally helpful. As paradoxical as it may seem, it is probably more useful to draw diagrams when teaching intonation than when teaching articulation.

The few examples which we have studied here show that careful contrastive studies are necessary before starting phonetic correction. Once mistakes have been predicted, they become easier to correct.

THE LEARNING PROCESS   Will students be able to learn pronunciation by themselves? If we are to believe the authors of many commercial materials and even an official booklet on the language laboratory: "By repeating the fine speech on the tape they unconsciously learn accent, pronunciation and intonation." With a few exceptions, however, most people do not completely lose their accent in a second language no matter how much effort they expend on the task. Consequently, it does not seem highly probable that merely by listening "unconsciously," even to very "fine" speech, will students acquire accurate pronunciation. Only children possess, to a great extent, the ability to imitate; adults are much less receptive, for their habits are too strongly imprinted in their minds. From this point of view, a human mind is already adult at early adolescence. Then, if left alone in a language laboratory, what can we expect from our adult students? Pimsleur (1959) states: "A student working alone can be expected to correct certain gross errors, that is, by listening to his speech and to the model." In this category we may include errors which correspond more or less closely to phonemic distinctions in the student's native tongue and features of stress and intonation. For example, he may learn by himself that the combination *oi* in French is pronounced /wa/, that in Spanish one says *teléfono,* and that a change of intonation suffices to change an Italian statement into a question. Since beginners will hear new sounds in terms of their own phonetic habits, our first task is to teach them to hear correctly in the new language. Theoretically this could be done with the aid of a programmed course in the language laboratory as well as in the classroom. Many things can be taught by a programmed course (Valdman, 1964), but as long as we are not able to have correcting machines capable of providing a visual display of phonetic errors (P. Léon, 1962), it will never be possible to rely entirely on the student's ability to judge his own pronunciation.

Thus, under present teaching conditions it seems more efficient to reserve the classroom for the traditional role of explanation and control and the laboratory for drill on the material previously presented by the teacher. During the class hour, the time devoted to pronunciation is to be determined by the student's needs. The essential thing is probably to create a phonetic awareness. Once a mistake has been pointed out, it must be indicated each time it appears again. But one must not try to correct everything at the same time. Let us repeat that the most important mistakes must be corrected first and that one difficulty a day probably will be enough, at least at the beginning. Teachers should also avoid drilling on the same phonetic problem for a long time; phonetic exercises must be short and intensive to be efficient. The phonetics class should start with a review of the preceding lesson; then the teacher should check that all students have completely understood the difficulty corrected in the classroom and drilled in the language laboratory period. A complete phonetic lesson should be divided as follows:

1. Presentation of the sound or general features to be drilled
2. Identification of this new sound or feature
3. Production and correction
4. Fixation

A new sound or a new general feature should be presented with a minimum of technical explanation. We have said that imitation itself will rarely succeed immediately, and most adult students want to understand what they are asked to imitate; several types of explanation could be used to this end. These explanations will be based on the same elements as the techniques of correction discussed above: articulatory, auditory, and linguistic. Articulatory diagrams might be particularly useful for the representation of consonantal articulations, but they would not be of great help when teaching vowels even if the point of articulation could be accurately represented.

The identification of new sounds must be checked by the well-known technique of "true or false." Checking must be rapid and at first should be done as a group activity. When possible, a choice among three alternatives is better than among two alternatives. For the production of sounds students are asked to repeat together, after the teacher, all the different oppositions. Group repetition frees students of inhibition and is preferable to individual repetition for work on rhythm or intonation. A trained teacher will recognize very easily where and by whom a mistake has been made. Of course, individual checking must be made as often as possible, but in a phonetics class all students must speak and repeat as many times as possible, and it would be very inefficient to spend much time in correcting a few students while leaving the others to await their turn. A good phonetics teacher elicits rapidly; since very good results are rarely obtained the first time, it is useless and psychologically unsound to drill on the same difficulty for a long period of time. Corrective phonetics is a cumulative process; it is a matter of practice and patience. Fixation of new sounds and features as habits is the last step.

A sound very rarely occurs in isolation. Vowels, however, can be isolated for analytical purposes, although they should never be taught extensively out of context. This is even more important in the case of consonants, which, as their name indicates, are sounds that accompany something else. For maximum fixation, it seems that vowels and consonants must be drilled not only in minimal pairs but also in short and useful sentences. Learning in minimal pairs useful ordinary sentences leads generally to good motivation. Some handbooks are based on this idea, but others prefer, on the contrary, to present the same difficulty many times in the same sentence, e.g., *Mimi a mis ses amis à Miami* or *rápido corren los ferrocarriles.* Such sentences may seem odd, hard, and of little practical use. They are sometimes amusing, however, and for this reason can be useful for memorization (Haac, 1960).

The order of presentation of material is a problem related to the psychology of learning as well as to linguistics—perhaps the linguistic point of view has been too much emphasized here. Theoretically, the ideal progression would start at the phonemic level exclusively, taking into account statistical indices of functional load and proceeding to the phonetic level only when all obstacles to audiolingual comprehension have been overcome. In contrast, according to Delattre's method (1946) all oral phonetic habits should first be mastered gradually. Valdman et al. (1964) also decided to present sound features gradually, postponing difficult sounds "until fundamental speech habits have been acquired." Both textbooks introduce meaning from the beginning. Morton (1960), however, chooses to teach sounds without any reference to meaning, but this within the context of a laboratory situation only. As Hockett put it (1950), "In theory it would be fine if we could first learn everything about pronunciation of a new language—master all the habits—and then go on actually to talk it. In practice, the first step would be so dull that all motivation would be annuled." When presenting new material, one must remember that of the two aspects of learning pronunciation, perception and production, the most difficult skill to acquire is probably a nativelike audiocomprehension. How this skill is acquired is still poorly understood, but it seems that we perceive first the general shape of the sentence (on the syntagmatic axis), making in case of "noise" the necessary corrections (on the paradigmatic axis). In fact, "Any act of perception is intimately tied up with the perceiver's background, i.e. his previous experiences, his memory, and his attitudes" (Malmberg, 1963b). This means that our students will be able to hear correctly, to understand perfectly, only when they will have mastered all the structure of the language! It could be said that we can hear if we already know what is likely to be said. This is still confirmed by Homer Jacobson, as quoted by Malmberg (1963b). Audiocomprehension should be taught by first training students to understand complete sentences, or at least groups of words, and then by using minimal pairs in order to train their ears to perceive important acoustical cues. Pattern drills of the substitution type would probably be the best way of achieving this goal. For instance, in French we might present sentences of similar structure like:

Ma mère m'a apporté du café.

_____ donné _____.

Mon frère _____.

_____ du thé.

etc. . . .

In this kind of exercise, the student is trained to perceive the general acoustic frame of the sentence and prepared to fill any slot with meaningful sounds of his previous experience. Since such exercises must be drilled intensively, the language laboratory becomes an indispensable tool in the teaching and testing of accurate pronunciation.

When students have mastered the phonetic difficulties of what has been considered here as the second level of instruction, they are ready for a third step: "phonostylistics," the study of phonic expressive means (P. Léon, 1962). At this last stage of instruction students will be taught to identify and eventually to imitate variations which make up an accent, belong to personality, or form a style. Studying these variations from standard speech will make students more conscious of linguistic reality. It will also be a good introduction to the study of stylistics in the written language, which uses as its main source the spoken language.

REFERENCES

Belasco, Simon. *Manual and anthology of applied linguistics.* U.S. Office of Education, 1960.

Bloomfield, Leonard. *Outline guide for the practical study of foreign languages.* Baltimore: Linguistic Society of America, 1942.

Bowen, Donald J., and Robert P. Stockwell. *Patterns of Spanish pronunciation.* Chicago: The University of Chicago Press, 1960.

Cárdenas, Daniel N. *Introducción a una comparación fonológica, del español y del inglès.* Washington, D.C.: Center for Applied Linguistics, 1961.

Catford, J. C. Langue maternelle et seconde langue. *Le français dans le monde,* 1963, **17,** 8–11.

Delattre, Pierre. *Principes de prononciation française à l'usage des étudiants anglo-américains.* Middlebury, Vt.: Vermont Books, 1946.

Delattre, Pierre. Un cours d'exercices structuraux et de linguistique appliquée. *French Review,* 1960, **33,** 591–603.

Delattre, Pierre. *The general phonetic characteristics of languages.*

Unpublished report. U.S. Office of Education, Language Development Branch, 1962.

Fouché, Pierre. *Phonétique historique du français: Introduction.* Paris: Klincksieck, 1952.

Fries, Charles C. *An intensive course in English for Latin American students.* Ann Arbor, Mich.: The University of Michigan Press, English Language Institute, 1947. 8 vols.

Grammont, Maurice. *Traité de prononciation française.* (1st ed.) Paris: Delagrave, 1934.

Haac, Oscar. Comments on methods and techniques. In Felix J. Oinas (Ed.), *Language teaching today.* Indiana University Research Center in Anthropology, Folklore, and Linguistics Publication No. 14. (Published as *International Journal of American Linguistics,* 1960, **26,** No. 2, Part I.)

Hockett, C. F. Learning pronunciation. *Modern Language Journal,* 1950, **34,** 261–269.

Jones, Daniel. *The pronunciation of English.* (Rev. ed.) London: Cambridge University Press, 1937.

Lado, Robert L. *Linguistics across cultures.* Ann Arbor, Mich.: The University of Michigan Press, 1957.

Léon, Monique. *Exercices systématiques de prononciation française.* Fascicule I, *Articulation.* Fascicule II, *Rythme et intonation.* Paris: Hachette/Larousse, 1964.

Léon, Pierre. *Laboratoire de langues et correction phonétique.* Paris: Didier, 1962.

Léon, Pierre, and Monique Léon. *Introduction à la phonétique corrective.* Paris: Librairie Hachette, 1964.

Malmberg, Bertil. *Phonetics.* New York: Dover Publications, Inc., 1963. (a)

Malmberg, Bertil. *Structural linguistics and human communication.* New York: Academic Press, Inc., 1963. (b)

Martinet, André. *Elements of general linguistics.* Cambridge, England: W. Heffer & Sons, Ltd., 1964.

Meyer-Eppler, W. In A. Moles and B. Valencien (Eds.), *Communication et langages.* Paris: Cauthier-Villars, 1963.

Morton, F. Rand. The language laboratory as a teaching machine. In Felix J. Oinas (Ed.), *Language teaching today.* Indiana University Research Center in Anthropology, Folklore, and Linguistics Publication No. 14. (Published as *International Journal of American Linguistics,* 1960, **26,** No. 2, Part I.)

Navarro Tomás, T. *Manual de pronunciación española.* (4th ed., rev.) Madrid: R. F. E., 1932.

Passy, Paul Edouard. *Petite phonétique comparée des principales langues européenes.* Leipzig: B. G. Teubner Verlagsgesellschaft, mbH, 1906.

Pike, Kenneth L. *Phonetics.* Ann Arbor, Mich.: The University of Michigan Press, 1947.

Pimsleur, Paul. The functions of the language laboratory. *Modern Language Journal,* 1959, **43,** 11–15.

Politzer, Robert L. Phonetics and pronunciation theory. *Applied Linguistics in Language Teaching,* 1954, **6,** 19–27.

Ripman, W. *Elements of phonetics: English, French and German.* London: J. W. Dew and Sons, Ltd., 1889.

Trager, George L., and Henry L. Smith. *An outline of English structure.* Norman, Okla.: University of Oklahoma Press, 1951.

Valdman, Albert. *Applied linguistics—French: A guide for teachers.* (Ed. S. Belasco) Boston: D. C. Heath and Company, 1961.

Valdman, Albert. Toward a redefinition of teacher role and teaching context in foreign language instruction. *Modern Language Journal,* 1964, **48,** 277.

Valdman, Albert, et al. *Drillbook of French pronunciation.* New York: Harper & Row, Publishers, Incorporated, 1964.

Varney-Pleasants, Jeanne V. *Phonetic French dictionary.* New York: Goldsmith Music Center, 1959.

5

APPLIED LINGUISTICS AND GENERATIVE GRAMMAR

SOL SAPORTA

Sol Saporta (1925–   ) received his undergraduate degree from Brooklyn College and his graduate degrees from the University of Illinois, under Prof. Henry Kahane. He taught at Indiana University and is currently professor of linguistics and Romance languages at the University of Washington. He was a fellow at the Center for Advanced Study in the Behavioral Sciences and in 1965 delivered the State of Oregon Condon Lectures. His publications reflect his interest in Spanish linguistics, linguistic theory, and psycholinguistics.

A central question in the application of linguistics to the teaching of foreign languages involves the conversion of a scientific grammar into a pedagogical grammar. What form the pedagogical grammar takes, whether drills or rules or some combination of the two, is presumably determined by some assumptions about the nature of learning in general, that is, by principles which are not primarily linguistic. On the other hand, the content of the grammar, that is, a specification of what it is that is to be learned, is narrowly linguistic.

Now, in principle, the strategy for improving pedagogical grammars might involve starting from either direction. One could take a pedagogical grammar which is known to be only partially adequate and, given a comprehensive learning theory, perform whatever operations of segmentation, recombination, and reordering that might be necessary to effect maximally efficient learning of essentially the same material. Or one could take the same partially adequate grammar and refine the linguistic description of the relevant data, leading, it would be hoped, to a closer approximation of the desired terminal behavior. Thus, a textbook writer who decides that examples should precede rather than follow statement of the rule is following the first strategy, based in this case on the assumed superiority of "inductive" learning; but a textbook writer who treats *he is easy to please* as representing a different construction from *he is eager to please* is providing a description which more accurately reflects the data and is therefore following the second strategy. Obviously, the two are not mutually exclusive.

Strangely enough, the impact of the descriptive linguistics of the forties and fifties on language teaching was primarily on the form and only incidentally on the content of pedagogical grammars. I think it is not unfair to say that with the possible exception of such features as stress and intonation—perhaps phonology in general—linguists by and large had little to say about the nature of the major languages that were being taught and somewhat more to say about how they were to be taught; with authentic models, initially via speech and subsequently via writing, through repetition, memorization, and manipulation of illustrative sentences, etc. In short, the influence of linguists was more on the goals and methods of language instruction than on the elucidation of the pertinent linguistic facts. Unfortunately, however, in keeping with the narrowly behavioristic tenor of the times, the learning theory which has served as the basis for the pronouncements about method has been the most inflexible form of stimulus-response formulation, which has suggested to language teachers that the probability of acquiring the unconscious control of a set of grammatical rules is merely a function of the frequency and reinforcement associated with sentences illustrating the rules.

Recent studies in generative grammar have had two consequences of some relevance in this connection. First, they have made explicit the kind of capacities a language learner must have if he is even to approximate the competence of a native speaker, capacities such as the ability to distinguish grammatical from ungrammatical sentences and to produce and comprehend an infinite number of the former, the ability to identify syntactically ambiguous sentences and more generally the interrelation of sentences, etc. Second, although a careful examination of these capacities does not necessarily provide an answer as to how they are acquired, it makes it clear that there are certain ways in which they are unlikely to be acquired. Specifically, it cannot be the case that learning a language merely involves successively closer approximations to the linguistic performance of some model, since this latter performance includes slips, mistakes, false starts, and a variety of nongrammatical behavior, which the competent speaker is able to identify as such, and, more important, the corpus to which the learner is exposed is nothing more than some small sample of the linguistic universe of grammatical sentences which ultimately characterize his competence.

One distinction in the aims of a pedagogical grammar and a scientific grammar must be made clear. A scientific grammar enumerates the grammatical sentences of a language and provides each with a structural description and a semantic interpretation. The pedagogical grammar ideally attempts to develop the native speaker's ability to recognize and produce sentences. That is, a speaker can accept an arbitrarily selected sequence of elements in his vocabulary, determine whether or not it is a sentence in his language, and, if so, assign to it its correct structural description and semantic interpretation. It is difficult even to formulate the analogous problem of speech production; yet clearly the speaker's capacities include the ability to integrate situationally appropriate verbalizations. An enumeration of the grammatical sentences, therefore, is considerably short of a sentence recognizer, for example, and it is fair to say that we are far from understanding the latter operation.

In this connection, the traditional translation grammar provided an explicit formulation of the relevant pedagogical aim by assuming that the semantic interpretation could be precisely specified by a sentence in the learner's native language. The recent tendency to distinguish translation from the skills a native speaker controls has been a healthy one, but the vague suggestion that the meaning of sentences is somehow derivable from observation of the situations in which they occur is quixotic and cannot be seriously considered as an alternative method for systematically providing the relevant semantic information. Indeed, such a proposal in effect precludes the possibility of understanding new utterances at all and hence fails by definition. One cannot help but conclude that the speaker's ability to provide a semantic interpretation for a novel sentence must somehow be related to his knowledge of the meaning of the constituent elements. This is not to imply that the meaning of sentences is derivable by a simple "additive" process, but the implication that it is not derivable at all is an extreme case of confusing baby and bath water. The problem may be viewed as one of specifying the metalanguage in which the semantic information is to be framed. The traditional language teacher chose the most obvious candidate for such a metalanguage, namely, the speaker's native language. The disadvantages are obvious, but little is gained by legislating the problem out of existence.

We find, then, that the traditional grammarians more closely approached the aims of language teaching by attempting to match a speaker's ability to understand and produce arbitrarily selected novel sentences. Their pedagogical failure was in the assumption that such abilities could be taught by the conscious application of the relevant abstract formulations. Applied linguists have noticed the irrelevance and, at times, the interference of verbalizing such formulations, and some have incorrectly assumed that the appropriate abilities could be achieved solely by judicious performance of carefully selected and ordered examples. Others have been willing to modify the latter procedure to include formulations of some unspecified sort of some syntactic and semantic information. They have, however, failed to make explicit the form, content, and alleged pedagogical function of such formulations, and until they do, the corresponding claims are difficult to evaluate.

Before examining the more concrete proposals which might be made regarding second language learning as a result of recent studies in transformational grammar, it may be appropriate to question the validity of some of the suggestions which linguists in general have made. My impression about these claims is that linguists by and large have generated more heat than light or at least have promised more than they have delivered.

The basis of all language teaching which pays even the most superficial lip service to linguistics is the primacy of speech over writing. This linguistic fact has been utilized in two ways. Some have converted it into an educational goal, claiming that if one is obliged to reduce one's aims, then concentration on speaking is more fruitful than concentration on reading. Others, unwilling seriously to alter their aims, nevertheless maintain that listening and speaking should be taught first, reading and writing next. The arguments which have been proposed for this position are essentially the following: (1) It reflects the way children learn their native language. (2) Writing is only an imperfect representation of speech; the former includes all the relevant distinctions, such as stress and intonation in English, whereas these are only unsystematically represented in writing. (3) The transfer in learning from the spoken to the written form is greater than the reverse.

The first of these arguments is largely irrelevant. It merely demonstrates that speaking before writing is the necessary order in first language learning, not that it is the only order nor even the more efficient in second language learning. Parenthetically, it may be instructive to reexamine in this connection the procedure by which a child acquires his native language; the argument that one might facilitate second language acquisition by reproducing in part the first language situation might backfire if, as seems reasonable, a native language cannot, in a sense, be taught at all. Evidence such as the fact that children exposed to rather different samples of a given language develop very similar linguistic capacities suggests that children are not taught their language but that rather one could not prevent a normal child from acquiring the language of his environment. What makes second language learning a problem is the fact that whatever ability, presumably innate, that the child has which permits him to perform this feat is apparently lost as he matures.

The second argument given above for teaching speaking before writing is partly an oversimplification. Writing systems are not always less explicit in marking relevant information; occasionally they include information even when it is absent in the acoustic signal. Let us consider, for example, the capitalization of German nouns or the use and position of grammatical markings like the apostrophe in *boys, boy's,* and *boys'*. More important, however, whatever relevance the second argument has is largely as a basis for the third; that is, it is assumed that if one form of the language makes a distinction which the other does not, it is more efficient to start with the more differentiated and proceed to the less differentiated rather than the reverse.

But when phrased in this way, a number of characteristics of the written form of a language like English emerge. Given the variety of morphophonemic alternations which can be provided by general rule, it seems quite appropriate to have different representations for the final phonological segments of *sum* and *condemn* in view of the corresponding nouns *summation* and *condemnation*. Similarly, there is nothing the matter with the orthography of forms like *electric, electricity,* or *democrat, democratic, democracy* since they enable the derivation of the correct pronunciation by general rules. On the other hand, the derivation of the orthographic representation of the unstressed vowels would be a task of some magnitude. Analogously the oft-cited French adjectives like *petit* and *gris* and German forms like *rund* and *bunt* maintain morphophonemic distinctions not present in the spoken form except, of course, in the related forms *petite, grise* and *runde, bunte.*

In any case, no matter how reasonable the assumption may be about speaking facilitating writing more than the reverse, the evidence seems to be largely anecdotal, coming from generations of language students who found little transferability from writing to speech. The attempts to demonstrate the validity of such an assumption have been inconclusive.[1] But quite apart from the validity of the position, it is not clear that it qualifies as a narrowly linguistic principle. In making such claims, linguists have argued as much as educators or psychologists as they have as linguists.

A second concern in applying linguistic notions to language teaching is the presentation and function of grammatical rules. What is unfortunately referred to by some as "the linguistic method" is usually characterized by basic conversational sentences for memorization, pattern-practice exercises, and grammar by induction. It is not obvious how any of these notions follow directly from any adequate theory of linguistic structure or, for that matter, from any but the most superficial learning theory. It seems clear that having somehow stored a very large number of sentences cannot be equated with having learned a language. It may be argued that no language teacher, no matter how linguistically unsophisticated, suggests that such an equation is valid. One cannot help but conclude, however, that certain methods and, indeed, precisely those methods most closely associated with linguistics do demand a considerable amount of such storage, in spite of the fact that a method which requires maximization of storage is self-defeating. This, then, is the incongruity in the alleged role of memorization as a technique for learning. The student who makes the most progress by adopting rote memory as a strategy will presumably be the most reluctant to abandon it, and failure to abandon it means failure to learn a language. One is led then to the paradox of second language learning. Language is rule-governed behavior, and learning a language involves internalizing the rules. But the ability or inclination to formulate the rules apparently interferes with the performance which is supposed to lead to making the application of the rules automatic. The curious consequence is that linguists whose central concern is precisely the formulation of accurate grammatical statements are identified with a method in which the value of such statements is limited to "summaries of behavior."

Phrased differently, underlying much of the current teaching of second languages is a confusion between the training schedule undergone by the learner and the structure of what it is that is ultimately learned. All models of learning based exclusively on imitation and reinforcement fail to account for the ability of anyone who has mastered a language to produce and understand novel utterances. The relationship between the

---

[1] For example, see Pimsleur and Bonkowski (1961) for evidence of the superiority of oral before visual presentation but Postman and Rosenzweig (1956) for results which can be interpreted to demonstrate the reverse. The author's research is supported in part by U.S. Office of Education Contract No. OE–2–14–010.

utterances to which the learner is exposed and the universe from which the sample is chosen is complex and poorly understood, but much of what passes for applied linguistics is based on the erroneous assumption that what is learned is merely a representative sample of sentences plus some vague notion like generalization. Specifically, the view that merely presenting sentences like *I eat meat, I eat fish,* and *I eat fresh meat* will automatically lead a learner to produce *I eat fresh fish* is an empty oversimplification. Such a view does not account for the obvious fact that the learner who has also been presented with *I eat well* presumably will not produce **I eat fresh well*. To say that new sentences are produced by generalization or analogy is of little help unless one can make explicit how a learner selects precisely the correct analogy. The ability to accept *I eat fresh fish* and to reject **I eat fresh well* implies command of an abstract grammatical rule, a rule which distinguishes *I eat fish* from *I eat well* and, incidentally, which makes the distinction without appeal to the acoustic signal. In short, the correct generalization implies knowledge, perhaps unverbalized, that nouns and not adverbs may be modified by adjectives, and that *fish* and not *well* is a noun. No amount of hand waving will obscure the fact that this is what has to be learned, and the appeal to generalization is vacuous since it presupposes knowledge of precisely what it is that is to be learned. On the other hand, having made this point explicit, we are no nearer understanding what the most efficient way is of learning it.

A third linguistic claim involves the role of contrastive analysis. Any observer is aware of the interference in second language acquisition which is due to application of first language rules. It seems reasonable, therefore, to assume that the optimal pedagogical grammar for a given target language, whether in the form of drills, rules, or some combination of the two, will be determined in part by the native language of the prospective learner. There can be little quarrel with the premise, but it is not clear how a systematic comparison of adequate grammars is to be affected or that the results of such a comparison would be significantly different from what a talented teacher might derive from, say, an examination of student errors. Independent of the mechanics of contrastive analysis is the fact that another factor, namely, the simplicity of the rules involved, interacts in ways which are not clear with the similarities and differences provided by systematic comparison. The extreme position regarding contrastive analysis is that if two languages were exactly alike, then the student would have no problems, regardless of how complex the system was.[2] But this implies, for example, that since English *be* has a particular

---

[2] This position is found, for example, in Stockwell, Bowen, and Martin (1965).

set of forms, the easiest learning situation for English speakers would be found in a language in which the equivalent was irregular in precisely the same way, as opposed to, say, a language in which the equivalent conformed to the same rule as all other similar forms. It seems unreasonable, however, to accept the conclusion that similarities and differences completely override questions of internal consistency and simplicity.

The reservations registered above about the claims of linguists and the interpretations of these claims are more or less independent of the particular kind of grammatical description involved. Since there seems to be little question that the recent investigations by Noam Chomsky and others on the nature of language and grammar provide the most coherent view thus far proposed, it may be of interest to inquire as to what specific implications for second language learning can be derived from the view that a grammar consists of a partially ordered set of rules which enumerate the set of grammatical sentences, assigning to each sentence its correct structural description.

First, however, the main contribution of generative grammar is precisely that to the extent that it provides the most meaningful statements about the relevant data, it enables textbook writers to base their material on the most adequate description. For example, Mary S. Temperley (1961) has pointed out the inadequacy of drills which suggest that sentences like *we elected Tom secretary* are expansions of *we elected Tom,* with *secretary* somehow to be understood as a modifier of *Tom.* That such an analysis is incorrect is demonstrated by the corresponding passive, which is *Tom was elected secretary,* not **Tom secretary was elected.* If linguistics has any contribution to make to language learning, it is this: to make explicit in general and in particular what is learned. To the extent that transformational grammar provides the best description, it by definition also provides the best basis for application. It is incongruous to argue that some less adequate formulation can be successfully applied where a more adequate one cannot. On the other hand, the possibility still exists that the difference between teaching based on a correct formulation and teaching based on no formulation is minimal.

One frequently made suggestion is that ordering in the scientific grammar might have some counterpart in the pedagogical grammar. At one extreme is the trivial case in which the presence of one distinction presupposes another and hence ordering is automatic. For example, if the distinction between transitive and intransitive verbs depends on the presence or absence of noun phrases, then clearly the distinction between the two types of verbs cannot be taught before the distinction between verb phrases (VP) and noun phrases (NP). At the other extreme is the obvious case in which ordering in the generative grammar cannot be understood as making a claim about pedagogy. Thus, some phonological rules presumably must be taught before some syntactic rules in spite of the fact that in general the former follow the latter.[3]

A generative grammar does, however, make some claims about the kind of information needed in the production and recognition of certain types of sentences. For example, in English the grammar maintains that knowledge of the passives with a deleted agent presupposes knowledge of the full passive, but not vice versa. Such knowledge is the basis of making the distinction between *the snow was piled up by the wind* and *the snow was piled up by the building*. More generally, the grammar makes explicit cases in which constructions are derived by deletions, e.g., *I eat* from *I eat NP*, which is what enables a speaker to distinguish *I eat well* from *I sleep well*.

But all such discussions[4] seem to be based on the assumption that somehow the order of presentation determines the order of application, an assumption which in its general form is demonstrably false, since no one wishes to claim that one cannot learn to use the brake on a car before learning to use the starter.

In spite of this reservation, however, it should be possible to test the proposition that it is easier to proceed in general from a formally marked distinction to a case of structural ambiguity (ambiguities resulting from deletion being a special case) than to proceed in the reverse direction. Of interest, then, is the consequence of such a position when it involves teaching infrequent or even nonoccurring forms. Thus, *John can jump higher than the Empire State Building* is ambiguous, but it is not clear what the pedagogical virtue might be of teaching *John can jump higher than the Empire State Building can jump* at all, let alone before the corresponding short form.

Presumably, the best scientific description provides the basis for the best pedagogical drills. Thus, most grammars of English would point out that whereas *the boy called up the girl* represents one structure, *the boy called up the stairs* represents another. This difference is made explicit by merely marking the constituent boundaries. Drills based on the different analyses might involve expanding the latter (*the boy called loudly up*

---

[3] Leonard Newmark (1964) points out that one might infer from the place of the phonological component that phonology might very well be taught last and that such a view "is at sharp variance with the attitudes of most applied linguists, but is in good agreement with our common sense feeling that it is more important to be able to speak a language fluently and to say a lot of things in it than to have marvelous pronunciation but not know what to say" (p. 7). Newmark, however, finds no evidence to assume that ordering or, for that matter, grammatical analysis of any kind is facilitative.

[4] More lucid than most is the one by Teeter (1963).

the stairs) but not the former (**the boy called loudly up the girl*) and, conversely, permuting elements in the former (*the boy called the girl up*) but not the latter (**the boy called the stairs up*).

On the other hand, the relation between *I like amusing stories, I like raising flowers,* and *I like entertaining guests* cannot be indicated merely by marking constituent boundaries. Understanding these sentences involves knowledge of the underlying structure, where the differences are marked. A drill for exploiting the difference might merely involve insertion of the article *the,* yielding *the amusing stories* but *raising the flowers* and both *the entertaining guests* and *entertaining the guests*. But let us notice again the incongruity in all such drills. The ability to perform the drill implies knowledge of the syntax. In short, it presupposes knowledge of precisely the information it attempts to teach. But this is not just a minor quibble: this is a crucial aspect of all second language learning. A drill which derives *his amusing stories* and *his raising flowers* from *his stories amuse* and *he raises flowers* can be done automatically; since the output does not distinguish the constructions, performance of the drill does not necessarily indicate discrimination of their underlying structure; that is, performance of the drill does not ensure learning. On the other hand, a drill which does the reverse, deriving *his stories amuse* from *his amusing stories* and *he raises flowers* from *his raising flowers* can be said to test but not to teach, since performance of the drill presupposes precisely the information to be taught.

Let us consider a similar example in Spanish. *Me permite comer* ("he allows me to eat") must be distinguished from *me quiere comer* ("he wants to eat me"). *Me* is subject of the verb *comer* in the first example but object of *comer* in the second.

This is a fact that any scientific grammar of Spanish must explain. But how command of the rules which explain this fact is to be achieved is not dictated by the form of the rules themselves. Thus, a reasonable formulation of the difference in structures might include underlying structures which differ in precisely what relation the first person pronoun has to the verb *comer,* say, something like:

$$\left.\begin{array}{l} \text{El quiere Comp} \\ \text{El me comerà} \end{array}\right\} \Rightarrow \text{El me quiere comer.}$$

but

$$\left.\begin{array}{l} \text{El permite Comp} \\ \text{Yo como} \end{array}\right\} \Rightarrow \text{El me permite comer.}$$

But the assumption that a formulation such as the above also prescribes the form of a pedagogical drill is unwarranted. Indeed, performing such drills can be done automatically. Performing the reverse of such drills, that is, identifying the underlying structure, presupposes exactly the distinction which is presumably being taught.

The aim of applied linguistics may be viewed as specifying what the input must be to a device which yields a sentence recognizer and producer of some second language as output. Much of the discussion has centered on whether the input should be in the form of drills, rules, or both, and if both, in what combination and order. It is not surprising that these efforts have had limited success when we consider that relatively little is known about either the device or the output. The internal structure of the device, i.e., the learner, has gone relatively unexplored, except to point out that one of its components is a grammar of the learner's native language. It has generally been assumed that the effect of this component has been inhibitory rather than facilitative. In spite of claims to the contrary, we must conclude that learning principles are largely unknown. Regarding the output of such a device, studies in generative grammar have only recently suggested what the problem is in understanding the nature of a sentence analyzer and describing the capacities that characterize it.

We see that we have now come full circle. The impact of modern linguistic theory must be to improve the content of pedagogical grammars. In this sense the traditional grammarians were on the side of the angels. Postwar linguists focused on the fact that ability to verbalize even adequate rules did not ensure performance and argued for the importance of practice. But the practice which has been devised is of two kinds, one of which can be performed automatically and hence may have only a minimal effect on the learner's competence and another which presupposes precisely the competence to be learned. The drill which serves as input to a naive student and which is somehow converted into command of precisely the appropriate rule is an illusion.

REFERENCES

Newmark, Leonard. Grammatical theory and the teaching of English as a foreign language. In David P. Harris (Ed.), *The 1963 conference papers of the English section of the National Association for Foreign Student Affairs.* NAFSA Studies and Papers, English Language Series, 1964, No. 9. Pp. 5–8.

Pimsleur, Paul, and Robert J. Bonkowski. Transfer of verbal material across sense modalities. *Journal of Educational Psychology,* 1961, **52,** 104–07.

Postman, Leo, and Mark Rosenzweig. Practice and transfer in the visual and auditory recognition of verbal stimuli. *American Journal of Psychology,* 1956, **69,** 209–226.

Stockwell, Robert P., Donald J. Bowen, and John W. Martin. *The grammatical structures of English and Spanish.* Chicago: University of Chicago Press, 1965.

Teeter, Karl V. Review of Elinor C. Horne, *Beginning Javanese Language,* 1963, **39,** 146–151.

Temperley, Mary S. Transformations in English sentence patterns. *Language Learning,* 1961, **11,** 125–134.

6

THE CONTRIBUTIONS OF PSYCHOLOGICAL THEORY AND EDUCATIONAL RESEARCH TO THE TEACHING OF FOREIGN LANGUAGES

JOHN B. CARROLL

John B. Carroll (1916–   ) became interested in linguistics as a result of his friendship with Benjamin Lee Whorf, whose writings he edited and published in 1956. Basically, however, he is a psychologist, with degrees from Wesleyan University and from the University of Minnesota. Since 1949 he has been on the staff of the Graduate School of Education at Harvard University, where he is now professor of educational psychology. He is the author of two books on language and the psychology of language, as well as the originator of the Modern Language Aptitude Test. In addition, he has conducted many studies of problems in the teaching of foreign languages.
A previous version of this paper was presented at the International Conference on Modern Foreign Language Teaching, Berlin, September, 1964.

In a period when many new developments and new ideas are brought forth, it is appropriate to think about the role of research and theory not only in guiding these new developments and new ideas but also in providing a sound basis for foreign language teaching in all its aspects. This paper will concern research and theory specifically in the psychological foundations of foreign language teaching; it will not treat the role of linguistic theory in this field.

We shall have to treat research and theory somewhat separately, for, on the one hand, certain kinds of research do not depend much on theory and, on the other, some kinds of theories are extremely difficult to test by any empirical research. But as I hope to show, the best research is based on theory and interacts with it, and the best theories are those that can be tested by empirical research.

Research is widely held to be a "good thing." Many industries allocate a certain percentage of their budgets to the support of research laboratories, and they generally find this an extremely rewarding thing to do. It has been proposed that education should imitate industry in this regard; the amount of money devoted to education in most advanced countries is so large that even a very small percentage of the educational budget should yield fairly large sums for research. Several countries, most notably the United States and the Soviet Union, have established extensive programs for research in education. The Soviet Union has set up a series of research institutes for various aspects of education, and these institutes are turning out interesting and useful reports as well as materials of instruction. In the United States, most educational research is performed by persons attached to the colleges and universities, and a very large proportion of it is now supported by government funds. We may take note of such programs as those of the U.S. Office of Education. Among these, the Cooperative Research Program supplies funds for educational research, both basic and applied, at all levels of the educational system and for all kinds of problems and subject matters. Under the National Defense Education Act (NDEA), there are two further programs of support for educational research: the so-called "Title VII program," aimed specially at supporting research on the use of "new" media, such as films, television, and programmed instruction; and, of special interest here, the Title VI Language Development Program, which, in addition to providing funds for the development of foreign language teaching materials and the training of teachers of foreign languages, makes funds available for fundamental research in the theory and methodology of foreign language teaching. Although the funds from Title VI first became available in 1958, there has been disappointingly little use of them for basic research in foreign language teaching methodology, primarily because of the shortage of qualified and interested research workers in this field. I shall, however, be able to cite several significant studies that have come out of this program.

At the same time, skepticism has been voiced in some quarters about the possibility of doing research that can make a significant difference in the conduct of foreign language programs. One complaint is that research is often so abstract or so far removed from the realities of the classroom that it would be difficult to apply the results in any practical way. Another variety of complaint is that even if the research is closely tied to real-life classroom situations, the variables are often so difficult to control that one hesitates to draw generalizations from the results. There is admittedly some basis for these complaints, but a deeper examination of the issues raised may lead us to the conclusion that valid and significant educational research in foreign language teaching is nevertheless possible.

One way of getting at the problem of the role of research in foreign language teaching is to consider who are the potential "consumers" of research results. For our purposes, I would identify four types of consumers: teachers, teacher trainers, educational policy makers, and authors of instructional materials. Let us consider first the teacher, who is, after all, at the heart of the educational process. There are various ways in which teachers respond to findings from educational research, largely depending upon their personalities, attitudinal systems, experience, and training. There is, of course, the standpat traditionalist who is quite sure that he is doing the best that can be done and wants no intrusion of research findings to disturb the fine techniques he has already developed. For all we know, many of these traditionalists are quite justified in their stand; others may be simply in a rut, consistently producing poorer results than they might be able to produce if they were to take account of research outcomes and newly developed materials. At the opposite extreme from the standpat traditionalist is the impressionable adventurer who will "try anything," particularly if it is the latest fad or fashion. A special subtype of impressionable adventurer is the "gadgeteer," the teacher who has an insatiable thirst for gadgets and other kinds of hardware, phonographs, tape recorders, hi-fi speaker systems, teaching machines, and the like. Somewhere in between these extremes I hope we find the majority of teachers, teachers who have convictions about the soundness of their teaching techniques but are open-minded and interested in new ideas, materials, and techniques that stem from research and development, with a readiness to try out these techniques in their classrooms.

The fruits of research that are easiest to apply in the classroom are of course the texts, films, teaching-machine programs, and other materials that already incorporate and embody the findings of research. Next in order come the gadgets and other pieces of equipment that are provided to render these teaching materials more accessible to the student. Another kind of research outcome immediately and directly applicable in the classroom would be one which indicates what kind of text or teaching material is most effective for a certain purpose, for the teacher has only to choose to use that text or material (assuming, of course, that he has the power and the means to choose). For example, research indicating the usefulness of particular types of audiovisual materials obviously has implications for the teacher. The kind of research result that is hardest for the classroom teacher to apply or even to understand, in many cases, is the one that demonstrates the effectiveness of a certain teaching *procedure* that must be carried out in some consistent manner by the teacher in the moment-by-moment conduct of a teaching session. For example, if research says, as it seems to, that an efficacious procedure for the teaching of pronunciation is the "shaping"—by gradual approximation—of behavior according to the principles worked out by the psychologist B. F. Skinner, the teacher must not only thoroughly understand these principles and how to apply them but also be able to carry out the procedures effectively in the classroom. Often teachers find it rather difficult to change their behavior on the basis of research findings, even when the procedure is exceedingly simple and obvious. For instance, although I do not know of any research that directly implies this, I believe that a good principle to follow in carrying out any teaching routine in which one wants to call on successive pupils is not to call on them systematically in a set pattern but to do so more or less randomly, so that pupils will maintain themselves in a state of alertness to be called on at any time. Yet I understand that efforts to get teachers to change from a systematic to a random calling procedure have sometimes met with failure, apparently because teachers are unable to change their characteristic modes of classroom behavior.

This leads us to the conclusion that *trainers* of teachers of languages should be avid consumers of educational research insofar as it yields information on what kinds of teaching procedures are most effective or desirable in other respects, because the best opportunity of getting teachers to learn to use these methods is at the point at which they are first trained to teach. We should remind ourselves that it is not only research specifically directed at modern foreign language teaching that teacher trainers need to know about but also the whole gamut of research on teacher behavior. This has been summarized in the recently published *Handbook of Research on Teaching,* edited by N. L. Gage (1963), and it has also been presented in various texts on educational psychology. For example, the teacher trainer should be mindful of research on the personality of teachers and its effect on classroom learning. One of the best-established findings of educational research is that a major source of variation in pupil learning is the teacher's ability to promote that learning. Exactly what this ability consists of is not certain, but we have strong evidence that along with knowledge of subject matter there is involved the teacher's ability to organize this content and present it with due regard for the pupil's ability and readiness to acquire it.

Another consumer of research is the educational policy maker. Of course, many people may contribute to the making of educational policy. In the United States, policy can be made by persons at almost any level, from the classroom teacher to the school superintendent, the school board, or even the United States Congress. Comparable situations exist in other countries. At whatever level, the maker of educational policy needs facts of various sorts on which to base his decisions. In the field of foreign language teaching, he needs facts about such questions as the following: What is the optimal age for being introduced to a foreign language? How long should foreign language instruction last to give the student a solid mastery of the language being taught? Is it best to spread out this instruction rather thinly over a number of years or to give the instruction intensively? Should there be any selection of who is to be given foreign language instruction, and, if so, how should the pupils be selected? It has seemed to me (Carroll, 1960) that one of the prime functions of educational research is to supply information of this sort to educational policy makers.

One other type of consumer of educational research is the person who has to do with the preparation of teaching materials, whether he is the author of a text, the producer of a film, the originator of a teaching-machine program, or whatnot. He needs research results concerning the content and optimal organization of materials of instruction. The textbook writer who is careful to seek the answers to such questions and then applies them competently in developing his material is rare indeed. There is a real problem in organizing and communicating the results of research in such a way that they will be readily understood and applied by this kind of consumer. Despite an enormous amount of research in the United States and elsewhere on improving the instructional characteristics of films, for example, the producers of educational films have in general failed to capitalize on these findings.

These remarks point up the problem of the linkage between the researcher and the consumer of research. How is the researcher going to communicate with the consumer of his research? Does he even know what his audience is and what his audience wants? We are all familiar with the fact that the researcher most typically publishes his results in some journal article that few of the potential consumers even know about, let alone have time to read or act upon. It is difficult for the researcher to reach his audience even through a teachers' convention, because of the competition for time and the fact that only a small fraction of the potential audience is able to attend such meetings.

I can pass on to you one suggestion for solution of this problem. It is not original with me; indeed, it has been discussed in many circles. The idea actually comes out of the history of American agriculture: the idea of the county agent, the person who by personal visitation communicates the findings of agricultural research (better seeds, better insecticides, better methods of crop rotation, etc.) to the farmer right at his door. There could be an analogue of the county agent in education: the individual who makes a specialty of communicating the findings of research to the potential consumer, the teacher, teacher trainer, educational policy maker, or preparer of instructional material. We have had a few instances in the United States of people who have functioned like county agents in helping schools install and use language laboratories. The idea could be extended to include specialists in other aspects of research and development. The major problem that would be encountered, at least in the United States, is the shortage of persons qualified to do this kind of educational liaison. The existing personnel are too much needed either as teachers or as researchers. Another problem that might be encountered, embarrassingly enough, is that the results of research and development might not be thought clear and definite enough to provide the would-be educational-change agent with a solid product to sell. That is to say, I am not sure that educational research in the teaching of foreign languages has come up with ideas, principles, and materials that are as well established as those the agricultural county agent has to communicate to the farmers on his rounds. But this is a matter that I wish to consider further in the remainder of this discussion.

A moment ago I alluded in passing to the kinds of research "products" that might be utilized by the consumer of research. A further consideration reveals that these products lie along a continuum from the most tangible to the most intangible: on the one hand, substantive materials like books, films, tests, teaching machines, and so forth that have the findings of educational research "built in," as it were, ready for use, just as a refrigerator embodies the results of the latest research in the science of refrigeration; and, on the other hand, ideas and principles that remain in the abstract until they have been applied, actualized, or acted upon by a skillful educator. This continuum corresponds to another continuum that differentiates the researcher whose main concern is with immediately practical problems from one whose efforts are directed chiefly toward understanding the kind of behavior he is dealing with. On the one hand, we have the researcher who wants to find a better way of teaching, who seeks to find the immediate cause of students' errors and difficulties, who wants to demonstrate the usefulness of a new technique, or who wishes to find the correct basis for reaching some particular practical decision. On the other hand, we have the researcher who is trying to build a science of learning, who would like to make precise predictions about the effects of a given teaching procedure, or who would be most pleased to confirm or deny a particular theory of learning. I would like to affirm that there is a place for both types of researchers, in fact, for workers at every point on the spectrum between the intensely practical and the intensely theoretical. It is easy to understand what the practical researcher is doing but not so easy to understand what the theoretical researcher is up to, at least in the behavioral sciences. I suppose that before nuclear fission was discovered there was a suspicious air about what theoretical physicists were up to, but this has been largely dispelled by now. I hope this air can become dispelled also in the behavioral sciences. We have already begun to achieve some really startling results from theoretical work in behavioral science, and I believe there will be much more to come.

Let me cite a brief example of some possible gains that may ensue from theoretical research in learning. One that is often used for this purpose is the research of Skinner with his pigeons: the fact that in the experimental laboratory situation pigeons can be "trained" to almost any stunt or series of stunts by the right "schedule of reinforcements," the reinforcers being rewards for particular movements. There is now considerable doubt as to how this principle can be applied in human learning, because it does not always work and other factors may be operating. Therefore, I shall try to select an example straight from human learning. Some of the work of a group of psychologists who call themselves *mathematical learning theorists* will furnish good examples. Recent work by a group at Stanford University suggests that one of the problems encountered in learning is that of converting short-time memories into long-term ones. Empirically, it is found that items that have once been presented or exposed to a learner for a short time quickly fade from memory, particularly when many additional items are immediately presented. This is true even though the learner may have the impression, each time a new item is presented, that he will never forget it. We are all conscious of having felt this way about some new name, fact, telephone number, or whatever, only to find that a few moments later the material has vanished. These are common observations; what the mathematical psychologists have been able to do is to propose exact equations for the rate at which material is learned or forgotten. Prof. Patrick Suppes (1964) of Stanford University is trying to apply these mathematical developments to the resolution of the classical "whole-part" learning problem for the special case of foreign language learning. In his view, the problem is one of the competition between learning and forgetting. If learning occurs faster than forgetting, it is better to devote more attention to learning new materials, and thus the whole method, in which one works over the whole of a list of vocabulary, let us say, is better than the part method, in which one attacks the list piecemeal. Suppes's research is not yet complete; tentative results suggest that actually learning and forgetting occur at about the same rates, and therefore the part and the whole methods are equally effective for the kinds of learning his subjects are doing. This result, however, happens not to agree with other results that suggest that part learning is increasingly efficient as the length of the list or material to be learned gets longer. Nevertheless, whatever the final result, it may possibly be relevant to foreign language learning, because one characteristic of this learning that may differentiate it from many other kinds is the sheer volume of the material to be learned. The foreign language teacher would be well advised to optimize the rate at which new words, phrases, syntactical patterns, and so on are introduced in the course of learning. Yet sheer empirical, trial-and-error methods of determining the optimal rates at which new material is to be introduced and then reviewed ("revised") are not enough; because the different combinations of possibilities are large in number, only a mathematical analysis has any real promise of disclosing the true optima. Therefore, I would urge support of theoretical research in learning even though the payoff may not be seen in any immediately practical outcomes.

Consideration of Professor Suppes's work gives rise to some other remarks about the relation between research in the laboratory and research in the classroom, for the work of Suppes that I have been describing is done exclusively in the laboratory. In his experiment the learner hears a different Russian word and its English equivalent every four or five seconds until the whole of a list of, say, 108 words has been presented; in the next round, the learner is told to try to say the English equivalent before he hears it, and so it goes, round after round, until the learner can anticipate all the correct answers. This kind of vocabulary learning is clearly very different from the kind that is typical in the classroom, where every word may be presented with ample meaningful context and a lengthy explanation of etymology or other matters. But Professor Suppes is not claiming that his method of vocabulary learning is superior to any other; I am sure he would admit that it is inferior to the method that is used in most classrooms. This is irrelevant, however, to the purpose of his experiment, which is concerned with a quite different set of problems. First, the laboratory setting is believed to be necessary to control the many extraneous variables that are inevitable in a classroom experiment; and, second, it is unlikely that the type of learning activity would change the *pattern* of results. Any results found concerning whole-part learning for the laboratory setting would in all probability have the pattern and general form that might also be found in a classroom experiment if this were feasible, but the laboratory experiment is very much cheaper and simpler to carry out.

If we can check the impulse to demand that laboratory research imitate the classroom learning setting in *all* respects and realize that this research usually seeks patterns of relationships among sharply delimited sets of variables, holding all others constant or at least under control, we shall be on the road to a better understanding of the role of research in the behavioral sciences. But we shall achieve an even higher degree of comprehension if we realize that the problems attacked in laboratory research, more often than not, stem from theory and the attempt to test particular theories, rather than from practical concerns. We are at such a really rudimentary stage in the development of theory in the behavioral sciences that there is enormous scope for theoretical developments. This is true not only for learning theory in general but also for the theory of foreign language learning. That is, we do not yet have either a good general theory concerning the conditions under which learning takes place or a general theory of language behavior that would enable us to select optimal components of a foreign language teaching system for any given case. This is not to say that we know nothing about learning—I would hold that we know a good deal about it on a descriptive, functional level, for we can state quite a number of generalizations and principles that, if followed, will help the teacher or learner improve the course of learning. My point is that no proved *theory* now exists to account for all the phenomena we can observe or even the phenomena that we can predict and control. We are in the stage in the history of our science that chemistry was in before molecular theory was well developed.

The lack of a proved theory becomes particularly acute when we try to understand the process of learning a second language. Examination of the practices of foreign language teachers and the writings of several theorists suggests that there are today two major theories of foreign language learning. One may be called the *audiolingual habit theory;* the other, the *cognitive code-learning theory.* The audiolingual habit theory, which is more or less the "official" theory of the reform movement in foreign language teaching in the United States, has the following principal ideas: (1) Since speech is primary and writing is secondary, the habits to be learned must be learned first of all as auditory-discrimination responses and speech responses. (2) Habits must be automatized as much as possible so that they can be called forth without conscious attention. (3) The automatization of habits occurs chiefly by practice, that is, by repetition. The audiolingual habit theory has given rise to a great many practices in language teaching: the language laboratory, the structural drill, the mimicry-memorization technique, and so forth. The cognitive code-learning theory, on the other hand, may be thought of as a modified, up-to-date grammar-translation theory. According to this theory, learning a language is a process of acquiring conscious control of the phonological, grammatical, and lexical patterns of a second language, largely through study and analysis of these patterns as a body of knowledge. The theory attaches more importance to the learner's understanding of the structure of the foreign language than to his facility in using that structure, since it is believed that provided the student has a proper degree of cognitive control over the structures of the language, facility will develop automatically with use of the language in meaningful situations.

The opposition between these theories can be illustrated by the way they would deal with the findings of contrastive linguistics. According to the audiolingual habit theory, information about the differences between the learner's native language and the target language is of use to the teacher in planning drills and exercises because it would pinpoint the student's difficulties, but it would confuse the student, who needs only to imitate the foreign language sounds and patterns until by practice he masters them. According to the cognitive code-learning theory, on the other hand, the differences between the native language and the target language should be carefully explained to the student, so that he may acquire conscious control of the target language patterns.

In practice, of course, some teachers act as if they believed in both of these theories, appealing to one of them for some of their teaching procedures and to the other for different aspects. But I would nevertheless insist that the two theories represent rather fundamental differences in teaching method and style that show up in the way textbooks are written and foreign language courses are taught. We need information on which of these theories is a better basis for foreign language teaching.

At this point the would-be researcher has an important strategy decision to make. One course open to him is to conduct a large-scale educational experiment in which the results of teaching based on the audiolingual habit theory are contrasted with teaching based on the cognitive code-learning theory. This kind of research is feasible but very expensive and difficult to control. The experimental design would call for some method of assuring that the students taught under the two theories are approximately equal in ability and motivation; ideally, students would be randomly assigned to the two methods, but educational realities may make this impossible. Separate and distinct courses and materials of instruction must be created, and the instructors must be trained to adhere closely to a certain style of presentation.

This, in fact, was the choice made by a research team at the University of Colorado, consisting of a foreign language professor, George A. C. Scherer, and a psychologist, Michael Wertheimer. The complete results of this experiment on the teaching of German at the college level are available in a book recently published (1964). The experiment contrasted an audiolingual method, based largely on the audiolingual habit theory, with a bilingual grammar-translation method of the traditional sort, based on some variety of the cognitive code-learning theory I have described above. Random assignment of some 300 students to the two methods was used. The "traditional" group was given reading material right from the start, while the use of reading materials in any form was delayed for twelve weeks in the case of the audiolingual group. At the end of the first year, the audiolingual group was significantly better in listening and speaking and was not far behind the traditional group in tests of straight reading and writing. Unfortunately, in the second year it was not possible to give the two groups differentiated instruction, but even so, at the end of this second year the audiolingual group was still slightly ahead in speaking ability, presumably because of its good early start in this skill. The traditional group was slightly better in writing ability, but the two groups no longer differed at all in listening and reading. On the whole, the average differences between the groups were small, small enough, at any rate, to suggest that it does not make any material difference whether one uses the audiolingual method as opposed to the traditional grammar-translation method. We can suppose in this experiment that there was good teaching in both methods, and perhaps this was really the major variable that held both groups up to a fairly high standard.

One is gratified that the Scherer-Wertheimer experiment has been performed (incidentally, under a grant from the U.S. Office of Education from the aforementioned NDEA Title VI Language Development Program), even though the results are in a sense disappointing. The dramatic superiority that an ardent audiolingual habit theorist might have predicted failed to appear. I would make the following comments on this experiment, and my comments are not wholly from hindsight, because I had privately predicted the general pattern of the results. First, it is almost impossible to control the techniques that the *student himself* will adopt to acquire a given skill, particularly over a long course of study. For example, even though the audiolingual method was presumably "monolingual" (i.e., conducted almost exclusively in German, the target language), many students undoubtedly adopted the strategy of translating the German material into English at every opportunity. Likewise, some students under the bilingual grammar-translation method would have found ways of indulging in audiolingual practice. Thus the two methods were not so sharply differentiated as they should be in an experiment. Second, it is doubtful that the theoretical bases for the teaching methods in the experiment were sufficiently well formed to make for high contrast. For example, the notion of audiolingual habit formation may not have been sufficiently exploited in the audiolingual group, and the notion of conscious cognitive control does not seem to have been explicitly employed in the grammar-translation group. Further, there was no precise formulation of the relevant theory. Scherer and Wertheimer were merely concerned with the general comparison of two widely used methods of teaching as they understood them. This in itself was laudable, but it should be noted that testing of theory was not their primary objective.

Another course of action available to the researcher is the setting up of more precisely controlled, small-scale experiments to check *hypotheses*. A theory implies an interconnected set of hypotheses, each of which can be tested in a separate experiment. The work of Suppes, in testing hypotheses about learning and forgetting rates, is an example of experimentation of this sort. In December, 1959, a conference of psychologists was held at the University of California at Los Angeles, chaired by Paul Pimsleur. This conference developed a number of plans for experimentation. Many were based on theory, and some of them have been carried out. I mention the final report of this conference as a source of ideas for research in foreign language teaching (Pimsleur, 1959).

In the space that remains I wish only to stress my feeling that if research in foreign language teaching is to be really productive, it must become better attuned to theory, both in psychology and in linguistics. Let me point out that neither the audiolingual habit theory nor the cognitive code-learning theory is closely linked to any contemporary psychological theory of learning. The audiolingual habit theory has a vague resemblance to an early version of a Thorndikean association theory, while the cognitive code-learning theory is reminiscent of certain contemporary gestaltist movements in psychology which emphasize the importance of perceiving the "structure" of what is to be learned, without really relying on such movements. Actually, neither theory takes adequate account of an appreciable body of knowledge that has accumulated in the study of verbal learning. Among these facts are the following:

1.   The frequency with which an item is practiced per se is not so crucial as the frequency with which it is contrasted with other items with which it may be confused. Thus, the learning of items in "pattern-practice" drills would be improved if instead of simple repetition there were a constant alternation among varied patterns.

2. The more meaningful the material to be learned, the greater the facility in learning and retention. The audiolingual habit theory tends to play down meaningfulness in favor in producing automaticity.

3. Other things being equal, materials presented visually are more easily learned than comparable materials presented aurally. Even though the objective of teaching may be the attainment of mastery over the auditory and spoken components of language learning, an adequate theory of language learning should take account of how the student handles visual counterparts of the auditory elements he is learning and help to prescribe the optimal utilization of these counterparts, such as printed words, phonetic transcriptions, and other visual-symbol systems.

4. In learning a skill, it is often the case that conscious attention to its critical features and understanding of them will facilitate learning. This principle is largely ignored by the audiolingual habit theory; it is recognized by the cognitive code-learning theory. It would imply, for example, that in teaching pronunciation an explanation of necessary articulatory movements would be helpful.

5. The more numerous kinds of association that are made to an item, the better are learning and retention. Again this principle seems to dictate against the use of *systems* of language teaching that employ mainly one sensory modality, namely, hearing. A recent experiment performed at the Defense Language Institute, West Coast Branch (Army Language School, Monterey, California) seems to show that dramatic facilitation of language learning occurs when words denoting concrete objects and physical actions are associated with actual *motor* performances involving those objects and actions. Thus, the student learns the meaning of the foreign language word for *jump* by actually jumping! Language teaching becomes a sort of physical exercise both for the students and for the instructor whose actions they imitate.

These, then, are a few examples of theory-derived principles that, if further examined and verified, could contribute to more effective ways of teaching foreign languages. It would be trite to say at this point that "more research is needed," although it is obviously the case. Actually, what is needed even more than research is a profound rethinking of current theories of foreign language teaching in the light of contemporary advances in psychological and psycholinguistic theory. The audiolingual habit theory which is so prevalent in American foreign language teaching was, perhaps, fifteen years ago in step with the state of psychological thinking at that time, but it is no longer abreast of recent developments. It is ripe for major revision, particularly in the direction of joining with it some of the better elements of the cognitive code-learning theory. I would venture to predict that if this can be done, then teaching based on the revised theory will yield a dramatic change in effectiveness.

REFERENCES

Carroll, John B. Wanted: A research basis for educational policy on foreign language teaching. *Harvard Educational Review,* 1960, **30,** 128–140.

Gage, N. L. (Ed.) *Handbook of research on teaching.* Chicago: Rand McNally & Company, 1963.

Pimsleur, Paul. *Psychological experiments related to second language learning: Report of the NDEA conference.* Los Angeles: University of California, 1959.

Scherer, George A. C., and Michael Wertheimer. *A psycholinguistic experiment in foreign-language teaching.* New York: McGraw-Hill Book Company, 1964.

Suppes, Patrick. Modern learning theory and the elementary school curriculum. *American Educational Research Association Journal,* 1964, **1,** 79–94.

7

PSYCHOLINGUISTIC PERSPECTIVES ON LANGUAGE LEARNING

MOSHE ANISFELD

Moshe Anisfeld (1934–   ) was born in Poland and received his high school and undergraduate training in Israel and his graduate degrees in psychology at McGill University. He spent two years in postdoctoral work at Harvard University with interruptions for summer appointments in psycholinguistics at the University of Washington and at Indiana University. He held the post of visiting assistant professor in the Psychology Department at McGill University and is currently assistant professor of psycholinguistics at Cornell University.

The purpose of this article is to present some ideas from psychology and linguistics that have particular relevance to language learning and teaching. Almost any psychological observation can be shown to relate to as complex a process as language learning, but limits have to be set for the purposes of this chapter, which will therefore be restricted to the psychological insights the writer finds most revealing with respect to language acquisition. Some equally important ideas have been omitted because they have already been treated in an excellent article by Lambert (1963). The reader is also referred to a recent book on the psychology of language teaching (Rivers, 1964).

Language teachers sometimes turn to psychologists for solutions to specific practical problems they encounter in the classroom or laboratory. No such solutions will be offered here, for it is felt that at the present stage of development of psychology large-scale applications to practical situations can be accomplished only by a superficial treatment of psychological subject matter and an oversimplified analysis of the nature of the problems for which psychology is consulted. At present a psychologist can suggest general guidelines for observing and understanding human behavior rather than prescriptions for curing specific ailments. Even with respect to general principles, however, the teacher is not asked to accept the authority of science but rather is invited to examine critically the ideas expounded. The professional psychologist has the benefit of relative familiarity with the literature of his discipline, but the language teacher has the advantage of insights gained from experience.

We shall now proceed to an exposition of the substance of this chapter under two major headings. The first section deals with the nature of language, and the second with psychological processes pertinent to language acquisition.

THE NATURE OF LINGUISTIC COMPETENCE

Language can be divided into two components: specific habits and general rules. In the first category falls mainly the lexicon of a language, including words, phrases, and idioms; in the second, grammar. The essential difference between the two categories resides in the degree of extendibility of the known to new situations. Knowing that in English a particular piece of furniture is referred to as *chair* does not provide information for inferring what the word would be for another piece of furniture, table, for example, but the structure of the sentence *this is a chair* is generalizable to *this is a table*. The attribution of specificity to the lexicon and generality to grammar is not an absolute matter but a relative comparison. Obviously, there are grammatical exceptions which, like vocabulary items, have to be learned one by one. And there are also broad regularities and restrictions in the realm of word formation. Thus, for instance, the units *two, three, . . . , nine* in English are arbitrary, and each one has to be learned separately; but the multiples of ten of these units are not, and speakers will generalize from knowledge of some to the rest. More generally, once a lexeme in one form is known, the other forms can be inferred; a verb can readily be turned into a noun, a noun into a verb, and so with other parts of speech.

General patterns underlying the lexicon are revealed as much by what speakers do not say as by what they do say. A native (monolingual) speaker of English would more readily accept **thrub* than **srub* as a new word (Greenberg & Jenkins, 1964; Whorf, 1956). The reason for this difference is that the first sequence obeys the sound-order rules of the language whereas the second does not.

Another indication of structure in the lexicon can be found in the results of phonetic symbolism experiments. Given two artificial words and asked to match them against a pair of antonyms, subjects belonging to one language community will tend to agree among themselves about the best match but often disagree with the match accepted by speakers of another language (Taylor, 1963). Apparently, in acquiring specific vocabulary items, speakers unconsciously abstract certain general features characteristic of these items.

Regularity can thus be found even in the lexicon of a language, but it is most glaring in grammar. For an understanding of the nature of language we therefore have to turn to grammatical rules. Our knowledge of the character of these rules has been much advanced by the work of Noam Chomsky and his associates on generative transformational grammar (Chomsky, 1957, 1965; Lees, 1960; Postal, 1964).

Philosophers of science sometimes describe scientific theories as grammars of science. A scientific theory hypothesizes certain elementary units (e.g., atoms, molecules, etc.) and rules for interrelating them. A theory is constructed on the basis of observed phenomena in a certain domain of nature. Its adequacy depends primarily on how economically it deals with these phenomena and how accurately it can predict new phenomena. The theory need not bear any superficial or obvious relation to the data it endeavors to explain. Thus the validity of the atomic theory does not depend on the direct observation of atoms in matter. Now, if such theories are called grammars, perhaps it is possible to construct grammars of natural languages that would have structures and functions similar to those of scientific grammars. This is exactly the task transformational linguists set for themselves. They construct their theories of language by postulating grammatical categories such as noun phrases, verb phrases, etc., and interrelating them by rules of formation and transformation. The formation component specifies the rules for forming simple declarative sentences (or more precisely, base phrase markers that underlie such sentences). The transformation rules are designed to derive different types of sentences from the declarative ones. Thus rather than treat the active, passive, imperative, interrogative, and negative sentences as independent frames with their own rules, transformational analysis interrelates them all.

This approach develops to its fullest the notion that language is a system. In a system all components are interdependent and coordinated with each other, and language in the hands of the transformationalists becomes such a system.

The main body of data that transformational theorists attempt to account for consists of the intuitive judgments of speakers concerning utterances in their language. They strive to answer such questions as the following: Why do speakers feel that certain utterances are permissible in their language while others are not, even though in both cases the utterances may not have been heard before? This is exemplified by the classic comparison (Chomsky, 1957, p. 15) of (1) *colorless green ideas sleep furiously* and (2) *furiously sleep ideas green colorless.* Transformational linguists attempt to provide an analysis that could explain the perceived difference between such pairs. That the account cannot simply state the prescribed order of grammatical markers (*-less, -s, -ly*) is shown by relating pairs 1 and 2 to the following two utterances (Chomsky, 1964) : (3) *harmless seem dogs young friendly* and (4) *friendly young dogs seem harmless.* The order of markers in utterance 3 corresponds to that of utterance 1, and that of utterance 4 to that of utterance 2; yet utterance 3 is not acceptable as grammatically well formed while utterance 4 is. This indicates that comprehension of language relies on a deeper level of analysis of sentence structure, which transformational grammar attempts to make explicit. The transformational analysis also claims success in explaining the possible alternative interpretations of such ambiguous sentences as *they are eating apples* and *the police were ordered to stop drinking at midnight.*

Transformational theory in about a decade of development has shown great power in explaining the underlying reasons for intuitive judgments of speakers. In basing itself on speakers' judgments rather than on their actual speech, the theory shows greater interest in the norms native speakers have acquired concerning what is appropriate in their language than in the extent to which they obey these norms. Consequently, the observation that in free speech people produce incomplete and ungrammatical sentences does not constitute evidence against the theory as long as the speaker, when asked, could judge the ungrammatical utterances as such. Obviously, what a person says does not necessarily reflect what he knows how to say, and the theory is concerned with the latter and not the former, i.e., with competence, not performance. Performance—what a person actually says in a particular situation—is not determined solely by linguistic competence. Other factors, such as motivation, nature of the situation, and immediate memory capacity, interact with competence to result in performance. Analogously, the observation of a driver going through a red light does not constitute sufficient grounds for the inference that he does not know what the sign means; in interpreting this behavior one has to take into account the driver's motivation to obey the rule, his other competing needs, etc.

Another possible objection to the theory must now be considered. It is clear that most speakers of a language could not make explicit the system of rules they are said to possess. Moreover, many speakers would not even understand these rules if they were explained to them. This situation, however, does not constitute evidence against the theory, for in nonlinguistic psychological realms as well people are not always aware of the determinants of their behavior. Sigmund Freud made this point forcefully with respect to motivation by pointing out that the reasons people give for their behavior may not be the true ones. The true reasons could be hidden in the unconscious and therefore be inaccessible to direct self-observation. A similar attitude underlies the rejection of introspection as a method for studying thought processes. People are not usually conscious of the mental steps they go through in solving problems. It is therefore not surprising that speakers are ordinarily not aware of the psychological processes that govern their use of language. The abstract and complex nature of these processes, as revealed by the deep-level analysis of transformational grammarians, makes the psychologist's task of discovering the mechanisms responsible for language acquisition and use especially difficult and challenging.

PSYCHOLOGICAL PROCESSES IN LANGUAGE ACQUISITION

Let us now examine the psychological work on learning and retention and on perception to assess its contribution to the understanding of language acquisition.

LEARNING AND RETENTION   The question of how, what, and why organisms learn and retain has been of major concern to psychologists. The best-developed theories in this area, however, are based on experiments involving the learning of simple tasks acquirable by animals and have limited relevance to the acquisition of such a complex and uniquely human behavior as language. It appears that learning theory has some applicability to the acquisition of specific linguistic habits but has very little to say about the acquisition of rules.

Language habits.   One type of learning, known as classical conditioning, has been investigated extensively in the animal laboratory, and we shall now turn to an examination of its relevance to the habitual aspects of language. This examination will be followed by a discussion of mechanisms for the acquisition of language rules.

Classical conditioning procedures endeavor to establish reliable links between environmental events (stimuli) and activities of the organism (responses) in such a way that a particular activity will come under the control of a particular stimulus. For instance, by use of classical conditioning procedures, a dog can be made to salivate to the sound of a bell. This is accomplished by sounding the bell and immediately following it by the presentation of food (which reliably leads to salivation). After frequent repetitions of this sequence the dog will salivate to the sound even in the absence of food. When this response has been achieved, the animal is said to have been conditioned. Conditioned links of this sort have been established between many other stimuli and responses besides the bell and salivation, and important insights into the associative process have been derived from such experiments. We shall now attempt to utilize these insights in discussing associative processes in language learning.

The associations involved in language can be classified into two categories: extralanguage associations and intralanguage associations. In the first category fall all links that have to be made specifically between environmental stimuli and linguistic units. Thus learning the word for a particular referent involves some kind of association, as does the learning of an appropriate expression for a particular occasion. The intralanguage category refers mostly to the integration of smaller language units into larger ones. The establishment of a word as an integrated whole is a result of linkage of its component sounds. On a higher level of integration, words associate with each other to form phrases and idioms.

The acquisition of meaning is a complex and little understood process, and it certainly involves more than just formation of associations between referents and words, but associative processes no doubt play a role here. For a child to learn the meaning of the word *skates,* say, he would have to have heard this word in the presence of the real skates or some pictorial or verbal representation of them. Often such pairing would need to be repeated several times before the association became well established. The association between the object skates and the word *skates* is not a single association but a complex of many associations. Various features of the skates (a sports item, has blades, worn on the feet, etc.) become linked in the associative transaction with various features of the word (beginning with an /s/ sound, a one-syllable word, etc.). Some of these links may be formed and retained more readily than others and give rise to errors, such as an interchange of the names for skates and skis.

A particular response becomes attached not only to the stimuli nominated by the experimenter or teacher but also to others present in the situation. This accounts for the observation that it is usually easier to recall a person's name if one encounters him in surroundings and attire similar to those that were present when the name was first learned. A name given when a person is introduced becomes associated not only with the person's face and figure (in themselves complex stimuli) but also with such supporting stimuli as the people who stood around, the house of the host, etc. If one cannot recall a name immediately, it therefore helps to reinstate in memory the conditions in which the name was heard. This observation has direct applications to education. A student who studies a particular material in one situation, such as a language laboratory, may not be able to reproduce it easily in other situations. Individuals are sometimes observed to have greater difficulty in speaking a foreign language in contexts removed from those in which they learned it than in similar ones. Apparently what happens is that during the learning process the new material becomes connected to many of the cues in the situation; therefore when the situation is faithfully reproduced, recall is easier than when it is not. Thus every new response appears to be bound by the specific stimulus context in which it was acquired.

This analysis would suggest that an item learned in a certain position in an ordered presentation would be easier to recall when the preceding items in the list are given than when they are not. Since in everyday life one has to use language not in any systematic order but in answer to needs that arise, it would seem that the teaching method should not fix any item in a certain position but should allow for its use in many different conditions in order to provide for flexibility and independence of language habits from specific contextual stimuli.

Now, let us turn to intralanguage associative processes. The integration of sounds into words and words into higher-order units is achieved only through repeated experience, in close contiguity, of the elements that make up the unit. Thus, for instance, English speakers have the phrases *go home, go to hell,* and *go away* available as units because they have heard and used them over and over many times. In constructing sentences such phrases are immediately available and do not need to be formed on the occasion they are used. This enables the speaker to construct grammatical utterances faster than if he had to work from scratch on the level of words. The formation of intralanguage associations is thus important for a full mastery of language. This fact suggests why drill in translation equivalents is bad practice. The explicit linkage of a word in one language with a word in another language may interfere with the facilitative effects of intralanguage associations. Thus, for instance, if a student repeats many times the pair *go-aller,* the association between the two will become so strong that the French word will come to the student's mind whenever he uses the English equivalent and inhibit the smooth transition from *go* to the other English words, a skill necessary for fluent speech.

Thus far we have been emphasizing the dependence of learning and retention on the external features of the learning conditions, but man is a self-regulating organism and is not wholly at the mercy of external stimuli. The learner can enhance his retention of learned material in various ways not entirely dependent on external conditions. Even if the material is presented in a very specific situation, the learner can free himself from its constraints by imagining different situations under which it may need to be available. A quotation from William James (1890, p. 662) should make this point clear:

> In mental terms, *the more other facts a fact is associated with in the mind, the better possession of it our memory retains.* Each of its associates becomes a hook to which it hangs, a means to fish it up by when sunk beneath the surface. Together, they form a network of attachments by which it is woven into the entire tissue of our thought. The "secret of good memory" is thus the secret of forming diverse and multiple associations with every fact we care to retain. . . . Briefly, then, of two men with the same outward experiences and the same amount of mere native tenacity, *the one who* THINKS *over his experiences most,* and weaves them into systematic relation with each other, *will be the one with the best memory.*

Since James's times, we have accumulated evidence which elaborates on the conclusion that the memorizer does not always store passively the information presented to him but has the capacity to weave it into a systematic organization. For instance, let us give a subject a list made up of animal and weapon words in mixed order and ask him to memorize the list and then write down all the words he can recall. Examining the order in which the subject recalls the words, we discover that he organized them by the two categories (Bousfield, 1953). In this case the subject spontaneously (whether consciously or unconsciously) structured the material. In cases in which the subject does not on his own hit on an organizational principle, proper instructions will readily lead him to employ it and facilitate his memory (Tulving, 1962).

Such observations, although interpretable in associative terminology, seem to be more elegantly handled by information-processing models (e.g., Yntema and Trask, 1963). These models conceive of memory storage as cross-classification analogous to the cataloging of books in a library under different subject headings. Each item entering memory for permanent storage gets tagged by the various categories. Such cross-categorization facilitates retrieval of information when needed. It would seem that good memory depends partly on the development and utilization of useful categories for tagging individual items. Categorization seems to account for the observation that often, especially in a foreign tongue, a person cannot think of the appropriate word but instead comes up with categorically related words. In English, for instance, an individual may not be able to recall the word *menu* but will remember that it fell in the same category as *list* or *food*. The categorization notion can also explain such errors as saying the opposite of what one intends to say, *left* instead of *right* and *down* instead of *up*, for example. Errors of this sort can be understood in terms of a system of hierarchical tags from general to specific. The main tag would place all four words in the category of items concerned with directionality. Second-order tags would indicate that one pair is concerned with horizontal direction and the other with vertical direction, and only third-order (or lower-order) tags would distinguish between the two members within each pair. This analysis makes it entirely possible for a speaker to take account of all the tags but the most specific and therefore to interchange antonyms.

It thus appears that even in the realm of linguistic habits association theories have to compete with information-processing models. The fate of association theories in the realm of linguistic rules, to which we now turn, is much worse.

Language rules. There have been many attempts to explain phenomena of grammar in terms of chains of word associations. According to this view, there is nothing unique in grammar; its apparent complexities can be reduced to associations among words. This view, however, has been shown to be completely inadequate (Chomsky, 1957; Lashley, 1951). Speakers are clearly able to produce, and hearers to understand, utterances composed of words which were never associated with each other before. It has become obvious now that the selection of each word in a sentence cannot be explained solely by reference to the preceding words; account has to be taken of superordinate rules of grammar that exert their influence not in a sequential left-to-right fashion but through a simultaneous process working from top to bottom.

Since the nature of linguistic rules has been described most completely in transformational grammar, it seems appropriate to ask how transformational grammarians conceive of the acquisition of such rules. The answer that emerges from the writings of Chomsky (e.g., 1962) and others is that the child is functioning as an implicit inductive scientist. The child collects data from his environment in the form of linguistic utterances he hears, classifies them into various grammatical categories, and constructs rules to account for the regularities he discovers. He then uses these rules in producing new utterances. The system the child develops is not static but subject to revision as new linguistic data become available in the course of development. Apparently, human beings are endowed with a program for analyzing linguistic input to discover a system of underlying regularities. The amazing thing about language acquisition is that out of a collection of random, unorganized, and often ungrammatical linguistic utterances the child manages to form a well-structured system of rules. Because such a phenomenal system is mastered in a relatively short time, it is suspected (e.g., Lenneberg, 1964) that the language analyzer is largely innate and that it makes a substantial contribution to the shape of the product of its analysis, i.e., to grammar. In other words, the acquisition of language depends not only on exposure to environmental stimulation but also on specific innate propensities of the organism.

These ideas were developed for first language learning by children, but similar processes of inference probably go on in second language learning by adults. It is possible, however, that the ability to formulate linguistic rules diminishes with increased age. This would explain the observations (e.g., Masson, 1964) that pre-teen-age children learn languages faster than teen-agers and adults. But whatever the degree of efficiency of the rule-abstracting process in postchildhood, there is little doubt that the learner encountered by the high school and college teacher of languages spontaneously organizes and analyzes in some way the material presented to him. It is crucial to find out what the nature of these analyzing processes is in order to take account of them in the structuring of teaching materials.

This analysis of language learning and retention has forced us to consider two major factors, the external environment and the internal processes of the learner and retainer. External stimuli were seen to provide cues for the retrieval of retained material and information for an internal analyzer which constructs a system of syntactic rules on the basis of this information. We shall now see that these two factors also have to be considered in the analysis of perception.

PERCEPTION Apart from learning and retention, perception is another major field of psychological inquiry, and we shall now relate some of the ideas developed in it to second language learning. Roughly speaking, perception refers to the processes that are initiated in the brain when the organism is stimulated by some external agent. There are three components in the perceptual process: the physical stimulus, the sensory stimulus, and the percept. The physical stimulus refers to the stimulating agent as it exists objectively in the environment. The statement "a wooden 10 x 5 x 2 board supported at a height of 5 feet from the ground by four metal poles" would constitute a description of a physical stimulus. The representation of a physical stimulus in one of the human senses constitutes the sensory stimulus. The sensory stimulus is not an exact replica of the physical stimulus: on any given occasion only some aspects of the physical stimulus are registered by the senses. For instance, the projection on the retina of the object described would vary from one situation to another depending on the angle of vision, illumination, and other factors. When the sensory input is interpreted by the higher centers of the brain, a percept is achieved. In the case described it is obvious that the interpretation involves the placement of the input in the conceptual category "table."

Thus far we have described perception as a one-way process leading from the physical raw materials through the sensory input to the final percept. This is an incomplete picture. Perceptual interpretation often begins before the complete accumulation of the sensory data and guides the search for relevant data. The perceiver is not passively awaiting the income of sensory raw material to start his interpretation but is active in forming hypotheses as to the category membership of a particular stimulus and looks for cues to confirm or reject them. The hypotheses can be based on probabilities of occurrence of certain events in certain environments, on motivational variables, on preliminary inspection of the stimulus, and on other factors. This view of the perceptual process is supported by many formal experiments (e.g., Bruner, 1957). The reader can convince himself of its validity by trying to insert a word or two in one language while carrying on a conversation in another. Most of his bilingual fellow conversants would not notice these words, and if they did notice them, understanding would not be guaranteed. The conversants would not expect to hear words in the other language and therefore would not be ready to perceive them.

The role played by the physical stimulus is limited not only by the factor of preparedness but also by the nature of the categories employed by the perceiver. Categories do not exist in nature; they are human inventions imposed on it to meet social needs. Certain features of objects are made prominent and given signal value for categorization while other features physically more imposing may remain in the background. Sapir (1951, p. 46) used a similar conception in his analysis of phonemes, as can be seen from the following passage:

> To say that a given phoneme is not sufficiently defined in articulatory or acoustic terms but needs to be fitted into the total system of sound relations peculiar to the language is, at bottom, no more mysterious than to say that a club is not defined for us when it is said to be made of wood and to have such and such a shape and such and such dimensions. We must understand why a roughly similar object, not so different to the eye, is no club at all, and why a third object, of very different color and much longer and heavier than the first, is for all that very much of a club.

The observation that percepts are joint products of environmental stimuli and of cultural categories for their classification can find examples in foreign language learning. Often a beginning student does not hear a particular phoneme in the new language as different from a close phoneme in his native tongue; i.e., he classifies the stimulus input into the wrong category. Obviously, proper categorization presupposes the availability of the appropriate categories. It is therefore important for the foreign language learner to build up phonemic categories appropriate to the new language.

Phonemic categories seem important not only for speech perception but also for speech production. Speech is more than an activity of the articulatory muscles. In voluntary control of speech, the speech organs must receive instructions from higher centers in the brain as to what sounds to produce. If a particular sound of a foreign language is not represented in the brain, such instruction is obviously not possible. This analysis may explain why training in sound discrimination can be more beneficial in the initial stages of language learning than training in speech production.

On the other hand, a particular phonemic concept need not develop solely via the auditory modality; it can develop through the kinesthetic modality, i.e., through the sensors in the muscles and tendons. That is, sounds are registered not only by our ears but also by mechanisms embedded in the muscles that deal with the feedback from their own activity. If, therefore, a new form of activity is employed in the production of a particular sound, the student may be able to recognize it accurately when he himself articulates it even though he is not able to hear it correctly when produced by others (see Lane, 1965).

SUMMARY

Language has been viewed as consisting of two components: specific habits and rules. The acquisition of specific habits can be explained partly by associative rote-learning principles, while rule learning requires the postulation of an information-processing device that induces rules from a limited corpus of examples. Perception is the mechanism that filters the raw material for this information analyzer. Perception itself is codetermined by the environmental stimuli and by the categories the perceiver has learned to use in his commerce with the environment.

REFERENCES

Bousfield, W. A. The occurrence of clustering in the recall of randomly arranged associates. *Journal of General Psychology,* 1953, **49,** 229–240.

Bruner, Jerome S. On perceptual readiness. *Psychological Review,* 1957, **64,** 123–152.

Chomsky, Noam. *Syntactic structures.* The Hague: Mouton, 1957.

Chomsky, Noam. Explanatory models in linguistics. In E. Nagel, P. Suppes, and A. Tarsky (Eds.), *Logic, methodology and philosophy of science*. Stanford, Calif.: Stanford University Press, 1962. Pp. 528–550.

Chomsky, Noam. Degrees of grammaticalness. In J. A. Fodor and J. J. Katz (Eds.), *The structure of language*. Englewood Cliffs, N.J.: Prentice-Hall, Inc., 1964. Pp. 384–399.

Chomsky, Noam. *Aspects of the theory of syntax*. Cambridge, Mass.: The M.I.T. Press, 1965.

Greenberg, J. H., and J. J. Jenkins. Studies in the psychological correlates of the sound system of American English. *Word*, 1964, **20**, 157–177.

James, William. *The principles of psychology*. New York: Henry Holt and Company, 1890. Dover Publications, Inc., 1950. Vol. 1.

Lambert, Wallace E. Psychological approaches to the study of language. *Modern Language Journal*, 1963, **47**, 51–62, 114–121.

Lane, H. The motor theory of speech perception: A critical review. *Psychological Review*, 1965, **72**, 275–309.

Lashley, K. S. The problem of serial order in behavior. In L. A. Jeffress (Ed.), *Cerebral mechanisms in behavior*. New York: John Wiley & Sons, Inc., 1951. Pp. 112–136.

Lees, R. B. The grammar of English nominalizations. *International Journal of American Linguistics*, 1960, **26**, No. 3.

Lenneberg, E. H. The capacity for language acquisition. In J. A. Fodor and J. J. Katz (Eds.), *The Structure of language*. Englewood Cliffs, N.J.: Prentice-Hall, Inc., 1964. Pp. 579–603.

Masson, L. I. The influence of developmental level on the learning of a second language among children of Anglo-Saxon origin. *Canadian Education and Research Digest*, 1964, **4**, 188–192.

Postal, P. Underlying and superficial linguistic structure. *Harvard Educational Review*, 1964, **34**, 246–266.

Rivers, Wilga M. *The psychologist and the foreign language teacher*. Chicago: The University of Chicago Press, 1964.

Sapir, E. The psychological reality of phonemes. In D. G. Mandelbaum (Ed.), *Selected writings of Edward Sapir*. Berkeley, Calif.: University of California Press, 1951. Pp. 46–60.

Taylor, Insup K. Phonetic symbolism re-examined. *Psychological Bulletin*, 1963, **60**, 200–209.

Tulving, E. Subjective organization in free recall of "unrelated" words. *Psychological Review*, 1962, **69**, 344–354.

Whorf, Benjamin L. *Language, thought and reality*. Cambridge, Mass.: The M.I.T. Press, 1956. Pp. 220–232.

Yntema, D. B., and F. P. Trask. Recall as a search process. *Journal of Verbal Learning and Verbal Behavior*, 1963, **2**, 65–74.

8

THE IMPLICATIONS OF BILINGUALISM FOR LANGUAGE TEACHING AND LANGUAGE LEARNING

JOSHUA A. FISHMAN

Joshua A. Fishman (1926–   ) is a social psychologist who has specialized in language and behavior, primarily in the area of sociolinguistics. He has been a fellow at the Center for Advanced Study in the Behavioral Sciences and is currently a member of the Social Science Research Council's Committee on Sociolinguistics. He is professor of psychology and sociology at Yeshiva University and dean of its Graduate School of Education.

It is my contention that language teachers (all language teachers but particularly foreign language teachers) are producers of bilinguals. As such, there should be a natural affinity between social psychologists of language, such as myself, and teachers of language. My colleagues and I are accustomed to pursuing various theoretical questions related to social behavior via empirical research on bilingualism. We are quite convinced that "there is nothing as practical as a good theory." On the other hand, foreign language teachers are accustomed to relating practical methods of instruction to individual differences in ability and style. Their work convinces me that "there is nothing as theoretically provocative as sensitive practice." Thus, it is my conviction that we have a great deal to learn from each other that leads me to offer the following observations.

WHAT IS BILINGUALISM?

I would define bilingualism as "demonstrated ability to engage in communication via more than one language." This definition is careful not to restrict bilingualism to any particular level of "demonstrated ability" or to any particular kind of "communication." Indeed, this definition strikes many people as being unduly permissive, so much so that students have often told me that "even they would be bilingual under this definition." It is important, however, to realize that under certain circumstances people can be bilingual without knowing it, just as many people can speak prose all their lives without knowing it.

There is a widespread assumption among Americans that bilingualism must be defined as *"equal* (balanced) and *advanced* mastery of two languages," but this assumption is subject to question on two counts:

1. To require that bilingualism be defined in terms of equal and advanced mastery is no more justifiable than to require that intelligence be defined restrictively as equivalent to genius or that health be defined restrictively as equivalent to the complete absence of any dysfunction. We know very well that both intelligence and health are matters of degree as well as of kind. In more general terms we recognize the logical fallacy of defining any behavioral manifestation in terms of an unusual degree or quality of the behavior in question. The same is true with respect to bilingualism, and language teachers must be particularly sensitive to its varying degrees and kinds.

2. To require that bilingualism be defined in terms of equal and advanced mastery is tantamount to excluding all *natural* bilingual populations, those of today as well as all those that have existed since the dawn of history, from meeting the requirements of the definition. Indeed, the only ones who could conceivably fit the bill of equal and advanced mastery are a few rather atypical translators and teachers. Certainly the hundreds of millions of Central and Eastern Europeans, the Africans, Asians, and Melanesians whom we usually think of as natural bilingual populations cannot be said to evince balanced and equal mastery.

It would seem that Americans hold so tenaciously to a balanced-and-equal-mastery definition of bilingualism because it is a definition which enables so many of them to disqualify themselves, i.e., to hide their own bilingualism from themselves and from others and to masquerade as monolinguals. Many Americans have long been of the opinion that bilingualism is "a good thing" if it was acquired via travel (preferably to Paris) or via formal education (preferably at Harvard) but that it is "a bad thing" if it was acquired from one's immigrant parents or grandparents (Fishman et al., 1965; Fishman & Nahirny, 1964). So reluctant are many Americans to show pride in their immigrant-based bilingualism that I find that once the equal-and-advanced-mastery camouflage is denied them, they tend to jump to the other end of the spectrum and to argue: "Well, then, everybody's bilingual!" This argument of "We're all in it together" is, however, no more valid than the "not-me" argument that preceded it. Although nearly everyone *is* bilingual (if only in the sense that he masters different "registers" appropriate to home, school, church, office, ball park, etc.), people still differ very greatly in the *degree* and in the *kind* of their bilingualism. Indeed, it is exactly this set of facts (that nearly everybody is bilingual but that the degrees and kinds of bilingualism differ very markedly) that has made bilingualism such a fruitful field for psychological and sociological study.

I shall conclude these definitional remarks by saying that even a much stricter definition of bilingualism (e.g., "demonstrated ability to engage in prolonged discussions concerning activities of daily life in more than one language") would still qualify more than half of the world's population today (and far more than half in earlier days) as bilingual. Moreover, even by such a definition we are dealing with an extremely widespread achievement, an achievement to which the work of foreign language teachers merely adds embellishment rather than basic components.

WHY STUDY BILINGUALISM?

Since language teachers are actively producing bilinguals (although few "teacher-made" bilinguals function at a level that meets the stricter definition mentioned above), it is their professional responsibility to be interested in what different degrees and kinds of bilingualism do to their pupils—intellectually, emotionally, and attitudinally. I plan to review recent findings pertaining to these very matters. Before doing so, however, I should like to point out that most social and behavioral scientists are interested in a bilingual's bilingualism for reasons quite different from those revealed by language teachers. Basically, we view bilingualism as a prism that breaks up the subtle and continuous spectrum of language behavior into more easily recognizable strands or rays. Whether a social or behavioral scientist is interested in language development, in habitual language use ("the ethnography of communication"), in sociocultural differences in language use, in behaviors toward language (such as language loyalty or antipathy), or in any one of the countless other topics that attract psychologists, social psychologists, and sociologists to the study of language-related behavior, it is often the case that bilingualism permits a clearer recognition of the processes that must be investigated. Bilingualism provides the investigator with benefits akin to those of binocular vision and binaural hearing when the latter are compared with monocular vision and monaural hearing. Far from being a complication in the field of language-related behavior, it frequently reveals such behavior with greater clarity than does monolingualism.

DEGREES AND KINDS OF BILINGUALISM

Teachers are understandably interested in questions pertaining to degrees of bilingualism. Frequently they want to know how they can make their pupils more bilingual. They want to know which methods will be most successful in accomplishing this goal and what the attitudinal consequences of greater degrees of bilingualism are. They also want to know whether pupil characteristics and method characteristics interact in ways such that some pupils can become more bilingual via certain methods whereas other pupils can become more bilingual only via other methods. When teachers ask social and behavioral scientists for answers to such questions as these, they find that (1) information is available concerning some of these matters but not concerning others and (2) it is available concerning other aspects of degrees of bilingualism than those that most teachers have usually considered. This is not an unusual state of affairs since any two disciplines working at different levels of abstraction cannot be expected to be perfectly attuned to each other's concerns. The two disciplines must, however, continue to ask questions of each other. Social and behavioral scientists become aware of additional problems for research when teachers ask them questions that cannot currently be answered. Teachers become aware of additional subtleties in their work when social and behavioral scientists give them answers that go beyond the questions that they have asked. This latter fact is amply demonstrated by the following summary of what social and behavioral scientists know about degrees of bilingualism.

There is no degree of second language achievement unrelated to particular kinds of bilingualism. When social and behavioral scientists refer to kinds of bilingualism, they have two different considerations in mind: contextual and processual.

THE CONTEXTS OF BILINGUALISM

The degree of an individual's bilingualism will rarely be the same in various *media,* such as speaking, reading, and writing. This is as true of natural bilinguals (those rendered bilingual by their total society) as it is of school-made bilinguals. Bilinguals who speak two languages quite well may nevertheless not read or write them both with similarily balanced facility. Indeed, in many natural bilingual settings only one of the languages spoken will be a language of reading and writing. This is true not only in Africa, where English, French, or some other language of wider communication rather than any of the local vernaculars is the language of literacy (Samarin, 1965; Stewart, 1965), but also in Europe, where, for example, Schwyzertütsch is widely spoken in Switzerland, although its speakers normally use High German for reading and writing (Weinreich 1951); South America, where, for example, Guaraní is widely spoken in Paraguay, although its speakers normally use Spanish for reading and writing (Rubin, 1965); and elsewhere. If the teacher is teaching a language which usually functions in a bilingual setting, he must certainly ask himself whether it is necessary to increase the bilingualism of his pupils in connection with all three media or only in connection with one or another of them. Even if the language in question normally functions in a monolingual (or primarily monolingual) setting, the teacher might well set up media priorities in terms of pursuing higher degrees of bilingualism in his pupils. The establishment of media priorities undoubtedly will have methodological consequences.

The degree of an individual's bilingualism will rarely be the same in various *roles,* such as comprehension (understanding messages from others), production (sending messages to others), and inner speech (talking to oneself, thinking out loud). This is also true of both natural and school-made bilinguals. Once again, the teacher must establish priorities (this time, role priorities) in conjunction with this determination that pupils attain a higher degree of bilingualism.

The degree of an individual's bilingualism will rarely be the same at various *formality levels,* such as intimate, casual, and formal levels. Normal bilinguals usually utilize only one of their two languages for intimate communications while reserving the other for formalized and ritualized communications (Geerz, 1965). Surely this must be equally if not more true of school-made bilinguals, and surely the language teacher must again arrive at a decision based upon priorities. In increasing the degree of his pupils' bilingualism, which is the most important: ability to engage in intimate, casual, or formal communication? Each level of formality requires a vocabulary, a sentence structure, and a set of attitudes toward oneself and one's interlocutors quite different from those required by the others.

The degree of an individual's bilingualism will rarely be the same in various *domains* of interaction. Walloon-Flemish bilinguals in Belgium may well speak Flemish to each other about hearth and home but utilize

French in speaking about art, music, and government. Certain sociocultural foci and certain relationships between individuals call for one
language rather than another in bilingual settings throughout the world.
The language of religion and poetry may not be the language of business
and family affairs; the language between nobleman and commoner may
not be the same as the language between nobleman and nobleman or
between commoner and commoner. The language teacher, particularly
one who is teaching a language that is utilized in a bilingual setting or
in a setting in which classical and colloquial variants of the same language
exist side by side (Ferguson, 1964; Stewart, 1965), must ask himself:
About what topics and *to* what range of social types do I want my pupils
to be able to communicate? Only after a decision has been reached with
respect to this question can greater degrees of bilingualism be pursued in
a realistic manner.

The four contextual decisions that have been independently enumerated above are actually related to each other in real life, whether that be
the real life of the natural bilingual setting or the real life of the classroom. The teacher must arrive at simultaneous decisions concerning all
these contextual factors. In doing so, he will have determined the *bilingual
dominance configuration* (Fishman et al., 1965) that he is seeking to
create in his pupils, for the bilingual dominance configuration—a topic
of overriding interest to behavioral and social scientists concerned with
bilingualism—is nothing more than a configuration derived from the
measurement of bilingual performance when such performance is viewed
in terms of the simultaneous interaction of media, role, formality, and
domain considerations. The dimensions of the configuration do not, however, define the performance per se: they merely provide a contextual
framework within which performance ("process") can be analyzed. This
then brings us to the second consideration that social and behavioral
scientists have in mind when they refer to kinds of bilingualism.

THE PROCESSES ("PERFORMANCES") OF BILINGUALISM

Obviously, degree of bilingualism must be recognizable, ultimately, in
terms of some sample of the pupil's language performance. There are,
however, a number of different ways in which any performance may be
evaluated. Linguists are inclined to evaluate bilingual performance in
terms of absence of interference (Haugen, 1956). From this point of view
an individual is more bilingual if his mastery of the phonology (sounds),
grammatical structure, and lexical repertoire of one language shows no
traces of the phonology, grammar, and lexicon of the other. Teachers
must decide whether this is also what they mean when they wish to pursue

higher levels of language achievement. If so, they may need to emphasize certain instructional procedures (e.g., "pattern practice") rather than others.

When psychologists refer to degrees of bilingualism, they tend to have in mind automaticity (rapidity) of response rather than lack of interference (Lambert, 1955). From this point of view facility (readiness and rapidity of flow) is the predominant consideration. Sociologists, on the other hand, are most likely to suggest frequency of use as a measure of bilingualism. From this point of view a pupil who uses a given second language most frequently (in terms of hours per day) is most bilingual, regardless of how effortlessly or how flawlessly he speaks (Lambert, 1955). Finally, there is an educational-testing approach to the evaluation of bilingualism which tends to stress size of repertoire as well as those criteria that are of interest to linguists and psychologists as mentioned above. Here we note a concern for vocabulary size and correctness of response (or of choice) relative to other pupils who have studied as long and presumably by the same methods (Manuel, 1963). All in all, the decision as to which kind or kinds of performance to recognize in evaluating degree of bilingualism is a difficult one. When this decision is added to the decisions required by the dominance configuration proper, it becomes clear why the attainment of higher degrees of bilingualism can never be removed from questions of educational philosophy and instructional methods.

In terms of the considerations introduced above the differences between "old" and "new" language instruction in the United States might be stated as follows: Years ago, language instruction emphasized *reading* ("medium") *comprehension* ("role") of *formal* texts dealing with *literary topics* and largely evaluated in terms of *repertoire size*. Today, most language instruction seems to emphasize the *production* and *comprehension* of *casual speech* dealing with *interpersonal and intercultural topics* and largely evaluated in terms of *lack of interference*. Today's language teachers are prone to declare that their predecessors did not develop well-rounded or natural bilinguals. This is undoubtedly true, but it is also true that today's teachers are emphasizing only certain cells of the entire dominance configuration. They too are limiting their goals and are producing bilinguals who differ in many ways from those produced by society outside the classroom.

TYPES OF BILINGUAL FUNCTIONING

Another difference between the old and the new schools of language instruction relates to the types of bilingual functioning that they each pursue. In this connection, psychologists and social psychologists concerned with bilingualism differentiate between two major types. One type of bilingual thinks only in one of his two languages, usually in that which is his mother tongue. When he produces communications (spoken or written) in his "other tongue," it is obvious that he is not thinking in that language from the degree of grammatical (not to mention lexical and phonetic) interference that his communications reveal. This type of bilingualism, which is based upon a neurological organization fused so that one language depends substantially on the same neurological components as the other, is referred to as *compound* (Ervin & Osgood, 1954) or *interdependent* bilingualism. It may be contrasted with a type of bilingual functioning in which the individual keeps each of his languages quite separate. He thinks in X when producing messages (to himself or to others) in X, and he thinks in Y when producing messages in Y. This type of bilingual functioning is referred to as *coordinate* or *independent* bilingualism.

In many ways it seems appropriate to equate the old approach to language teaching with the compound type of bilingual functioning and the new approach with coordinate bilingualism. Actually, however, such an equation is not entirely justified since most bilinguals manifest both compound and coordinate functioning from minute to minute, from topic to topic, from one interlocutor to another (Fishman et al., 1965). A "normally coordinate bilingual" may have been a compound bilingual initially, when he was just learning his second language. He may revert to compound bilingualism if an atypical occasion arises in which language X is called for, although the domain involved is clearly dominated by Y (e.g., when a bilingual Englishman tries to discuss the fine points of cricket in French). He may revert to compound bilingualism if it becomes necessary to speak X to a person with whom he would ordinarily speak Y about any topic (e.g., when two bilingual Englishmen who have been lifelong friends in English must speak French to each other because they are in the company of a monolingual Frenchman). Thus, the distinction between compound and coordinate bilingualism is not an absolute one that is settled once and for all in the brain of either a natural or a school-made bilingual. Nevertheless, it remains true that more modern ("direct") instructional methods have adopted the coordinate model as their own and that many teachers who are strongly convinced of the merits of the direct method explicitly aim at students who can keep their two languages apart, who can think independently in each, and who can "speak like natives" in each. This being the case, it might be of interest to such teachers to inquire into the cognitive and emotional consequences for the learner when such goals and the methods that are derived from them are vigorously pursued.

SOME CONSEQUENCES AND CONCOMITANTS OF THE "DIRECT" METHOD OF SECOND LANGUAGE LEARNING

Every teacher knows that pupils differ in their motivation for second language learning. Even when the intensity of motivation is equally strong, pupils still differ in the nature or origin of their motivation. Some pupils study other languages for *utilitarian* reasons (occupational advancement, scholarly interest in literature or in history, etc.). Others study languages for *integrative* reasons (e.g., cross-cultural sympathies and appreciations, a liking for other cultures and peoples). Although these kinds of pupils may be of equal language learning ability and have equally strong motivation, they will nevertheless tend to learn differently (Lambert, Gardner, Barick, & Tinstall, 1963). Those students propelled by integrative motives will be most successful in learning by the direct method. They will learn a great deal from out-of-school experiences (such as trips and visits and motion pictures). Those whose motivation is instrumental will tend to profit more from classroom instruction. They will do particularly well in connection with formal conjugation, translation, and other materials emphasized by the older instructional methods.

Ordinarily, pupils with integrative motivation gradually adopt various attitudes and self-views which characterize native speakers of the language that they are learning (Lambert, 1963; Lambert et al., 1963). In many ways they behave as if they wanted to become members of the other group, as if they wanted to adopt not only another language but a complete culture and all its behavior patterns. Undoubtedly their disposition to weaken their own-group ties and to strengthen other-group ties facilitates their learning. This widespread tendency does not, however, hold in one very important case: that of children learning an ethnic mother tongue with which they still have at least passive familiarity. In this case (and this is an extremely important one in the second language classroom in the United States and in immigration centers throughout the world) learners benefit most from pride in their own-group (ethnic-group) membership rather than from a desire to take on characteristics of another group (Anisfeld & Lambert, 1961; Brault, 1964).

These subtleties should be of great interest to the teacher who is devoted to the direct method, for they indicate that method may well have to take second place to other considerations: the learner's motivation, his background, and, indeed, even the degree of success he experiences. As the integratively motivated learner progresses in his studies, his attraction to "the other group" may become so strong as to embarrass or alarm him and his associates. He may come to experience considerable chagrin as his ties to his own group weaken. He may also experience considerable anxiety as he draws closer and closer to entry into a relatively strange group whose members may not like him nearly so much as he has come to like them. Indeed, feelings of *anomie,* homelessness and uncertainty and dissatisfaction (with respect to both one's own and the other group), may become so severe that it is precisely the more advanced, integratively oriented students who may seek opportunities to withdraw from the pressures of the direct method and from overly intense interaction with the other group. Having overreached themselves, they must draw back to minimize anomie and to reassert their identity. The sensitive teacher, however, will recognize this as a problem rather than as failure of the intensive-direct method.

THE PAINS AND PLEASURES OF BILINGUALISM

Although I do not mean the remarks made above to be mistaken for a critique of the intensive-direct method of producing bilinguals, I do think that it is appropriate for language teachers to realize that second language learning and bilingualism more generally may not be entirely matters of mutual goodwill on the part of students and teachers. More so than most school-imparted skills, school-based second language learning may require difficult cognitive and emotional readjustments, which may be beyond the limits of some personalities. School-based bilingualism, particularly that which proceeds via the intensive-direct method, requires that relatively mature organisms return briefly to childish ways of talking, of thinking, of groping for words, of admitting helplessness. At the same time, we know that the learner's personality consolidates as he passes the great adolescent watershed. Thereafter it becomes increasingly difficult for him to imitate perfectly sounds that are strange to his mother tongue. Although this particular difficulty is due primarily to physiological rigidity, emotional and intellectual rigidities also develop during these years, and not everyone can succeed in overcoming them.

Those who succeed more fully in dropping the barriers that impede school-based bilingualism may do so too completely, too naïvely, too rapidly. They may have to pay for their flexibility by suffering the pangs of rootlessness (anomie). This is by no means a fatal illness, however, and when it recedes, it reveals new facets of the self. Not only does the bilingual master two different codes, but he masters two different selves, two different modes of relating to reality, two different orders of sensitivity to the wonders of the world. These are the very reasons why bilingualism has been treasured by social and intellectual elites throughout the world and throughout the ages. By working together more effectively than we have in the past, teachers of languages and professional students of language-related behavior can make the benefits of bilingualism more widely available and more easily attainable to those who have not yet partaken of them.

REFERENCES

Anisfeld, Moshe, and Wallace E. Lambert. Social and psychological variables in learning Hebrew. *Journal of Abnormal and Social Psychology,* 1961, **63,** 524–529.

Brault, Gerald J. Some misconceptions about teaching American ethnic children their mother tongue. *Modern Language Journal,* 1964, **48,** 67–71.

Ervin, Susan M., and Charles E. Osgood. Second language learning and bilingualism. *Journal of Abnormal and Social Psychology,* 1954, Suppl. **49,** 139–146.

Ferguson, Charles. Diglossia. In D. Hymes (Ed.), *Language in culture and society.* New York: Harper & Row, Publishers, Incorporated, 1964.

Fishman, Joshua A. et al. *Language loyalty in the United States.* The Hague: Mouton, 1965. (See Chap. 15, "Language maintenance in a supra-ethnic age.")

Fishman, Joshua A., and Vladimir C. Nahirny: The ethnic group school and mother tongue maintenance in the United States. *Sociology of Education,* 1964, **37,** 306–317.

Geerz, Clifford. Linguistic etiquette. In J. A. Fishman (Ed.), *Readings in the sociology of language.* The Hague: Mouton, 1966.

Haugen, Einar. *Bilingualism in the Americas: A bibliography and research guide.* American Dialect Society Publication No. 26. University, Ala.: University of Alabama Press, 1956.

Lambert, Wallace E. Measurement of linguistic dominance of bilinguals. *Journal of Abnormal and Social Psychology,* 1955, **50,** 197–200.

Lambert, Wallace E. Psychological approaches to the study of language, Part II. *Modern Language Journal,* 1963, **47,** 114–121.

Lambert, Wallace E., R. C. Gardner, J. C. Barick, and K. Tinstall. Attitudinal and cognitive aspects of intensive study of a second language. *Journal of Abnormal and Social Psychology,* 1963, **66,** 358–368. (Also see R. C. Gardner and Wallace E. Lambert. Motivational variables in second-language acquisition. *Canadian Journal of Psychology,* 1959, **13,** 266–272.)

Manuel, Herschel T. *The preparation and evaluation of inter-language testing materials.* Report of Cooperative Research Project No. 681. Austin, Tex.: University of Texas, 1963.

Rubin, Joan. Bilingual usage in Paraguay. In J. A. Fishman (Ed.), *Readings in the sociology of language.* The Hague: Mouton, 1966.

Samarin, William J. Lingua francas with special reference to Africa. In J. A. Fishman (Ed.), *Readings in the sociology of language.* The Hague: Mouton, 1966.

Stewart, William A. A sociolinguistic typology for describing national multilingualism. In J. A. Fishman (Ed.), *Readings in the sociology of language.* The Hague: Mouton, 1966.

Weinreich, Uriel. *Research problems in bilingualism with special reference to Switzerland.* Unpublished doctoral dissertation, Columbia University, 1951.

9

PROGRAMMED INSTRUCTION AND FOREIGN LANGUAGE TEACHING

ALBERT VALDMAN

Albert Valdman (1931–   ) received his early schooling in France and holds degrees from the University of Pennsylvania and Cornell University. He has taught at the Foreign Service Institute and Pennsylvania State University and is presently chairman of the Department of Linguistics at Indiana University. His publications include books and articles in the areas of French linguistics and the application of linguistics to problems of second language learning.

In the course of the last two decades foreign language instruction has been revolutionized by the impact of two sets of external developments. On the one hand, society has inexorably pressed toward the extension of instruction to more and more of its members, including the culturally underprivileged and the intellectually ungifted, and has changed objectives of foreign language study from exclusive concern with reading-translation to emphasis on audiolingual skills. Concurrently, the development of new pedagogical materials and techniques based on the findings of an emerging science—structural linguistics—and the widespread use of electromechanical devices has resulted in more efficient instruction, particularly the newly added training in comprehension and speaking.

But concentration on such external components of foreign language teaching as materials, techniques, and devices has diverted attention from more fundamental components: time, the role of the teacher, the nature of the learning process, the structure of the teaching environment, and the student himself. It must be remembered that it was not primarily by the application of their specialized knowledge to the preparation of materials or the elaboration of teaching techniques that structural linguists were to influence the course of foreign language instruction. Rather, it was by the modification of the traditional foreign language teaching context: (1) reduction of class size, (2) intensive contact, (3) specialization of teaching function (a linguist to provide explanation and guidance and a native informant to serve as a drilling machine), and (4) variation in class size depending on activity. Like traditional foreign language teachers, however, linguists failed to realize that some teaching functions can be assumed by the learner himself. Consequently, the intensive method programs directed by linguists retained the conventional class organization, which keeps all students in lockstep and fails to accommodate individual variations in linguistic aptitude, motivation, attitude, and previous experience in the target foreign language. If we are to continue to provide audiolingual training to the constantly growing heterogeneous masses of learners that are given access to our secondary schools and colleges, it is imperative that we experiment with more flexible organizational frameworks and curricular patterns radically different from the present one-teacher and one-classroom systems. We must make foreign language instruction more efficient, more economical, and more flexible so that it will accommodate individual differences in aptitude, background, and motivation.

But to break the lockstep we must have at our disposal materials that make self-instruction possible at all levels of language acquisition. Before planning curricular modifications we must first consider the application of programmed instruction to foreign language learning problems and review those concrete results of this application that are currently available or in preparation.

PROGRAMMED INSTRUCTION

What is programmed instruction? Stated most simply, it is an educational technique which starts from the premise that learning results from the shaping of behavior toward some predetermined criterion by way of a technique through which optimum process is determined by student behavior. Programmed instruction can best be understood in terms of the general framework the Harvard psychologist B. F. Skinner developed for the description of behavior. Skinner divides animal responses into two classes: *respondents* and *operants*. The former are responses elicited by specific stimuli and subject to the laws of classical conditioning, such as involuntary reflexes; the latter are responses for which no obvious stimulus can be discovered and which are said to be *emitted* rather than *elicited*. Skinner (1957), through experimentation principally with rats and pigeons, discovered that the rate of emission of operants increased if followed by certain types of stimuli. In a classical experiment, a hungry pigeon is placed in an enclosed rectangular box containing a disk-shaped key that operates an automatic food magazine. Eventually, and in the absence of any directly observable causative stimulus, the pigeon will peck at the key, causing the magazine to release a pellet of food. The pigeon will peck again, and again will receive food. In Skinnerian terms, the pecking of the pigeon is said to operate on the environment and is termed an *operant response*. The consequence of the pigeon's pecking, the release of food, is termed a *reinforcing stimulus* or *reinforcer*, since it causes the rate of response to increase. If the pigeon's pecking is not reinforced with food, it will soon cease or be *extinguished*. By carefully scheduling the administration or withholding of reinforcement, Skinner was able to cause pigeons and rats to learn very complex behavior. The technique involves reinforcing any emitted responses that approximate the desired response and proceeding by successive approximation until the desired terminal response has been emitted. This technique, *shaping*, also involves forming discriminative behavior by reinforcing a given response in the presence of a given stimulus. For instance, a pigeon can be made to peck a key only when a 100-cycle-per-second (cps) tone is sounded by reinforcing it immediately with food and by withholding food when any other tone, say a 200-cps tone, is sounded. Although Skinner's paradigm for learning is derived from his laboratory observations of animals, he is confident that it applies also to human verbal learning (1957, p. 3):

> The basic processes and relations which give verbal behavior its special characteristics are now fairly well understood. Much of the experimental work responsible for this advance has been aired out on other species, but the results have proved to be surprisingly free of species restrictions. Recent work has shown that the methods can be extended to human behavior without serious modifications.

It has been suggested persuasively that Skinner's theory of human behavior cannot readily account for the way in which a child acquires language or in which a native speaker understands the sentences of his language because it fails to take into consideration innate processes and structures (Chomsky, 1959). It has also been pointed out that, to the extent it proclaims that a complex body of knowledge is learned best when it is broken down into its smallest components, programmed instruction does not originate with Skinner but is exemplified by the Socratic dialogue and is implicit in the oft-quoted passage from Descartes's *Discours de la méthode:* ". . . to divide each of the difficult points . . . in as many bits as possible and as is necessary to resolve them better," etc. A careful distinction is sometimes made between the concept of the teaching machine or automated instruction and programmed learning. Nonetheless, to equate programmed learning merely with the division of the subject matter into small steps and the immediate confirmation of the learner's response is to fail to recognize that the central concept of that approach is the definition of the teaching process in terms of control of student behavior through proper reinforcement. The desirability of teaching machines follows logically from this definition since, better than any other presentation device, they permit a more rigorous control of student behavior by withholding reinforcement when desired responses are not emitted. Equating learning with control of the subject's operant responses presupposes that in the final analysis it is the student himself, not the programmer, who determines the optimum sequence of learning steps, for as will be recalled, only responses emitted by the subject can be reinforced and shaped. It is, therefore, essential that a detailed record of student responses be kept and that the latter be induced to make as many observable responses as possible. A program is an accumulative repertoire of responses organized in a chain of small steps representing increments of successive approximation to the desired terminal behavior. The first step in the preparation of the program, then, is a statement of the desired terminal behavior as well as the initial behavior exhibited by the student, since only if the beginning and the end points are clearly stated can intervening behavior be shaped. Finally, another important principle of programmed instruction is the observation that errors resulting from intermediate steps that are too large have an aversive effect which lowers the rate of responding. The step increments of a program should allow the student to progress through a program with a minimum of errors.

Any material or pedagogical technique which exhibits the following characteristics may be said to be programmed:

1. Rigorous specification of terminal behavior
2. Division of the subject matter to be taught in a gradual sequence of optimum minimal steps
3. Immediate confirmation and reinforcement of student responses
4. Active mode of response on the part of the student

5. Revision and modification of the materials to accommodate individual student differences

TERMINAL BEHAVIOR

Much of the controversy with regard to foreign language teaching can be attributed directly to the lack of careful specification of final objectives and the confusion between description of course content and description of terminal objectives. Since the sequence of responses that the student will be trained to make is determined by the desired terminal behavior, a very detailed specification must be prepared of the skills, knowledge, and attitudes the student is expected to achieve upon completion of the program. This specification must take the form of operational, observable, and measurable entities. An operational definition of terminal behavior should identify and name the overall behavior act, state the important conditions under which the behavior is to occur, and define the criterion of acceptable performance. To say, for example, that a course is expected to train the student to speak Spanish fluently without making glaring errors and without any marked foreign accent is hardly useful. To be capable of more precise observation and measurement, the terminal behavior for a complete two- or three-year foreign language course should be expressed in terms of a series of objectives at various linguistic levels: auditory discrimination, pronunciation accuracy, and control of a stated set of structural features and lexical items.

The control of these components should also be stated for specific rates of production and perception and at defined noise levels, for it is a well-known fact that a student's rate of utterance in the target language will be lower than in his native language and his comprehension ability will not resist as high a noise level. For instance, in a study of the French spoken by native Wolof speakers in Senegal, Calvet (1964) reports that their rate of utterance is 30 percent slower in French.

Fernand Marty (1962, p. 2) gives the following definition of the pronunciation accuracy to be achieved by students having completed a programmed French course he is currently developing at Hollins College, Virginia: " . . . a pronunciation sufficiently accurate to handle effectively the morphological and syntactical contrasts of the language." This is still a very approximate yardstick, but he sets up a sample list of contrasts that the student must discriminate and differentiate: /ü/ versus /u/; /ẽ/ versus /èn/; /r/ versus /rr/, etc. He also requires that the student be able to phonate at a rate found acceptable by natives, namely, 150 syllables per minute, and to reply with a maximum latency of three seconds. Terminal auditory comprehension performance is specified as identifying 200 syllables per minute against background noises.

The description of near-native pronunciation in operational and, by definition, measurable terms is a task that must precede any attempt to formulate rigorous terminal behavior in this area. Most linguists would begin, as Marty does, by listing an inventory of phonemic contrasts which the student should hear and maintain. Depending on the speaker's geographical and social provenience, the style used, and position in the phonological phrase, French exhibits from seven to sixteen vowel phonemes (Table I).

A statement of desired terminal behavior would be required to specify whether the student was expected to discriminate and differentiate between the units of the maximum or the minimum inventory. A more demanding program might insist on the proper distribution of allophones or on a shift from one style to another under appropriate circumstances. It is important to note here that programmed instruction prescribes no view of the subject matter and that the technique is not inherently audio-lingually oriented; a program can only reflect the programmer's views concerning the subject matter treated and the terminal behavior he has specified. It is no more "right" for a program to aim at native phonological accuracy than at a pronunciation which barely makes it possible for a native speaker to decode the message. What we must establish is the degree to which various linguistic components—phonemic accuracy, speed

Table I

		i	ü	u
		é	œ́	ó
è:	è	è	œ	ò
			a ǀ â	

ẽ	õ
œ̃	ã

Vowels separated by solid lines constitute the minimum inventory; the nasal vowels separated by -.- broken lines do not occur in Southern French; vowels separated by --- broken lines are in free alternation or complementary distribution in many dialects; vowels to the left of dots (...) occur only in formal style.

of response, etc.—contribute to the naïve layman's very valid impression of fluency, grammatical accuracy, stylistic congruity, and accent. As we shall see later, rigorous specification of terminal behavior is purely academic unless the program provides for effective control of student response through reinforcement.

The statement of the initial behavioral repertoire of the student is equally important since it determines the sequence of step increments leading to the desired terminal behavior. The need to define rigorously initial behavior suggests that there are many areas in foreign language instruction in which the preparation of suitable programmed materials will be thorny indeed. I refer particularly to the teaching of English as a foreign language in American universities. Since in an average class students will differ with regard to their relative proficiency in spoken and written English and since, furthermore, they do not share the same native language, it is impossible to write a single program for all students. What will probably be more effective is a series of self-contained programs dealing with individual features of pronunciation and grammar which can be used in conjunction with classroom activities of a more conventional type. These remarks apply *mutatis mutandis* to advanced or remedial foreign language courses.

DIVISION OF THE SUBJECT MATTER TO BE TAUGHT IN A GRADUAL SEQUENCE OF OPTIMUM MINIMAL STEPS

The subject matter of the course of instruction must be organized and presented in a sequence of minimal steps carefully designed so that each step is made easier by virtue of the assimilation of material presented in previous steps. Step size is not determined exclusively by contrastive linguistic analysis of the features involved; teaching experience, insights into the learning process, and, above all, observation of students are probably equally significant. Step size should be so planned that the student progresses toward the terminal behavior while making a minimum of errors in the process. As opposed to much conventional learning, programmed learning is "trial-and-success" rather than trial-and-error learning. While it is possible to insult the intelligence of the learner by breaking up a learning task into too many steps, most subject-matter specialists who try programming tend to make steps much too large; paradoxically, the greater the number of frames a program contains, the faster students work through it. Although ideal step size must be determined by student performance, useful insights are obtained from prior analysis of the components of a given linguistic feature and the determination of possible areas of interference.

One of the most important techniques of programmed instruction is shaping new responses from responses the student already emits. In conventional pronunciation drills the student is expected to acquire new sounds by simple mimicry or, in more refined methodologies, by contrast drills, either target language oppositions (French, *russe/rousse;* Spanish, *sera/seda;* German, *kennen/können*) or target-native language pairs (French, *tout*/English *too*). But veteran teachers know that most students can be guided to the acquisition of sounds not present in the inventory of their native language. Most teachers scorn tricks that lead to inter-mediate sounds which are neither native language sounds nor accurate renditions of the target language sound; these are precisely the tricks the programmer seeks.

In devising shaping sequences the programmer must examine the passive as well as the active inventory of the learner. For example, in the teaching of English /θ/ to French speakers it is customary to instruct a student to place his tongue between the upper and lower front teeth and to produce a friction noise. This procedure requires him to produce a new voiceless fricative distinct from the French fricatives /f/ and /s/ as well as the dental stop /t/ in a single step. Many French children and some adults lisp (French *zézayer*), as such tongue twisters as *combien sont ces six saucissons-ci, Monsieur Sans-souci?* attest. French lisped /s/ is acoustically similar to English /θ/ and is within the passive and—for purposes of mock imitation—within the active inventory of all French speakers. This suggests a pedagogical sequence that starts with the shaping of English /θ/ from a lisped French /s/ and ends with contrasting the newly acquired sound class to English /f/, /s/, and /t/ in minimal pairs like *thin/fin, thin/sin, thin/tin.* Shaping underscores an important differ-ence between behavioral and contrastive analysis. In classical contrastive analysis the analyst focuses on the points of difference between two lan-guages or, in other words, on probable negative transfer from the native to the target language. The programmer, on the contrary, seizes upon positive transfer. In programmed as in conventional instruction thorough and expert linguistic analysis must precede the preparation of materials.

The thorniest problem in the application of programmed instruction to foreign language teaching problems is the determination of learning steps. Some programmers consider that a language is composed of "a finite number of basic arbitrarily meaningful and contrastive significant patterns" often referred to as "acoustic signifiers" (Morton, 1960). According to this view the vowel /o/ in Spanish is considered the acoustic signifier for first-person actor (e.g., *hablo* versus *habla*), and the con-sonant /n/ is the acoustic signifier for third-person plural (e.g., *habla* versus *hablan*). But it is difficult to see how this approach could be generalized and how such units could be enumerated in a consistent and simple fashion. For instance, in French, to relate the adjective forms *petite* /pEtit/ and *petit* /pEti/ does one posit as a meaningful unit the grammatical category "feminine" or does one list a set of processes that relate feminine and masculine forms? Should one prefer to follow the currently fashionable generative model, one might be tempted to define a step increment as equivalent to the application of an individual rewrite or transformational rule. For example, with regard to the derivation of the appropriate form of French adjectives such as *petite/petit* that exhibit contrasting feminine and masculine forms, one would start from the feminine singular form and account for all others by rewrite rules as follows:

1. /pEtit/ ---- masculine, prevowel ⟶ /pEtit/
    (no change)

2. /pEtit/ ---- masculine, general ⟶ /pEti/
    (loss of final consonant)

3. /pEtit/ ⟩ -- plural, general ⟨ /pEtit/
   /pEti/   (no change)   /pEti/

4. /pEtit/ ⟩ -- plural, prevowel ⟨ /pEtitz/
   /pEti/   (+ /z/)   /pEtiz/

Mastering adjectives like *grande/grand* or *fraîche/frais,* whose masculine prevowel forms differ from the feminine base form (e.g., /grãd/ versus /grã/ and frèš/ versus /frèz/), or those with nonpredictable generalized masculine forms (*belle/bel/beau* /bèl/ versus /bó/) would require additional learning steps.

The production of English yes-no questions would require three steps, each corresponding to the application of a transformational rule:

1. Verb form replaced by verb base
   You like tea.   You like tea.
   He likes tea.   He like tea.
2. Insertion of modal *do*
   You like tea.   You do like tea.
   He like tea.   He does like tea.
3. Inversion of subject and modal *do*
   You do like tea.   Do you like tea?
   He does like tea.   Does he like tea?

Let us note that learning the appropriate forms of so-called "irregular" verbs like *do* entails additional steps. Alternatively, it might prove pedagogically simpler to consider English verb phrases as basic and present- and past-tense forms as derived from them by transformations. Starting from *I do go,* one could derive *I don't go* and *do I go?* and generalize to obtain *I'm going, I want to go,* etc.; *I go* and *I went* would be presented at a later stage. It is apparent that were this procedure followed rigorously, the structure of English would need to be stated in terms of several thousand rules, to hazard a very conservative guess.

Surely the relative frequency of occurrence and relative generality of linguistic features should bear heavily on the establishment of step-increment sequences. Thus in French the aforementioned adjectives of the *petite/petit* type, whose pattern of derivation applies to a long list of other adjectives, should be presented before those like *belle/bel/beau, molle/mol/mou,* and *vieille/vieil/vieux,* which constitute unique instances of a single pattern of derivation. One should, however, caution against too literal an application of linguistic theory in the determination of optimum learning steps and in the ordering of steps into pedagogically efficient sequences. Ultimately, learning steps are determined on the basis of student response, and one should not expect necessarily a close correlation between the results of linguistic and behavioral analysis.

A characteristic feature of minimal step increment is the introduction and gradual removal of prompts called *fading* or *vanishing.* In teaching students the days of the week in Italian one might simply have students repeat the list or, what amounts to the same thing, substitute the days in basic sentences:

> Vanno a Roma   lunedì
> martedì
> mercoledì
> jovedì
> venerdì
> sàbato
> domènica

A programmed sequence would first isolate nouns ending in *-dì.* They would first be presented in full, next only the dissimilar elements would be given (*lune-, marte-, mercole-*), then only the first syllable (*lu-, mar-, jo-*), and finally the student would be expected to provide the entire word upon presentation of the English equivalent.

The following programmed sequence illustrates prompting and vanishing techniques in the teaching of spelling rules in French, specifically, the rule which states that intervocalic /z/ is represented by *s.* The sequence also reviews the rule stating that pronounced final consonants are spelled with a final consonant letter + *e.* (The material is part of a

CONFIRMATION	INSTRUCTIONS AND STIMULUS	STUDENT RESPONSE
	5.53 Write the vowel sounds. *cousine*	/ / / /
/u/ /i/	5.54 The /z/ sound between two vowel sounds is written *s*. Write *s*.	/u/ /z/ /i/ ↓ —
↓ *s*	5.55 *Cousine* The vowel sound *ou* is spelled *ou*. Copy the missing letters and repeat: *cousine*	c _ _ s i n e
c o u s i n e	5.56 Write the missing letters and repeat: *cousine*	c _ _ s _ n e
c o u s i n e	5.57 A /z/ sound between two vowel sounds is written *s*.	True False
True	5.58 Write the missing letters and repeat: *cousine*	c _ _ _ _ n e
c o u s i n e	5.59 Write and repeat: *cousine*	_ _ _ _ _ _
c o u s i n e		

programmed French course prepared for Sutherland Educational Films and utilized in conjunction with a partially self-instructional French course at Indiana University; see Valdman, 1964, 1965).

IMMEDIATE FEEDBACK AND REINFORCEMENT OF STUDENT RESPONSE

In programmed instruction practice does not make perfect unless the desired behavior is reinforced immediately. Unreinforced practice can be dangerous, for it may lead to the overlearning of undesired responses. After each step the student must have a *confirmation* of the correctness or incorrectness of his response, as the case may be. The smaller the time span between response and confirmation, the more effective the reinforcement or extinction of the response. There is a high degree of interdependence between appropriate step size and efficacy of confirmation; if steps are too large, there can be no confirmation.

It is quite easy to confirm responses when the student's task is limited to discrimination or the construction of written answers: one need only provide the correct response. But how can oral responses be confirmed? Three choices present themselves:

1. The instructor
2. An evaluating device
3. The student himself

The first alternative is excluded by definition since the ultimate goal of programmed instruction is self-instruction: one can hardly conceive of generalized private tutoring in an age when the shortage of qualified teachers is a universal problem. A speech-analyzing computer? Unfortunately an operational, let alone an economically viable, language-evaluating device is still in the realm of science fiction. There remains the student himself.

Pioneers in the field of programmed foreign language instruction have taken up the challenge of having the student actively participate in the entire learning process. Starting from the assumption that the ability to discriminate between two sounds leads directly to the ability to differentiate them, they train the student to distinguish between native and target language near equivalents, on the one hand, and to classify target language phonemic units correctly, on the other. Most researchers report that this assumption is proving to be generally valid; surprisingly, the most noteworthy feature of self-instructional programmed foreign language courses is the degree of accuracy in pronunciation attained by the subjects.

Recent experimentation also lends support to empirical evidence.

William A. Henning (1964) exposed three groups of American undergraduates, comparable with regard to language aptitude as measured by the Carroll-Sapon and the Seashore tests (Carroll & Sapon, 1959; Carl E. Seashore et al., 1939), to three different self-instructional programs presenting five French phonological features of both the phonemic and the subphonemic types. Group A was exposed to differentiation training only and group C to discrimination only, while group B received a mixed treatment consisting of half of treatment A and half of treatment C. Surprisingly, Group C scored significantly higher in differentiation and the ability to evaluate correctly pronunciation errors. More research and more widespread testing of programs are necessary, however, before it can be claimed that any student, no matter how low his linguistic aptitude, can function as an accurate self-evaluator and acquire a flawless pronunciation in any language through self-instruction alone.

ACTIVE MODE OF STUDENT RESPONSE

In programmed materials the student working individually is given the opportunity to react actively by imitating a model, performing oral transformations, engaging in a dialogue with the program, or constructing written responses of varying length. While in the conventional classroom the individual student performs solo at most a dozen times with diffuse or nonexistent confirmation, in his tête-à-tête with the program he produces several hundred responses in a single class period. Programmers have discovered that requiring the student to respond actively—orally, in writing, or by pushing a button—in a long series of graduated steps forces him to spend more time on a particular learning task and ensures *total,* that is, "real" learning.

APPROACHES TO FOREIGN LANGUAGE PROGRAMMING

The application of programmed instruction to foreign language teaching is still in its infancy, and many of the techniques employed by even the most experienced programmers are still exploratory. Except for the majority of programs distributed commercially, which are based on unsophisticated versions of the grammar-translation method, programmers aim at a high degree of audiolingual proficiency on the part of the learner and must devise manners of reinforcing oral responses.

F. Rand Morton's work represents by far the most orthodox and uncompromising application of Skinnerian principles to programmed instruction. Morton (1960) began experimenting with full self-instructional materials in Spanish at Harvard University in 1953 and, with the help of various collaborators, has extended his techniques to French, Russian, Chinese, and Thai (Morton, 1964). He believes in a rigorous separation of various phases of language learning and in the mechanical, unthinking character of the acquisition of foreign language skills (Morton, 1964, p. 3):

> As with most other language skills, it [discrimination] requires no intelligence. (The less you "think" about the sounds and the more you "hear" them, the easier it will be.) It can be accomplished most quickly if the student makes a conscious effort to "automize" himself—turn himself into a non-thinking "machine" whose only responsibility is to respond immediately, mechanically, AUTOMATICALLY to an external, physical stimulus.

Morton's Spanish Audio-lingual Language Programming (ALLP), a revision and development of his earlier course and the most representative of the ALLP courses, proposes itself the following terminal behavior:

1.   Mastery of the standard phonological system of language as demonstrated by use of discriminatory abilities in echoic vocal behavior similar to those of a ten-year-old native speaker

2.   A manipulative ability in the language permitting an appropriate vocal response to any verbal behavior with which confronted within the typical repertory of a ten-year-old native of the language

3.   Active standard vocabulary of no less than 1,275 lexical items

4.   The ability to expand immediately the terminal linguistic repertory with experience in a foreign country where the language is spoken

ALLP starts with a *phonematization* phase designed to train the student to discriminate among Spanish phonemes and between Spanish sound features and phonetically similar English near equivalents. After the student can demonstrate the ability to identify Spanish phonemes and sound features with an accuracy of about 90 percent, he begins to *vocalize* sound features in isolation and within utterances. The next phase, *acoustic signifiers,* trains him to manipulate abstract phonic signals carrying grammatical function in utterances whose meaning is not revealed to him. This activity rests on the questionable premise that all meaning not purely semantic, i.e., lexical, is cued by acoustic features. For example, to the question *¿quiere usted que hable yo?,* the student is expected to reply, *si, quiero que hable usted.* He is also trained to make certain gestures to accompany signifiers, for example, "finger poking" to accompany first-person verbal suffixes or "eyebrow furrowing" to accompany interrogative structures.

In the ALLP French program the discrimination, vocalization, and acoustic-signifier phases are combined, and the student successively is trained to discriminate between accurate renditions of a French phoneme and variants distorted by American English articulatory habits, to distinguish the phoneme from other French phonemes, to echo only upon presentation of an accurate rendition of it, and to produce it upon hearing some other French phoneme. He is also taught to associate the phoneme with an arbitrary symbol that differs from the conventional orthography (*dictation*) and, conversely, to convert the symbol to the appropriate articulatory features (*textual behavior*). Finally, in the syntax phase "grammatical" meaning is attached to the phoneme, and the student proceeds to manipulate morphemes determined by its presence. This phase is illustrated by Frame 334 below, which involves the contrast /ẽ/ versus /ün/ and the grammatical function of this contrast as masculine-feminine forms of the indefinite article.

FRAME 334

GENDER CONTRAST: /ẽ/-/ün/   CONFIRMATION

---

1. The English determiner *my, his, your* corresponds in French to two sets of determiners: /mõ/, /ma/, etc. These sets are characterized by two sounds, /_/ and /_/.   /õ/, /a/

2. These two sets are maintained with the determiners which correspond to the English *an* as in *an oogle*. /ma bag/ becomes /ün bag/; /mõ vó/ becomes /ẽ vó/. Which are the two signals corresponding to English *an* as in *an oogle?* /_/ and /_/.   /ün/, /ẽ/

3. /ün/ is used with the set characterized by the /_/ sound. /ẽ/   /a/
is used with the set characterized by the /_/ sound.   /õ/

4. /ta vaš/ becomes /_vaš/;   /ün/
/tõ fis/ becomes /_fis/.   /ẽ/

Change the stimulus according to the following pattern:

  S: /ma vaš/   /mõ vó/   /il a mõ vó/
  R: /ün vaš/   /ẽ vó/   /il a ẽ vó/

Let us note that the only semantic information available to the student is that /ün/ and /ẽ/ mean "a" or "an." He is unaware of the fact that /vaš/ means "cow" and /vó/ "calf."

In ALLP French and Spanish meaning is attached to utterances in the next phase, "Structural Patterns." Morton admits that of the five stages of "tasks" of his program this one is the most difficult to handle and that its pedagogical presentation exhibits the least ingenuity. It appears to follow quite closely the basic-sentence and variation-drill approach of conventional New Key materials. In the last phase, "Generative Verbal Behavior," an attempt is made to simulate conversational situations.

Another group of programmed materials currently available or in preparation differs from Morton's chiefly by the fact that sound and meaning are paired as soon as possible. Like the ALLP, they aim at a high level of audiolingual proficiency and control pronunciation accuracy indirectly through discrimination training, but the learner is introduced simultaneously to units at several levels of the linguistic hierarchy: phonology, morphophonemics, syntax, and lexicon. The presentation of linguistic features is carefully graded, and these materials exhibit perhaps a stricter adherence to Skinnerian programming principles and techniques than do Morton's programs. This group includes Stanley Sapon's Spanish A, published by Encyclopaedia Britannica Press, and two elementary French courses currently being prepared, one by Fernand Marty at Hollins College, Virginia (Marty, 1962; Marty, 1965), and the other under my direction at Indiana University. I shall illustrate this group with my own program, Sutherland Educational Films Elementary French Programmed Course, which, for the sake of convenience, I shall refer to henceforth as SEF French.

SEF FRENCH PROGRAMMED MATERIALS

SEF French is a formally programmed course consisting of 8,414 frames displayed by a programmed workbook and accompanied by thirty-three hours of recorded tape. It is divided into twenty-two units varying from 41 to 812 frames and from 5 to 187 minutes of playing time. Strictly speaking, like Sapon's Spanish A, SEF is a linear program, but since students may be shunted to preceding steps in the program on the basis of their performances on criterion frames and since some of the frames have a loop structure, it may be considered cyclical too. A typical SEF French unit consists of the following:

1. A dialogue spoken by native speakers at normal conversational tempo.

2. A varying number of programmed sets introducing phonological features, spelling rules, grammar patterns, and vocabulary items. The step-by-step progression exhibited by these sets also provides for the reintroduction of material presented in preceding units.

3. A second presentation of the dialogue. Since the programmed sets force the student to manipulate the structures contained in the dialogue, the latter is, in effect, learned by the time this stage has been reached and the student is merely expected to recombine learned elements into a complete dialogue.

4. Questions on the dialogue employing structures unfamiliar to the student but to which he can reply by incorporating new structures in his acquired repertory.

5. A comprehension drill consisting of a short narrative presented only by the recorded program and followed by questions in English. In later units additional questions are introduced in French and are to be answered by choosing one of several alternate written French responses.

6. A final test consisting of a series of questions covering all the material presented. These are to be answered both orally and in writing. When the student fails to respond to a question accurately or fluently, he is shunted back to a specific sequence.

In SEF French the presentation of the phonology is gradual, and the order of presentation of phonological features determines the introduction of grammatical structures and lexical items. Every sequence of frames purports to lead the student to assimilate a sentence—by sentence is meant here not only a string of physically observable phenomena but an abstract structure on the basis of which many other functionally similar but physically different utterances can be produced. For instance, the sentence *Jacques va à Nice* is not only the string /žak va a nis/ but also a realization of the syntactic structure "subject + predicate + adverbial." After the student has been presented with a complete base sentence, he is led to discriminate and differentiate a small number of French phonemes and to produce them with accurate control of secondary articulatory features, particularly those that differ markedly from features of American English. Criterion frames require the student to produce the phonemes under consideration within complete sentences used in meaningful situations; in other words, new pronunciation habits must be so thoroughly acquired as to resist deterioration under the interference of higher levels of language structure.

Grammatical patterns are assimilated by the use of question-answer interaction between the student and the machine displaying the program rather than by pattern drills. The following illustrative sets oppose two types of modal auxiliary phases, the *aller* + infinitive construction, which is used exclusively to express futurity, and the *vouloir* + infinitive construction. (The numbers refer to units and frames, respectively; the portion of the frame in italics represents the oral stimulus provided by a tape recorder and is not seen by the student.)

Frame 13.392 is a criterion frame in which the student is instructed to record his response and evaluate it with the help of the following scoring checklist. On the basis of his self-evaluation he either proceeds to the next set or repeats the material.

Most foreign language programs are *linear,* but they are so devised that only the most gifted or well-prepared students can proceed through them without backing up and repeating individual frames or sequences

WRITTEN CONFIRMATION		STUDENT RESPONSE
	13.369 Answer aloud and write out your answer. *Vas-tu pêcher?*	

ORAL CONFIRMATION:
Oui, je vais pêcher.

| Oui, je vais pêcher. | 13.370   Answer aloud and write out your answer. *Veux-tu pêcher?* | |

Oui, je veux pêcher.

| Oui, je veux pêcher. | 13.371   Answer aloud and write out your answer. *Veux-tu jouer au tennis?* | |

Oui, je veux jouer au tennis.

| Oui, je veux jouer au tennis. | 13.372   Answer aloud and write out your answer. *Vas-tu jouer au tennis?* | |

Oui, je vais jouer au tennis.

| Oui, je vais jouer au tennis. | 13.373   Give the French for "I want to play tennis." | |

Je veux jouer au tennis.

WRITTEN CONFIRMATION		STUDENT RESPONSE
Je veux jouer au tennis.	13.374 Give the French for "I am going to play tennis."	

Je vais jouer au tennis.

Je vais jouer au tennis.	13.389 Answer aloud and write out your answer. *Qui habite à Nice?*	

Jacques habite à Nice.

Jacques habite à Nice.	13.390 Answer aloud and write out your answer. *Qui va habiter à Nice?*	

Suzy va habiter à Nice.

Suzy va habiter à Nice.	13.391 Answer aloud and write out your answer. *Qui veut habiter à Nice?*	

Paul veut habiter à Nice.

Paul veut habiter à Nice.	13.392 Answer aloud and write out your answer. *Habites-tu à Nice?*	

Non, j'habite à Vichy.

Non, j'habite à Vichy.		

STOP YOUR TAPE. Switch to listen. Rewind enough tape to be able to listen again to this last frame. Check (1) speed, (2) rhythm, (3) spelling.

	FIRST ATTEMPT	SECOND ATTEMPT	THIRD ATTEMPT
GOOD:	1 2 3 ⬛ Proceed to frame 393.	1 2 3 ⬛ Proceed to frame 393.	1 2 3 ⬛ Proceed to frame 393.
POOR:	1 2 3 ⬛ Go back to frame 375.	1 2 3 ⬛ Go back to frame 375.	1 2 3 ⬛ Report to your instructor.

Switch back to record

of frames; most students need to repeat a sequence of frames several times. Morton's programs may be characterized as cyclical: each sequence of frames is designed on the principle of the memory drum, wherein a series of learning items is presented repeatedly until a stated criterion has been met. John B. Carroll (1963) has experimented with a more formally cyclical program in which the presentation is made in two modes: a *familiarization* mode followed by a *learning* mode. His Mandarin Chinese Program is used with a complex audiovisual teaching machine called the Audio-visual Instruction Device (AVID), represented in layout form in Figure I. Each frame on the projection screen is divided into three areas—*presentation, question,* and *answer*—and the frames are organized into *loops* (forty or fifty frames each). In the familiarization mode the presentation of each frame is as follows: the presentation area is exposed, giving information or practice on a new step of instruction; next, the question area is exposed (with the presentation area remaining exposed), requiring the student to perform a task or answer a question; finally, after the student has responded, the answer area is exposed, providing reinforcement. The visual presentation is accompanied by a synchronized tape recording in which the recorded portion of a frame likewise may be divided into three parts. In the learning mode the presentation area and its accompanying tape recording are omitted.

The other type of programming paradigm is *branching.* Unlike linear programs, branching programs are sensitive to individual differences since the sequence of frames to which a student is exposed is determined by his responses. Generally, branching programs are composed of frames requiring multiple-choice responses, but with ingenuity it is possible to construct branching programs calling for constructed responses (Spolsky, 1965). While multiple-choice responses are adequate to induce discrimination behavior (e.g., differentiating among various

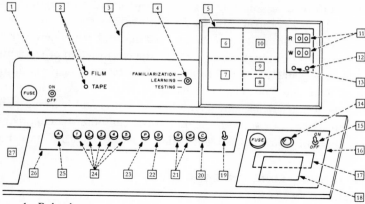

1 Relay box
2 Buttons for manually advancing film and tape loops to permit synchronization
3 Loudspeaker (optional; interchangeable with headphones)
4 Three-position switch for setting mode
5 Projection screen
6 Presentation area (P)
7 Question area (Q)
8 Answer area (A)
9 Prompt area (Pmt)
10 Reference area (Ref)
11 Counters for "Right" and "Wrong" responses
12 Counter reset button
13 Master on-off switch
14 On-off light
15 Switch for activation of paper feed mechanism
16 Writing surface panel
17 Transparent plastic coverplate
18 Paper tape (moves upward with each successive frame)
19 Three-position switch:
    Forward: interrupt tape
    Middle: normal
    Backward: (planned) repeat tape
20 C button: advance to next frame
21 R and W buttons: subject uses these to score his own responses
22 B button: advance to answer phase
23 P button: expose Pmt area in learning mode
24 Multiple-choice response buttons
25 A button: advance to Q area.
26 Response button panel (each button contains a small bulb which is lighted whenever the button is available for response)
27 Optional position for writing surface panel

FIGURE I. **Layout of console of AVID.** (Redrawn from John B. Carroll, *Programmed self-instruction in Mandarin Chinese: Observations of student progress with an automatic audio-visual device.* Wellesley, Mass.: Language Testing Fund, 1963. Used by permission.)

acoustic stimuli or distinguishing between well-formed and ungrammatical sentences), only constructed responses will train a student to produce the complex oral and written behavior that natural languages require. But only some sort of branching can lead to the construction of computer-based programs, which alone will fulfill the ultimate goals of programmed instruction: complete control of the learner's behavior, involving immediate and reliable feedback and adaptation to individual learning habits at each step along the way. An example of a computer-based program providing this full control of student behavior is provided in Chapter 10.

EVALUATION OF FOREIGN LANGUAGE PROGRAMMED MATERIALS

The criteria used to evaluate textbooks cannot be applied in assessing the effectiveness of a programmed course (Sapon, 1962, pp. 103–104) :

> When a teacher choses a text for use in his class, he is considering a source, or a resource, for himself, and his students, of facts, economically stated information, sample readings, guides for drills, suggestions for exercises, etc. It would be unusual for the teacher to expect the textbook to actually teach the students. The actual teaching will be done *by* the *teacher*. His job will be facilitated by a variety of aids, ranging from textbook through blackboards, slide projectors, pencils and chalk, but none of these aids can be evaluated independently from the teacher. It is what the teacher does with his assortment of aids that determines whether, and how well, his students perform. For this reason, a teacher looks at a new text with an eye to how he, the teacher, will use it as aid to his teaching. He can overlook areas he feels are weak, knowing that he can compensate such weakness by his own personal attention, and he can, and frequently does, disregard the sequence of chapters, rearranging them in his own preferred order of presentation.
>
> A teaching program is also an aid to the teacher's goals, but the goals are somewhat different from those involved with the use of a textbook, and the aid is different, not only in magnitude, but in kind. A program purports to do a stated amount of actual teaching, and leaves the student with a demonstrable degree of control of either a skill or a body of knowledge. Since this is what the teacher himself seeks to accomplish in his class, he is faced not with the evaluation of a teaching aid, but rather with the evaluation of another teacher and his promises.

In assessing the pedagogical effectiveness of programmed materials two sets of yardsticks are used: internal and external validation. Internal validation includes first a review of frames to make sure that:

1. Observable responses are required.
2. Responses are immediately reinforced.
3. Reinforcers cannot be obtained without the emission of the desired responses.

4. The observing behavior is controlled: i.e., the student must pay attention to the items in order to emit the correct responses.
5. The responses are selected to provide a gradual progression toward the terminal behavior.
6. Responses are adequately prompted.
7. There is sufficient fading or stimulus support (i.e., fading of prompts) as the student progresses toward the terminal behavior.

The next step is the tabulation of error rate: frames which are missed consistently must be eliminated or revised. But tabulation of error rate is practical only for short programs used by large groups of subjects. For foreign language programs, which typically contain many frames and which must be elaborated in field trials on small numbers of subjects, it is more useful to collect student comments which point out unsuitable or questionable items (Saltzman, 1963).

External validation consists primarily of comparing the results attained by the use of the program with those attained by the use of other programs or conventional instruction. Programmers have been loath to use this yardstick for several reasons. First, such comparisons are extremely difficult to perform with adequate controls, and even under the best conditions results are often inconclusive since, as has been pointed out, the premises of programmers and those of conventional teachers differ. Tests of foreign language proficiency at our disposal are still very inaccurate and inconclusive. They measure achievement at the time the tests are administered, but they fail to measure latency of skill and knowledge and the degree of automaticity of response, both of which are of extreme importance in predicting the likelihood of transfer of language skill to normal conditions of use. Despite the difficulties inherent in rigorous comparison of the proficiency attained through the use of programmed and conventional materials, only in this manner will prospective users be convinced.

Since the preparation and use of foreign language self-instructional materials are still in the exploratory phase, not much attention is being paid to the cost factor. The development and production of audiolingually oriented self-instructional materials is very expensive: the standard figure for the computation of the cost of a marketable programmed course of the type specified above is about $15 per frame. This sum provides for the preparation of both the text and the recorded program, as well as field testing and editing, but not for any special presentation device. A programmed course equivalent to a first-year college foreign language course would contain at the very least 10,000 frames and cost about $150,000. It is possible that as our experience in applying programmed instruction techniques to foreign language teaching grows, production costs will be reduced; but these hard facts suggest that it is the programmer's burden to demonstrate that, by the increased efficiency of instruction or the reduction of staff needs they make possible, programmed materials are worth the sizable initial outlays of hard cash they require.

A promising area for the use of self-instructional materials is research in foreign language instruction. One of the factors that has reduced the validity of much of what purported to be research in our field is the difficulty in isolating dependent variables and, particularly, of eliminating the contaminating effect of the teacher variable. Short self-instructional programs make it possible to study the effect of single variables on specific foreign language skills and to ask such questions as the following: Does the sequence lead to the specified terminal behavior? Are the theoretical assumptions underlying the sequence valid? What does the sequence teach in addition to the criterion behavior? When the same questions are asked about a textbook, the answer rests on the authority of the author or the teacher who uses it. In programmed instruction the student, on the basis of his learning, is the sole authority. As Sapon states (1962, p. 103), " . . . programmers must be made of stern stuff indeed if their egos are to survive. . . . The programmer must accept *a priori* that it is possible to teach what he sets out to teach. If the results are not as he hoped for, then he must recognize his own inadequacy, and seek the source of his errors."

Emphasis on the preparation of materials suitable for self-instruction should not divert our attention from the most important component of language instruction, the teaching environment. Even if efficient self-instructional programs become available in the immediate future, they will have little impact at the level of classroom application unless an appropriate environment is devised for their use and unless teachers accept a redefinition of their role. It has become a convention in discussions of self-instructional materials, on the one hand, to promise administrators reduced instructional costs and staff needs and, on the other, to assuage teachers' fears of technological unemployment. It has been shown in this paper that "language laboratories as teaching machines" at our disposal today can assume the following foreign language teaching functions: providing the native model, pronunciation and grammar drill, comprehension practice, explanation of structure, testing, and constant review. In other words, control and manipulation of language structures is perhaps best imparted through self-instruction. In the elaboration of audiolingual methods we have come to remember belatedly that parroting dialogues and performing mechanical pattern drills do not constitute use of language and that only if a student can comprehend and produce sentences he has never heard before and transfer his skills and knowledge to a normal communication situation can language learning be said to have taken place. Skillful elicitation of authentic conversation without straying from the confines of known patterns or succumbing to the temptation to explicate or drill is the mark of the experienced and gifted foreign language teacher and precisely what the teaching machine cannot do. The successful teacher must lead the student to *use* the language in a near-natural context and stimulate him to *behave* the language. The minimum requirements that this ability presupposes are a good but not native pronunciation, the ability to generate with automaticity grammatically correct and stylistically appropriate sentences in the target language, some insight into the learning process, a working knowledge of the structure of both the native and the target languages, and the ability to interact and empathize with students. Unless language teacher training and certification practices are revised so that foreign language teachers meeting these qualifications are made available in sufficient numbers at all levels, the machine indeed will take over, but the type of language instruction that will result will fall quite short of developing in our youth "a sense of values—personal, human, social—so that they may become discriminating, free individuals" (Mildenberger, 1962).

REFERENCES

Calvet, R. Phonétisme français et wolof. In J. Goliet (Ed.), *Études sur le français au Sénégal*. Centre de Linguistique Appliquée de Dakar, No. 4, 1964. (Mimeographed.)

Carroll, John B. *Programmed self-instruction in Mandarin Chinese: Observations of student progress with an automated audio-visual device*. Wellesley, Mass.: Language Testing Fund, 1963.

Carroll, John B., and Stanley M. Sapon. *Modern Language Aptitude Test*. New York: The Psychological Corporation, 1959.

Chomsky, Noam. Review of B. F. Skinner, *Verbal behavior*. *Language*, 1959, **35,** 26–57.

Descartes, René. *Discours de la méthode*. Paris: Mignot, 1929.

Henning, William A. *Phonemic discrimination training and student self-evaluation in the teaching of French pronunciation*. Unpublished doctoral dissertation, Indiana University, 1964.

Marty, Fernand. *Programming a basic foreign language course: Prospects for self-instruction*. Roanoke, Va.: Audio-visual Publications, 1962.

Marty, Fernand. *Active French: Foundation course*. Roanoke, Va.: Audio-visual Publications, 1965.

Mildenberger, Kenneth W. Problems, perspectives, and projections.

In Edward Najam (Ed.), *Materials and techniques for the language laboratory.* Indiana University Research Center in Anthropology, Folklore, and Linguistics Publication No. 18. (Published as *International Journal of American Linguistics,* 1962, **28,** No. 1, Part II.)

Morton, F. Rand. The language laboratory as a teaching machine. In Felix J. Oinas (Ed.), *Language teaching today.* Indiana University Research Center in Anthropology, Folklore, and Linguistics Publication No. 14. (Published as *International Journal of American Linguistics,* 1960, **26,** No. 2, Part I.)

Morton, F. Rand. *Audio-lingual language programming project.* Unpublished report, Contract No. OE–3–14–012. U.S. Office of Education, Language Development Branch, 1964.

Saltzman, Irving J. Programmed self-instruction and second-language learning. *International Review of Applied Linguistics in Language Teaching,* 1963, **1,** 104–114.

Sapon, Stanley. *Programmed learning and the teacher of foreign languages: Final report of the Seminar in Language and Language Learning.* Seattle: University of Washington, Department of Romance Languages and Literatures, 1962.

Seashore, Carl E. et al. *Seashore Measures of Musical Talent.* Camden, N.J.: Rádio Corporation of America, 1939.

Skinner, B. F. *Verbal behavior.* New York: Appleton-Century-Crofts, Inc., 1957.

Skinner, B. F. *Teaching machines.* Science, 1958, **128,** 969–977.

Spolsky, Bernard. Computer-based instruction and the criteria for pedagogical grammars. In Paul L. Garvin (Ed.), *Computation in Linguistics: A Case Book.* Bloomington, Ind.: Indiana University Press, 1966.

Valdman, Albert. Toward self-instruction in foreign language learning. *International Review of Applied Linguistics in Language Teaching,* 1964, **2,** 1–36.

Valdman, Albert. *The implementation and evaluation of a multiple-credit self-instructional elementary French course.* Indiana University, 1965. (Multilith.)

10

A SELF-INSTRUCTIONAL
DEVICE FOR
CONDITIONING
ACCURATE PROSODY

HARLAN LANE
ROGER BUITEN

Harlan Lane (1936–   ) received graduate degrees in psychology from Columbia and Harvard Universities and has served as research assistant at the Haskins Laboratories. He is presently director of the Center for Research on Language and Language Behavior at the University of Michigan, where he holds the rank of associate professor. He has been associated with research projects in the area of the application of programmed instruction to language learning and has published extensively in the field of speech perception, psycholinguistics, and programmed instruction.

Roger Buiten (1936–   ) received degrees from Calvin College, Grand Rapids, Michigan, and the University of Michigan in preparation for his activities as research engineer for the Center for Research on Language and Language Behavior at the University of Michigan. His interests are man-machine communications as related to the computer and the technical development of the related interface. The following paper is adapted from Progress Report No. 6, Report No. 05613–3–P, prepared by the Behavior Analysis Laboratory, University of Michigan, with support from the Language Development Program, U.S. Office of Education, and from the National Science Foundation.

The achievement of nativelike fluency in a second language is as uncommon and arduous as it is essential to effective social behavior in a foreign land. Social custom generally accords the novice who is acquiring a set of skills—whether in sports, cooking, warfare, or education—both indulgence and encouragement, but this is not the fare of a novice speaker of a second language. Native speakers of the language view him at best with suspicion and at worst with ridicule and hostility. Perhaps this is because of the central importance of language in almost every aspect of social life. Indeed, philosophers have contended that language is the defining property of man; the layman's tendency to view his *own* language as the defining property of man may have the same sources. Mark Twain entertainingly reveals the vital social role of fluency in the language of the community in this dialogue between Huck Finn and his friend Jim:

> "Looky, here, Jim; ain't it natural and right for a cat and a cow to talk different from us?"
> "Why, mos' sholy it is."
> "Well, then, why ain't it natural and right for a Frenchman to talk different from us? You answer me that."
> "Is a cat a man, Huck?"
> "No."
> "Well, den, dey ain't no sense in a cat talkin' like a man. Is a cow a man?—er is a cow a cat?"
> "No, she ain't either of them."
> "Well, den she ain't got no business to talk like either one er the yuther of 'em. Is a Frenchman a man?"
> "Yes."
> "Well, den! Dad blame it, why doan' he talk like a man? You answer me dat!'"

What can be done to teach a Frenchman, or an American, or a Yugoslav to "talk like a man" when he is among men who talk in a language different from his own? Clearly, the speaker must master the component speech sounds of the second language, their permissible patterns in grammatical utterances, and the appropriate occasions for these utterances. Without these complex skills he will often be unintelligible (Lane 1963a), and so it is these skills that receive the lion's share of research and pedagogy. Intelligibility, however, is only a part of the story of fluency in a foreign language. This report of research is concerned with another set of skills, relatively independent of the first, which contributes little to intelligibility and everything to fluency and thus to social acceptance. Nativelike fluency in a second language is predicated on a mastery of its patterns of intonation, stress, and rhythm, in short, on a mastery of its prosody.

Phonetic descriptions of numerous and diverse languages reveal a variety of highly stylized patterns of stress and intonation. The novice speaker of a second language who employs the prosody of his native tongue is most likely to sound foolish, even if his first and second languages have common historical roots and belong to the same language family. Recent acoustic studies of language prosody[1] confirm and amplify the phonetic descriptions. Again, the theme is diversity between languages and stereotypy within them. Delattre (1962b), for example, has extracted the characteristic intonation contours for declarative sentences shown in Figure I from spectrographic analyses of conversations in four languages. Among other contrasts, American intonation seems to be characterized by a recurrence of falling contours, whereas the motif of German, Spanish, and French is the rising contour. Similarly, there are characteristically different patterns of stress among languages. Concerning these four languages, for example, Delattre provides evidence that in French the stress is characteristically on the final syllable, whereas in Spanish it falls on the next-to-last syllable, while in English and German it varies between these two loci. The temporal patterns of responding, or rhythmic characteristics, of diverse languages have received little study, but the covariance of duration and stress in several languages is well documented (e.g., Lieberman, 1960), and it is not unlikely that future research will also reveal stylized patterns in the temporal spacing of speech segments.

It is axiomatic for the present report, then, that languages differ in their prosody and that the speaker who has not mastered the prosody of a second language is not fluent in that language. Before describing our approach to conditioning prosodic skills in a second language, it is desirable to review briefly the alternative approaches that have been employed —largely unsuccessfully—in the past. We restrict our attention to teaching prosodic accuracy to an adolescent or an adult while he resides in his native land, with all the sources of resistance to the learning of new habits of speech that this implies (Lane, 1962c). First, and most common, there are the techniques available to the language teacher in the traditional classroom setting. In this case, prosodic skills literally go by the board; they are rarely acquired well. Several constraints on language learning in the classroom militate against the acquisition of prosodic skills: the widespread conviction among college students that a language block is a place of execution; the broad objectives of the language course, often ranging from culture through literature to spelling; the large number of students confronting each teacher; the eddy of second language behaviors created amid a sea of first language habits; and so forth (Lane 1964a;

---

[1] Dreher (1951); Goodman (1952); Fry (1955, 1958); Malmberg (1956); Bolinger (1958a, 1958b); Bascom (1959); Jassem (1959); Garding and Gerstman (1960); Lehiste (1960, 1961); Lieberman (1960); Delattre (1961, 1962a, 1962b); Goldman-Eisler (1961); Hadding-Koch (1961); Rigault (1962); Lindblom (1963); Magdics (1963).

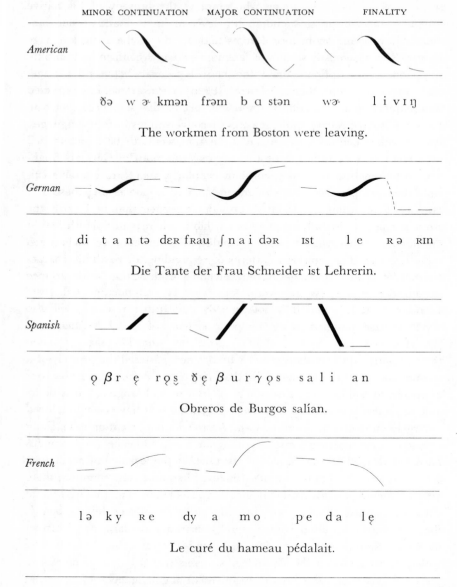

FIGURE I.   Characteristic intonation contours of declarative sentences spoken in American English, German, Spanish, and French. (From Pierre Delattre, *The general phonetic characteristics of languages.* Unpublished report. U.S. Office of Education, Language Development Branch, 1962. Used by permission.)

1964b). Rarely are the avowed ingredients of learning in evidence: active responding by the individual student, differential feedback or "reinforcement" depending on the accuracy of his responses, and careful sequencing of each component task according to the student's individual level of proficiency at the moment (Lane, 1963b). Moreover, the intrinsic complexity of prosodic features, extending as they do over several segments of an utterance, presents a special measure of difficulty to their attainment by classroom instruction. Little wonder if the language teacher is pleased when in two or three years a student learns the segmental sounds, some vocabulary, and the elements of reading and writing in the second language. If he does not sound like an authentic Frenchman, well, after all, he is not one.

When choral work in the language classroom is supplemented by sonic treatments in the language laboratory, the gain in learning is small.[2] Simple exposure is no more effective than it is plausible as a basis for learning (Lane, 1962a). In a few language laboratories there is provision for active responding by the student, and in a lesser number he may even hear his poor pronunciation played back to him repeatedly. The student is typically in no position to evaluate his pronunciation, however, since the novice speaker is usually a novice listener. Even if the student were able to discriminate between good and poor pronunciation, these have no differential effects in the immediate environment. When audible differences do not make a difference, both discrimination and production fail.

The third and most recent approach to language pedagogy is programmed instruction (Lane, 1964b). The application of programmed instruction has necessarily involved a molecular functional and linguistic analysis of the behaviors involved in language learning. Based on this analysis, new techniques for controlling the learning process have been applied to rendering it more effective and efficient. Once again, however, the conditioning of prosodic features has largely been overlooked. None of the language programs described in several recent and comprehensive surveys explicitly states prosodic accuracy as an objective, nor does any of these programs explicitly provide for the conditioning of the prosodic features, although all, of course, do battle with the segmental features and with vocabulary. The obstacles to employing programmed self-instruction as a means for conditioning prosodic accuracy are these: the student must be taught to discriminate between accurate and inaccurate prosody in the first place; then, these discriminations must be maintained during the acquisition of productive skills; finally, the student must apply the discriminations to his own vocal behavior—reliably and validly. No language program has yet tackled, no less has overcome, these obstacles.

From the ashes of these unsuccessful methods for conditioning pro-

---

[2] Lewis (1961); Reichard (1962); Keating (1963); Hutchinson and Gaarder (1964); Scherer and Wertheimer (1964).

sodic accuracy in a second language arises the image of a pedagogical phoenix with the following plumage. An instructional method is required that will (1) provide the student with rapid, reliable, and valid evaluations of his prosodic accuracy; and (2) adapt the learning sequence in accord with the student's proficiency at each step along the way. These pedagogical requirements led to the development, at the Behavior Analysis Laboratory, the Speech Auto-instructional Device (SAID).

SAID is an electromechanical device which performs three significant functions in conditioning prosodic accuracy in a second language. First, it presents to the student tape-recorded pattern sentences that are considered standards in prosodic performance. These sentences are programmed in the best-known sequence for teaching prosody in the target language to a speaker of a given native language. The student is instructed to imitate the pattern sentence after he hears it. Second, SAID processes the student's imitation and instantaneously evaluates its acceptability on the basis of its three distinct prosodic features: pitch, loudness, and tempo. Third, SAID immediately displays to the student the degree to which his imitation is unacceptable and demonstrates how he must modify his next imitation, in the prosodic feature under consideration, in order to make it more acceptable. This process of presentation-evaluation-

FIGURE II.   Experimenter's console, SAID system. The photograph shows the computer base of the system with teleprinter output (*left*), tape-reader input, monitoring equipment, parameter extractors, and tape recorder (*extreme right*).

display repeats itself until the prosody of the student's imitation is acceptable.

The first phase of the threefold machine process is the presentation of the tape-recorded pattern sentences. The sequence of patterns presented to the student is controlled by the computer base of SAID (see Figure II), which instructs the tape recorder to rewind when the imitation is unacceptable or to play the next pattern when the imitation is accurate.

The second phase, evaluation, is accomplished both by the computer and by analogue electronic equipment. The speech signals from the tape recorder and the student's response microphone are channeled to analogue extractors of the acoustic parameters (see Figure III). The conceptual bases for the parameter extractors were contributed by the University of Michigan's Communication Sciences Laboratory. The fundamental frequency, the major contributor to the perception of pitch in speech (Lane, 1962b), is extracted by filtering each of the speech signals into two ranges within the entire fundamental-frequency spectrum of the human voice. The range containing the fundamental is selected by

FIGURE III. Analogue electronic equipment, SAID system. (*Top to bottom, left to right:* test oscilloscope, mixer, frequency-to-voltage converter, monitor recorder, playback amplifier, amplifiers for parameter extraction, intensity extractor, error monitor meters, computer input amplifier, voice-operated relay, power supply, switching circuitry and filter bank for extraction of fundamental frequency, switching circuitry for mode selection, tape recorder.)

switching circuitry, and the signal from the selected range is sent to a frequency-to-voltage converter. The output of the converter is a direct-current voltage that varies linearly with the fundamental frequency of the speech signal. In this form it is digitized and processed by the computer.

The intensity of the speech signal, the major contributor to the perception of loudness (Lane, Catania, & Stevens, 1961), is extracted by rectifying and filtering. This produces a direct-current voltage which varies linearly with the peak instantaneous voltage of the speech signals. This voltage is digitized and processed by the computer. While processing the intensity parameter, the computer also records the time elapsed between successive intensity peaks.

The student has not been trained, and therefore is not able, accurately to interpret changes in frequency, intensity, and temporal spacing, since changes in these physical parameters do not produce simply corresponding changes in their apparent or psychological values. The student can, however, be expected to discriminate readily variations in the psychological effects of these physical parameters: pitch, loudness, and tempo. Therefore, the computer samples the output of the parameter extractors, selects one representative (peak) value of frequency and intensity for each burst of speech energy (usually a syllable), measures the time between intensity peaks, and compares psychological units according to the psychophysical functions for speech production and perception determined in earlier research (Lane, 1962b). The variation of these psychological values more accurately represents the prosodic features of speech from the point of view of the student and his language community. While the pattern sentence is presented to the student, the values of its psychological parameters are stored away in the memory of the computer. While the student is imitating the pattern, the psychological parameter values of his imitation are compared with corresponding stored values of the pattern, and three error scores are generated.

To perform this operation, the computer solves the following equation:

$$e = [\log S_i - \log S_o] - [\log M_i - \log M_o]$$

where e is the error fed back to the student on his panel meter, S_i is the ith value of the student's imitation for the feature being evaluated, S_o is the *first* imitation value to which all others are referred, and M_i and M_o are corresponding values of the modal pattern. It is this manipulation that makes the error readings for each speaker relative to his own first utterance; the pitch, loudness, and tempo values are normalized so that conditioning is based on the dynamics of prosody rather than on the absolute acoustic values of prosodic parameters. The error scores are compared with preset criteria of acceptability for the three features. The results of these acceptance tests determine the sequence of presentation and display.

The third phase of the machine process involves displaying the results of the comparison of pattern and imitation and the results of the acceptance tests. The display of the comparison difference is made on a zero-center meter, so that both the direction and the magnitude of error score can be monitored readily. The student's error score for one of the three features is displayed to him immediately after the error has been made as his imitation proceeds (see Figure IV). A neon indicator on his panel shows him which feature is being displayed on each trial. When the student's imitation is acceptable (that is, within preset tolerance) in pitch, for example, the device advances to the next feature, loudness, and the cycle of presentation-evaluation-display is repeated for his feature. Ultimately, the imitation is acceptable with respect to all three features, whereupon the next pattern sentence in the program is presented.

To illustrate the operation of the SAID system we may follow the student through one complete learning cycle. The student, seated in the sound-insulated booth shown in Figure IV, listens to the presentation of the pattern sentence. A light on this indicator panel tells him to imitate

FIGURE IV. Student booth, SAID system. The photograph shows the loud-speakers for presentation of the pattern sentence, the microphone that receives the student's imitation, and the student console (*left to right:* respond light, error display, mode indicator).

the "pitch" contour of the pattern. While he is making his imitation, the meter on his panel is swinging to the right when his response is too high in pitch and to the left when his response is too low. In a triad of utterances, for example, two error values are displayed, since there can be no error reading for the first utterance ($S_1 = S_o$; $M_1 = M_o$). If his largest error indication is greater than the tolerance for accurate imitation, the device will rewind the tape recorder and present the pattern sentence again. Assuming that the student's imitation has been acceptable on this second attempt, the device turns on the "loudness" light, rewinds the tape recorder, and again plays the pattern sentence. SAID then repeats the sequence for loudness as for pitch, and for tempo when loudness has been acceptably imitated. Finally, the three features must be acceptably imitated concurrently on three successive trials before the device advances the student to the next pattern sentence in the program.

The criteria for accurate imitation have been set at less than a 6 percent error for pitch, a 20 percent error for loudness, and a 10 percent error for tempo. These criteria were selected initially on the bases of acoustic-phonetic research and preliminary experiments with SAID. Ultimately, the choice of criteria must come from systematic listening experiments with native speakers of the target language.

The computer's teleprinter (Figure II) keeps a running record of the behavior of SAID and the student. When the cycle begins, the teleprinter types the word *pitch*, indicating the feature which the student is trying to imitate. Just before the pattern sentence is played to the student, the teleprinter types the letter P; the letter S is typed just before the device processes the student's imitation. After the imitation, the result of each comparison of pattern and imitation is typed out. If the student's imitation is acceptable, the teleprinter types the next feature (in this case, *loudness*); it then types the letter P for pattern again, and the sequence is repeated. When the imitation is thoroughly acceptable, the student is ready to move on to the next pattern in the program. The teleprinter then types out a table of results for all three features for each of the preceding trials before advancing.

A graphic analysis of the learning that has taken place is readily prepared from these records. When pitch, loudness, or tempo differences between the pattern and the imitation are plotted as a function of successive trials, several kinds of trends may be observed; the most obvious is the rate of learning to effect control over the prosodic features. The student's consistency and short-term retention and the relative difficulty of the prosodic features are also revealed by the plots of error versus trials. We use the term *consistency* to refer to the degree to which the error is steadily reduced prior to reaching criterion behavior and the term *retention* to refer to the degree to which low-error performance is maintained thereafter.

Preliminary experiments are under way to evaluate the effectiveness of the SAID system in conditioning prosodic accuracy. In one experiment, tape recordings containing triads of synthetic vowels were prepared. Within each triad, the vowel stimuli varied in fundamental frequency, formant frequency, relative intensity, and duration or temporal spacing. The error functions for a typical subject are shown for each of the three prosodic features in Figures V, VI, and VII. These data were obtained with a pattern of three vowels that varied only in fundamental frequency: 160, 120, and 160 cycles per second (cps). The stimulus duration was 250 milliseconds (msec); interstimulus duration was 500 msec; intensity was constant at about 70 decibels (SPL); and the formant frequencies were 300 and 900 cps, respectively.

In the plot of pitch error versus successive trials (Figure V), the filled squares represent those trials on which the student's error in pitch was displayed to him. The solid line connects error values associated with the change in pitch from the first to the second utterance, and the dashed line those associated with the change in pitch from the first to the third utterance. This student, like several others, finds the task of imitating the pitch of the vowel pattern quite simple under the supervision of the SAID system. Within a few trials, he achieves and retains a level of accuracy that is well within tolerance.

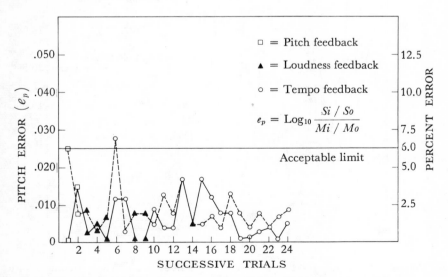

FIGURE V. **Pitch Error versus Successive Trials.** The difference, with respect to changes in pitch, between a triad of vowels, presented aurally, and its imitation on repeated trials by one student.

The SAID system then advanced to loudness evaluation and error display. The student's performance with respect to this prosodic feature is shown in Figure VI. The filled triangles indicate the error in relative loudness on those trials for which loudness error was displayed to the student. The solid and dashed lines connect normalized error values associated with the second and third loudness values, respectively. Although the student is much less consistent in imitating the loudnesses of the pattern than in imitating its pitch, continued attempts at imitation with visual display of error soon bring the loudness feature of his prosody within the acceptance limits. It is noteworthy that there is an increase in loudness error when the student first turns his attention to imitating loudness. Retention seems to improve with training; the trend of the function approaches a point well below the acceptance limit.

Finally, the SAID system advanced to tempo evaluation and display. The student's performance is shown in Figure VII, in which the filled circles indicate the error in tempo on those trials for which tempo error was displayed. Since there are only two tempo intervals in a triad of utterances and the first serves as the reference or normalizing value, there

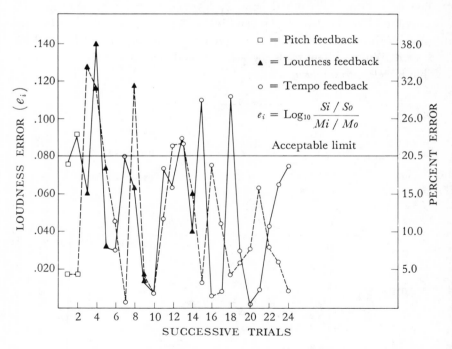

FIGURE VI. **Loudness Error versus Successive Trials.** The difference, with respect to changes in loudness, between the triad of vowels and its imitation. The trials are the same as those indicated in Figure V.

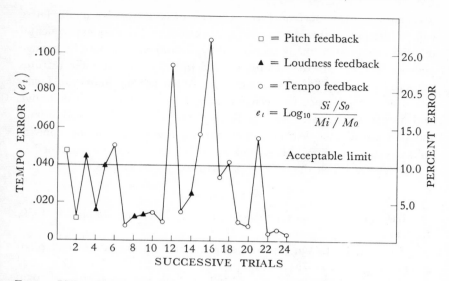

FIGURE VII. **Tempo Error versus Successive Trials.** The difference, with respect to changes in tempo, between the triad of vowels and its imitation. The trials are the same as those indicated in Figures V and VI.

is only one reading of tempo error per triad. This student, like several others, is consistent in his imitations of tempo and quickly brings this feature of his prosody within tolerances, but his retention of accurate tempo is poor. The latter finding may be attributable in part to the fact that stimulus duration, interstimulus interval, and intensity distribution within each stimulus all may contribute to the perception of tempo. The student whose data are shown in Figures V, VI, and VII is typical in that tempo was easier to master than loudness but more difficult to master than pitch.

Inspection of Figure VII reveals another programming feature that is presently a part of the SAID system. When the student achieves an acceptable imitation of tempo, the device tests the other two prosodic features concurrently. If the error associated with either feature is greater than criterion, the system recycles to evaluation and error display of the unacceptable feature. If both of the other features are within criterion, a light is flashed on the student's panel. This procedure is repeated until the student accurately imitates all three features on three successive trials. Then, the next pattern in the program is presented.

The capability of the SAID system to provide rapid, reliable, and valid evaluations of prosodic accuracy and to adapt the learning sequence in accord with the student's proficiency at each step, as well as the findings of initial experiments with the system, holds promise of improving and accelerating an important facet of second language learning. These capabilities and findings, however, raise certain preliminary experimental questions that are normally overlooked by traditional methods of language pedagogy: What are the quantitative tolerances of the prosodic features for nativelike fluency within a language? What are the sources of facilitation and interference between prosodic skills in a given pair of native and target languages? How well are newly acquired prosodic skills retained outside the learning environment, and what can be done to enhance this retention? These and related questions will be examined in future research with the Speech Auto-Instructional Device.

REFERENCES

Bascom, J. Tonomechanics of Northern Tepuhan. *Phonetica,* 1959, **4,** 77–88.

Bolinger, D. L. On intensity as a qualitative improvement of pitch accent. *Lingua,* 1958, **7,** 175–182. (a)

Bolinger, D. L. A theory of pitch accent in English. *Word,* 1958, **14,** 109–149. (b)

Delattre, Pierre. La leçon d'intonation de Simone de Beauvoir: Étude d'intonation déclarative comparée. *French Review,* 1961, **35,** 59–67.

Delattre, Pierre. A comparative study of declarative intonation in American English and Spanish. *Hispania,* 1962, **45,** 233–241. (a)

Delattre, Pierre. *The general phonetic characteristics of languages.* Unpublished report. U.S. Office of Education, Language Development Branch, 1962. (b)

Dreher, J. *A comparison of native and acquired language intonation.* Unpublished doctoral dissertation, University of Michigan, 1951.

Fry, D. B. Duration and intensity as physical correlates of linguistic stress. *Journal of the Acoustical Society of America,* 1955, **27,** 765–768.

Fry, D. B. Experiments in the perception of stress. *Language and Speech,* 1958, **1,** 126–152.

Garding, E., and L. J. Gerstman. The effect of changes in the location of an intonation peak on sentence stress. *Studia Linguistica,* 1960, **14,** 57–59.

Goldman-Eisler, Frieda. The significance of changes in the rate of articulation. *Language and Speech,* 1961, **4,** 171–174.

Goodman, A. C. *Imitation of intonation patterns.* Unpublished doctoral dissertation, University of Michigan, 1952.

Hadding-Koch, K. *Acoustical-phonetic studies in the intonation of Southern Swedish.* Travaux de l'Institut de Phonétique de Lund III. Lund-Gleerup, 1961.

Hutchinson, Joseph C., and A. Bruce Gaarder. *A brief analysis of the Keating Report.* Unpublished report. U.S. Office of Education, Language Development Section, 1964.

Jassem, W. The phonology of Polish stress. *Word,* 1959, **15,** 269–282.

Keating, Raymond F. *A study of the effectiveness of the language laboratory.* New York: Institute of Administrative Research, Teachers College, Columbia University, 1963.

Lane, H. L. Experimentation in the language classroom: Guidelines and suggested procedures for the classroom teacher. *Language Learning,* 1962, **12,** 115–123. (a)

Lane, H. L. Psychophysical parameters of vowel perception. *Psychological Monographs,* 1962, 761 (Whole No. 563). (b)

Lane, H. L. Some differences between first and second language learning. *Language Learning,* 1962, **12,** 115–123. (c)

Lane, H. L. Foreign accent and speech distortion. *Journal of the Acoustical Society of America,* 1963, **35,** 451–453. (a)

Lane, H. L. Specifications for auditory discrimination learning in the language laboratory. *International Journal of American Linguistics,* 1963, **29,** 61–69. (b)

Lane, H. L. Acquisition and transfer in auditory discrimination. *American Journal of Psychology,* 1964, **77,** 240–248. (a)

Lane, H. L. Programmed learning of a second language. *International Review of Applied Linguistics,* 1964, 249–301.

Lane, H., and R. Buiten. *A preliminary manual for the speech auto-instructional device.* Unpublished report. University of Michigan, Behavior Analysis Laboratory, 1964.

Lane, H. L., A. C. Catania, and S. S. Stevens. Voice level: Autophonic scale, perceived loudness, and effects of sidetone. *Journal of the Acoustical Society of America,* 1961, **33,** 160–167.

Lehiste, I. An acoustic-phonetic study of internal open juncture. *Phonetica,* 1960, **5,** Suppl.

Lehiste, I. Some acoustic correlates of accent in Serbo-Croatian. *Phonetica,* 1961, **7,** 114–147.

Lewis, E. N. *Experimentation on the development of more effective methods of teaching foreign languages by making extensive use of electro-mechanical aids.* Unpublished report. U.S. Office of Education, Language Development Section, 1961.

Lieberman, P. Some acoustic correlates of word stress in English. *Journal of the Acoustical Society of America,* 1960, **32,** 451–454.

Lindblom, B. Spectrographic study of vowel reduction. *Journal of the Acoustical Society of America,* 1963, **36,** 1773–1781.

Magdics, K. Research on intonation during the past 10 years. *Acta Linguistica,* 1963, **13,** 133–165.

Malmberg, Bertil. Observations on Swedish word accent. *Studia Linguistica,* 1956, **10,** 1–44.

Reichard, J. R. *Experimentation on the development of more effective methods of teaching foreign languages by making extensive use of electro-mechanical aids.* Unpublished report. Project No. 69. U.S. Office of Education, Language Development Section, 1962.

Rigault, A. Rôle de la fréquence, de l'intensité et de la durée vocalique dans la perception de l'accent en français. In A. Sovijarvi and P. Aalto (Eds.), *Proceedings of the 4th International Congress of Phonetic Sciences.* The Hague: Mouton, 1962. Pp. 735–748.

Scherer, George A. C., and Michael Wertheimer. *A psycholinguistic experiment in foreign-language teaching.* New York: McGraw-Hill Book Company, 1964.

11

TESTING FOREIGN LANGUAGE LEARNING

PAUL PIMSLEUR

Paul Pimsleur (1927–   ) received his Ph.D. degree in French from Columbia University and a subsequent M.A. degree in statistics and test construction from Teachers College, Columbia University. He taught at the University of California, Los Angeles from 1957 to 1961 and since 1961 has been director of the Listening Center at the Ohio State University. He is the author of numerous articles; of programmed courses in several languages, including modern Greek; and of a series of aptitude and proficiency tests in French, Spanish, and German to be published by Harcourt, Brace & World, Inc. This paper was originally prepared for oral presentation at the Seminar for College Teachers held at Indiana University July–August, 1964.

I. Language Aptitude

Studying aptitude for foreign languages is not the way to win popularity in the era of the New Key. An early but quite presentable form of my aptitude test was shown some time ago to an eminent authority of the movement. He commented: "Take that out in the backyard and burn it." Thus encouraged, I later showed the same test to another New Key leader. The opinion, though less vividly expressed, was essentially the same: I should abandon the whole thing, the sooner the better.

175

It may surprise you that I should take pains to report these unflattering opinions of the experts. Then it will surprise you still more to learn that I agree with them. What I presume they meant to censure was the pernicious notion that some children just are not suited for language study and that a low score on an aptitude test provides an excuse or a justification for depriving a child of his opportunity to study a foreign language. I, too, condemn such practices and defend the right of every child to have a look at the world he inhabits through more than one-eyed, monolingual glasses.

Exclusion, however, is only one of the functions an aptitude test may serve, and certainly not the most useful. Our purpose here is to examine its more positive functions. These helpful and fascinating functions may be named in two words: *prediction* and *diagnosis*.

I speak of fascination in connection with this apparently ascetic, statistic-laden subject because in fact few intellectual games are as exciting as that of making predictions and then seeing them confirmed or refuted. You marshal your evidence, apply your judgment and experience to weighting it correctly, and commit yourself to a forecast of what is going to happen. Not the least of this game's attractions is the risk involved in committing yourself to a specific prediction before the event; you place your bets on your own judgments, knowing that a time of reckoning, when it will be shown how right or how wrong your judgments were, is not far off.

PREDICTION

Prediction of aptitude for language study is currently practiced very widely and quite badly. While no actual figures are available, it is safe to say that a very substantial number of schools have selection procedures for language classes: procedures to help determine who may begin a language in the seventh grade and who must wait until the eighth or ninth grade, who will be placed in an "able" class and who in a "regular" one, who may study French and who Spanish. In most instances, the selection is made in ways which can readily be shown to be unfair to many students. Two of the most commonly used predictors are IQ and English grades. Let us see how well they and other predictors correlate with actual success in language learning.

The figures in Table I show both IQ and English grades to be inferior to other means that might as easily be employed. Schools should at least use grade-point average (a composite of the student's performance in a number of subjects), rather than IQ or English grades, since this average is a better predictor and is available without additional testing. There is,

TABLE I

PREDICTOR	CORRELATION WITH LANGUAGE GRADES
IQ	r = .46
English grades	r = .57
Grade-point average (GPA)	r = .62
Aptitude battery	R = .62
GPA plus aptitude battery	R = .72

however, a still better alternative. Let us notice what happens to the correlation when both grade-point average and the aptitude battery are used together: it rises to .72, a significant increase in the accuracy of the predictions. Clearly both predictors should be used together for most accurate results.

Much more is at issue here than simply picking up a few points in a statistical measurement. The higher the correction coefficient, the fewer the students who will be misplaced. The fewer will be such errors as barring a student from a class in which he would have succeeded or placing him in one in which he will not succeed. It is important for schools to use the best available means of placing language students, not only in fairness to the majority of students but also in fairness to those few whose only chance for scholastic distinction lies in their talent for language learning and who will be passed over by anything less than the most specialized measuring devices.

Moreover, the more audiolingual the language class, the more a specialized aptitude battery is needed to predict success in it. This is so because an audiolingual class calls into play audiolingual abilities which the student has not had to exercise in his other subjects.

DIAGNOSIS

The second function an aptitude test may serve is diagnosis. We may want a diagnostic instrument to help us find the *overachiever,* the student with especially good audiolingual ability. Or, as is more likely, we may want to diagnose the *underachiever.* As a recent study (Pimsleur, Sundland, & McIntyre, 1963) has shown, in most language classes between 10 and 20 percent of the students are underachievers. These are not just the poor achievers, those who do equally poorly in all their school subjects, but the underachievers, those who have significantly less success in language study than in their other courses. They may be B students who get D's in French or C students who fail it. They are a source of particular frustration to themselves and their teachers because their performance in the language class is below the level they and their parents have come to expect. It may be possible to help such students if we can identify them in advance, before they have gotten so far behind the class that it is impossible to catch up and before they have developed such a "block" where language learning is concerned that even the best teacher cannot reach them. In order to identify them in advance, we must have a diagnostic test.

There is a further implication in what has been said. To predict a learner's achievement and to diagnose his strong and weak points, we must know what abilities it takes to learn a foreign language. An additional reason for studying aptitude, then, is that as we learn more about it, we learn to understand the individual differences among language learners and perhaps to cope with them.

HISTORY

The history of foreign language aptitude testing can be described very briefly, because in a sense it began only a few years ago. Though a variety of such tests has existed since the 1920s, known usually by the names of their authors—Stoddard (Stoddard & Vander Beke, 1925), Symonds (1930), Luria and Orleans (1928; 1930), Hunt (Hunt, Wallace, Doran, Buynitzky & Schwarz, 1929), etc.—these tests were chiefly concerned with the prediction of a kind of achievement, namely, analytic manipulation of the written language, which is now passé. It takes quite a different kind of test to determine who will be good at understanding and speaking a language. Only one such test other than my own has appeared, namely, the Modern Language Aptitude Test by Carroll and Sapon (1958; 1959). A brief description of these two tests will help familiarize the reader with them.

Carroll-Sapon Modern Language Aptitude Test

Part 1: Number Learning. By tape recording, the examinee is taught an artificial system of number expression utilizing nonsense syllables. He is then asked to write down the Arabic numeral equivalents of a list of three-digit numbers in the artificial system, spoken at a fairly rapid pace on the tape. Fifteen items; approximately fourteen minutes.[1]

Part 2: Phonetic Script. The examinee learns a series of phonetic symbols for some of the phonemes of English by listening to pronunciations recorded on tape and following syllables printed in phonetic

---

[1] Total time, including instructions.

symbols on the test paper; after every five items, he is tested on the material just learned. All the phonemes are in English, and no fine phonetic discrimination is required. Thirty items; twelve minutes.

Part 3: Spelling Clues. The examinee chooses which of five words has the same meaning as the word represented in abbreviated form. Sample: kataklzm = (1) *mountain,* (2) *disaster,* (3) *sheep,* (4) *chemical reagent,* (5) *population.* Thirty items; five minutes.

Part 4: Words in Sentences. Each item consists of a "key sentence" with a word or phrase printed in capital letters, followed by another sentence with words and phrases underlined and numbered. The examinee is directed to pick the word or phrase in the second sentence which does the same thing in that sentence as the capitalized word does in the key sentence. Forty-five items; fifteen minutes. Sample:

He spoke VERY well of you.
Suddenly the music became quite loud.
    1   2   3   4

Part 5: Paired Associates. The examinee studies a list of twenty-four "Kurdish-English" vocabulary equivalents for two minutes; in the next two minutes he practices recalling the English meanings, and in the final four minutes he completes from memory a multiple-choice test of the presented vocabulary. Twenty-four items; eleven minutes.

The complete Modern Language Aptitude Test (MLAT) takes a little over an hour to administer. A short form, consisting of the last three parts, takes about forty-five minutes.

PIMSLEUR LANGUAGE APTITUDE BATTERY

Part 1: Grade-point Average (GPA). The examinee enters on the answer sheet his most recent year-end grades in English, mathematics, science, and history (or social studies). Four minutes.

Part 2: Interest. The examinee indicates, on a 5-point scale provided on the answer sheet, the degree of his interest in studying a foreign language. 1½ minutes.

Part 3: Vocabulary. A twenty-four item test of English vocabulary knowledge. Five minutes.

Part 4: Language Analysis. The examinee is given a number of forms in a foreign language (Kabardian) and their English equivalents. From these, he must conclude how other things are said in this language. Fifteen items; twelve minutes. Sample:

shi gader le = the horse sees father
shi gader la = the horse saw father
             be = carries

Q. How would you say "the horse carried father"?

1. shi gader be
2. shi gader ba
3. gade shir be
4. gade shir ba

Part 5: Sound Discrimination. The examinee is taught, by tape recording, three words in a foreign language (Ewé); they are similar though not identical in sound. He then hears sentences said in Ewé and must indicate, for each sentence, which of the three words it contains. Thirty items; eight minutes.

Part 6: Sound-Symbol. The examinee hears a bisyllabic or trisyllabic English nonsense word. He is to identify, from among four similar-appearing words printed on his answer sheet, the one which was said. For example, he hears ['tarpdɛl] and chooses among (1) *trapled,* (2) *tarpled,* (3) *tarpdel,* (4) *trapdel.* Twenty-four items; nine minutes.

The entire Language Aptitude Battery (LAB) takes approximately thirty-nine minutes to administer. As with the MLAT, the instructions and timing are on the tape.

RELIABILITY AND VALIDITY

The two questions usually asked concerning a test are: Is it reliable? Is it valid?

Reliability concerns, roughly speaking, the accuracy of a measuring instrument. This is largely a technical matter. Other things being equal, the longer a test is, the more reliable it will be. The reliabilities of the five parts of the Carroll-Sapon MLAT, as administered to ninth-, tenth-, and eleventh-grade students, are reported in the test manual to vary from a low of .55 for Part 2 to a high of .89 for Part 5. The median reliability is approximately .86. Reliabilities have been computed for the Pimsleur LAB; using a sample of 100 junior and senior high school students, the reliability of the "Language Analysis" part was .71, the Vocabulary Test had a reliability of .91, and the Sound-Symbol Test .82. The Ewé "Sound Discrimination" part is new to the battery, replacing a similar test using the Chinese language; the former test had a reliability of .73. These figures reflect the relative shortness of each subtest. The advantage, of course, is that the entire battery can be administered in a class period.

In my judgment, it is worth sacrificing a little reliability for the sake of this convenience and in order to include an additional subtest.

Validity has to do with how well a test actually measures what it purports to measure, in this case, language aptitude. An estimate of validity may be obtained by correlating the test scores with the students' actual performance in the language class; such figures are called validity coefficients. The MLAT was correlated against course grades of eighteen groups of French, Spanish, and German students, in grades 9 to 11. The eighteen validity coefficients ranged from .25 to .78; the median figure was .53. The LAB, used with a similar group of junior and senior high school students, yielded a coefficient of .71. With another sample, it yielded a coefficient of .55 for predicting scores on the Cooperative Spanish Test and one of .86 for predicting scores on the Cooperative French Test. At the college level, the MLAT manual reports twenty-four validity coefficients ranging from .13 to .69; the median coefficient is approximately .47. The only comparable figure available for the LAB is a correlation of .65 with Cooperative French Test scores among 200 students at the University of California, Los Angeles.

In evaluating these findings, one must remember two influences which worked in favor of the LAB's validity data. For one thing, the criterion of achievement in some of the LAB studies was the Cooperative Test, a standardized instrument of high reliability. All the MLAT figures were based on teacher grades, which are notably less reliable, and thereby probably lowered its validity figures. Second, in most of the studies in which the LAB was used, a new set of weightings was calculated each time so as to produce the highest validity for the particular sample in question. In actual use in the field, the test will have only one set of weightings (or at most two or three, e.g., for males and females) which will be applied to all samples, fitting each more or less well but rarely as well as a formula made up for the occasion would fit. The MLAT presumably used the same formula throughout the validation studies. Some "shrinkage," as it is called, may be expected to lower the LAB validity coefficients in new samples.

CONCLUSIONS CONCERNING PREDICTION

To summarize the findings on predictions, I conclude that (1) the MLAT and the LAB are approximately equal as predictive instruments, if one considers only the parts on which the student's actual performance is measured, that is, if Parts 1 and 2 of the LAB are ignored. (2) The inclusion in the LAB of two important factors (grade-point average and interest) not included in the MLAT, however, gives it an important degree of additional predictive validity. (3) Most parts of the MLAT are more reliable than those of the LAB, by virtue of their greater length. (4) The class-period length of the LAB, accomplished without sacrificing measurement on auditory tasks, may be attractive in situations in which testing time is at a premium. Apart from the matter of length, the two tests are equally easy to administer.

CONCLUSIONS CONCERNING DIAGNOSIS

Turning from prediction to diagnosis, we must consider briefly how these two tests came into being. Each is the result of some five years of research, in which a large number and variety of different tests were tried out experimentally. In both cases, the details of the research have been reported quite fully in the professional literature (Carroll, 1958; Carroll, 1962; Pimsleur, 1961; Pimsleur, 1962; Pimsleur, 1963; Pimsleur, 1964; Pimsleur, Mosberg, & Morrison, 1962; Pimsleur, Stockwell, & Comrey, 1962). Methodologically, the experiments bear considerable similarity, particularly in their use of such statistical techniques as factor analysis and multiple-correlation analysis. Such resemblances are not coincidental, for I was led to my own interest in aptitude testing by reading Professor Carroll's reports of his work. My test also profited from Professor Carroll's work in another way. Much of the problem in this kind of testing lies in breaking down the characteristic to be tested. The beginning of the work is to ask yourself these questions: What is language aptitude made up of? How can I best define its components so as to test them one by one? Since Professor Carroll had already reported several factor analyses, my collaborators and I knew, to some extent, which factors we ought to devise tests for. We were therefore able to devise so-called "single-factor" tests, each of which measures a specific, well-defined factor.

The theory underlying the LAB test, a theory derived empirically through analysis of experimental data, is that the "talent" for learning foreign languages consists of three components. The first is verbal intelligence, by which is meant both familiarity with words (this is measured in the LAB by the "Vocabulary" part) and the ability to reason analytically about verbal materials (this can be measured by the part called "Language Analysis"). The second component is motivation to learn the language, which is measured by the "Interest" part. The third component of language learning ability is called "auditory ability" and is measured, in two different aspects, by the "Sound Discrimination" and the "Sound-Symbol" parts of the LAB. Auditory ability was identified in a recent study (Pimsleur, Sundland, & McIntyre, 1963) as the main factor differentiating normal achievers from underachievers in foreign language learning. It is hypothesized to be the factor which accounts for differences in people's language learning ability which are not explainable by intelligence or interest.

Diagnosis is an individual matter, a matter of finding out the strengths and weaknesses of particular students in advance, so they can be helped. Let us examine several actual cases, exhibited in the sample diagnostic profiles shown on p. 184, to see how the LAB scores serve the diagnostic function. Each student's scores on the last four parts of the LAB are indicated on the profile charts by X's. The distance of the X from the horizontal center line indicates approximately how many standard deviations above or below the mean the score is. In the first case, that of junior high school student R. P., the scores in all four tests are substantially above the mean. The diagnosis, which is given to the right, was self-evident. It was later confirmed by the teacher that this student was indeed one of the two top students in the class.

The next case, that of D. J. M. was more complex. His scores on the first two tests, which measure aspects of verbal intelligence, were about average. His scores on the last two tests, which measure aspects of auditory ability, were both below average. The diagnosis therefore was that he would not be a very good student in any respect but that he might be worse in oral than in written work.

The next case, that of C. C., was quite different. It appeared she might be better at audiolingual learning tasks, such as listening comprehension, pronunciation, and speaking, than at grammar-translation tasks. This diagnosis was essentially confirmed, though not as strikingly as her test scores led us to suppose. I might suspect that this girl had some special difficulty on the second test, such as not understanding the directions or entering her answers in the wrong spaces. This could not be confirmed, since the study was conducted by mail; I have never met either the girl or her teacher.

The next girl, M. E., was in the same French class, but her profile is quite different. She appears completely average, except for the unusually low score on the "Sound-Symbol" part. This led to the statement in the diagnosis that she might have trouble in the audiolingual area. This was confirmed by the grades she received; the diagnosis had correctly indicated the direction of the difficulty but had not foreseen that it would be extreme enough to cause her to receive a failing grade in her oral work.

These cases illustrate diagnostic uses of the LAB. This is by no means to say that the test always tells us what we want to know about a student. Nevertheless, I think it can be fairly claimed that it gives useful diagnostic information and is one of the few means presently available by which

Sample Diagnostic Profiles

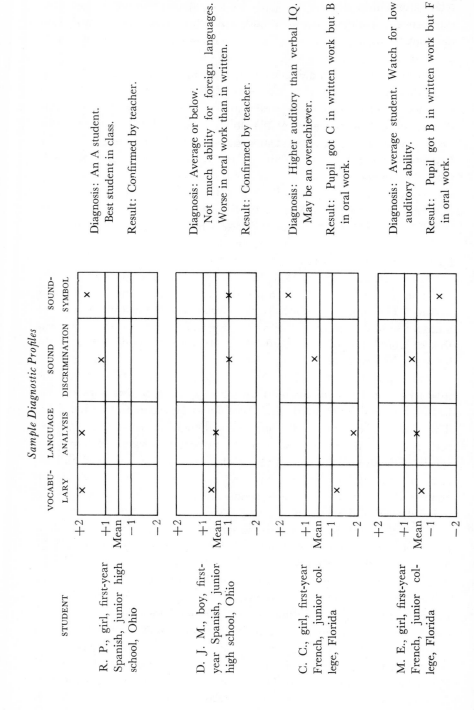

STUDENT		VOCABU-LARY	LANGUAGE ANALYSIS	SOUND DISCRIMINATION	SOUND-SYMBOL	
R. P., girl, first-year Spanish, junior high school, Ohio	+2	×	×	×	×	Diagnosis: An A student. Best student in class. Result: Confirmed by teacher.
	+1					
	Mean					
	−1					
	−2					
D. J. M., boy, first-year Spanish, junior high school, Ohio	+2					Diagnosis: Average or below. Not much ability for foreign languages. Worse in oral work than in written. Result: Confirmed by teacher.
	+1	×	×			
	Mean			×	×	
	−1					
	−2					
C. C., girl, first-year French, junior college, Florida	+2				×	Diagnosis: Higher auditory than verbal IQ. May be an overachiever. Result: Pupil got C in written work but B in oral work.
	+1			×		
	Mean					
	−1	×				
	−2		×			
M. E., girl, first-year French, junior college, Florida	+2					Diagnosis: Average student. Watch for low auditory ability. Result: Pupil got B in written work but F in oral work.
	+1	×	×	×		
	Mean					
	−1				×	
	−2					

such information may be obtained. Its diagnostic accuracy will grow as experience is acquired in its use and as it profits from further trials and revisions.

I hope that the preceding section has demonstrated to the reader the fascination that lies in predictive and diagnostic testing, but I hope also that it has convinced him on two issues: (1) No child should be barred from the opportunity to study a foreign language; certainly this is not the purpose of aptitude testing. (2) Screening a student for language study is like performing a surgical operation on him: nothing less than the best instruments will do.

REFERENCES

Carroll, John B. A factor analysis of two foreign language aptitude batteries. *Journal of General Psychology,* 1958, **59,** 3–19.

Carroll, John B. The prediction of success in intensive foreign language training. In Robert Glazer (Ed.), *Training research and education.* Pittsburgh, Pa.: The University of Pittsburgh Press, 1962.

Carroll, John B., and Stanley M. Sapon. *Modern Language Aptitude Test, Form A.* New York: The Psychological Corporation, 1958, 1959.

Hunt, Thelma, F. C. Wallace, S. Doran, K. C. Buynitzky, and R. E. Schwarz. *George Washington University Language Aptitude Test.* Washington, D.C.: Center for Psychological Services, 1929.

Luria, M. A., and J. S. Orleans. *Luria-Orleans Modern Language Prognosis Test.* New York: Harcourt, Brace & World, Inc., 1928, 1930.

Pimsleur, Paul. *A study of foreign language learning ability.* Monograph Series on Languages and Linguistics, No. 14. (Ed. Michael Zarechnak) Washington, D.C.: Georgetown University, Institute of Languages and Linguistics, 1961.

Pimsleur, Paul. Predicting achievement in foreign language learning. *International Journal of American Linguistics,* 1962, **29,** 2.

Pimsleur, Paul. Predicting success in high school foreign language courses. *Educational and Psychological Measurements,* 1963, **33,** 2.

Pimsleur, Paul. *Language Aptitude Battery.* (Experimental ed.) New York: Harcourt, Brace & World, Inc., 1964.

Pimsleur, Paul, L. Mosberg, and A. Morrison. Student factors in foreign language learning: A review of the literature. *Modern Language Journal,* 1962, **46,** 4.

Pimsleur, Paul, R. P. Stockwell, and A. L. Comrey. Foreign language learning ability. *Journal of Educational Psychology,* 1962, **53,** 1.

Pimsleur, Paul, D. M. Sundland, and R. McIntyre. *Underachievement in foreign language learning: Final report.* Contract No.

OE–2–14–004. Columbus, Ohio: The Ohio State University Research Foundation, May, 1963.

Stoddard, G. D., and G. E. Vander Beke. *Iowa Placement Examination*. Series FAI, Revised A. Iowa City, Iowa: State University of Iowa, Iowa City Extension Division, 1925.

Symonds, P. M. *Foreign Language Prognosis Test*. New York: Bureau of Publications, Teachers College, Columbia University, 1930.

II.   Listening Comprehension

A decade ago, in a "state-of-the-art" review of foreign language achievement tests, John B. Carroll (1954) felt impelled to assure his readers that, far from being impossible to construct, as had often been alleged, tests of listening comprehension were really no more difficult to make up than tests of reading. It is a measure of the progress made since then that a reviewer of today would no longer need to justify the feasibility of auditory testing. (Parenthetically, it may be added that similar apprehensions now apply to speaking tests, which still are far short of having achieved general acceptance among foreign language teachers.)

The year 1954 was a turning point. One year earlier, Edna Furness, reviewing auditory tests in Spanish in the *Modern Language Journal*, concluded that there was as yet not a single aural-oral test which had been validated, on which item analyses had been performed, and for which reliability data were reported. The same conclusion was essentially justified for all the languages. Although serious attempts at measuring the listening skill had been made by Tharp (Cole & Tharp, 1937), Rulon (1943), Sandri and Kaulfers (1946), Bovée (1948), Agard and Dunkel (1948), and Lado (1950), none had yet reported the kind of supporting data that Miss Furness had rightly demanded.

It was in that year, 1954, that the first of the modern tests of auditory comprehension was tried out. Its author was Nelson Brooks (1955), and the test subsequently saw the light of day both as a part of the College Entrance Examination Board tests and under its own identity as the Cooperative French Listening Comprehension Test. It was modern in availing itself of certain statistical techniques of test construction, at least item analysis and the use of norms, though its manual is weak in reporting the test's reliability and entirely lacking in evidence of the test's validity. It was modern, too, in eschewing all translation techniques. Not only is English absent from the items; it is absent from the entire test, since even the instructions are given in French.

Première Partie
Après avoir lu le numéro, je lirai deux fois une des cinq phrases qui con-

stituent la question. Vous devez reconnaître la phrase que j'aurai lue et l'indiquer sur la feuille imprimée. Par exemple, je dis: "Jean nageait. Jean nageait." Vous avez devant vous: "J'ai nagé. Je nageais. Jean nageait. Jean a nagé. Je nagerai." Puisque j'ai dit "Jean nageait", c'est la troisième réponse qui est juste et qui est marquée dans la colonne de gauche.

My own feeling is that it was a mistake to give the instructions in French, because, as the French say, *de deux choses l'une:* Either the task is self-evident, in which case why have the instructions at all? Or else it requires explaining, in which case why run the risk that a substantial number of students will not know what is expected of them? Let the student's comprehension of French be tested by the items, not by the instructions. When I used this test with my classes, I took the liberty of giving all the instructions in English, whereupon I found the test quite satisfactory. This test is more than a decade old now, and the swift changes in textbook vocabulary during the last few years may call for its revision, but it will be evident as this demonstration progresses how much is owed to it by more recent listening tests.

A most noteworthy recent even in foreign language testing was the publication of two complete sets of standardized tests, both sponsored by the Modern Language Association (MLA, 1962; 1964). One set is for testing the proficiency of teachers; the other, for testing the proficiency of students. Certainly both sets can be called "complete," for they cover the five commonly taught languages and include tests of all pertinent skills, at appropriate ability levels, and with alternate forms. We shall examine the manner in which listening comprehension is measured in these new tests.

Part A of the MLA Listening Test, Form LA, presents pictures from among which the student is to choose. He sees four pictures and is to select the one which corresponds to a sentence spoken by a taped voice in the foreign language. For example, he hears: *Estoy aquí con mi hermana. Ella es mayor que yo.* He is supposed to choose the picture in which the girl is bigger than the boy. This type of item is used in the lower-level tests, but not at the middle level.

In the next part of the test, the student chooses from among four sentences the one which best answers the question asked by the taped voice. Here are some examples from a lower-level Spanish test, Form LA.

(VOICE: ¿Están Vds. cansados?)

     f.   No, en el centro.

     g.   Amigos, nada más.

     h.   Tenemos muchos.

     j.   Sí, un poco.

(VOICE: ¿A qué hora tenemos que volver a casa?)

   a. A las cinco.

   b. Vuelven mañana.

   c. Sólo tengo una.

   d. Tres y cinco son ocho.

The remainder of the test, Parts C through F, uses approximately the same format. The student overhears, as it were, a snatch of conversation in the foreign language and is then asked questions about it. Here are several examples from the lower-level tests.

19.   VOICE: —Papa, *mira* el cartero.

          —Ah, corre a darle esta carta, Tomás.
          Date prisa, ¿eh?

   QUESTION: ¿Quién es Tomás?

          a. El hijo.

          b. El padre.

          c. El cartero.

          d. La persona a quien se escribe.

20.   VOICE: —Dispense Vd. ¿Puede decirme cómo se llega al correo?

          —Con mucho gusto, señorita. Siga Vd. dos cuadras más por esta misma calle.
          Si me permite, podría acompañarla.

   QUESTION: ¿Qué quiere el joven?

          f. Comprar unos cuadros.

          g. Saber dónde está el correo.

          h. Ir al correo con la señorita.

          j. Llevar las cartas al correo.

The reliability of this test requires little discussion. Reliability is largely a function of a test's length and of the statistical care exercised in selecting the items; since both of these factors are favorable, the tests are of more than adequate reliability. Figures above .90 are reported for all forms. Incidentally, all reliability and validity figures to be given here are for the teacher tests, rather than the classroom tests, from which the samples were taken. This information is not yet available for the latter set, but let us assume it will be equally satisfactory.

A test's validity is more difficult to establish than its reliability, for validity must be demonstrated in a variety of ways, all of which answer the same question: Is this test really measuring what it is supposed to measure? One kind of evidence establishes so-called "statistical validity"; that is, each item is examined by item analysis procedures to determine whether it distinguishes adequately between those who do well on the total test and those who do poorly. By this criterion, these tests are statistically valid. This method, however, is based on the assumption that the total score itself is valid. The truth of this assumption must be verified by independent means, often, as in this case, by seeing whether an individual's score on the test correlates well with some other measure of the same skill. Such a study was done, by Myers and Melton (1964), correlating MLA Listening Test scores with ratings of the same individuals' listening skill. The ratings were made at National Defense Education Act (NDEA) institutes by faculty members. Correlations of .70 are reported for both French and Spanish samples; the extent of this agreement is convincing evidence of the test's validity.

If we turn now to the Listening Comprehension Test of the Pimsleur French Proficiency Tests (Pimsleur, 1964), one difference is immediately apparent, namely, that two quite separate aspects of the listening skill are being tested. In the MLA tests we have just seen, all the parts tested comprehension of meaning in the foreign language. I consider it important also to test the student's ability to discriminate the foreign sounds and other auditory features, such as stress and intonation. Consequently, Part I of this test is devoted to this type of item. The student sees four sentences on his answer sheet; they are quite similar in sound. He hears the taped voice say one of them and must identify which was said.

5. C'est un bel état.
C'est un bébé.
C'est une beauté.
C'est un bel été.

13. C'est un jeu si amusant.
Ce sont des yeux amusants.
Ce sont des jeux amusants.
C'est un jeu amusant.

The purpose of these items is to sample the student's mastery of the acoustic features which signal semantic differences in the foreign language, in other words, the segmental and suprasegmental phonemes. Here, we wish to measure his ability to receive and decode them, just as in one part of a speaking test we wish to measure his ability to encode and produce them. This means we must begin with a relatively complete inventory of such features, so that we can sample them adequately, with particular attention to those which may be especially difficult for our American students. In this task, the fruits of linguistic science are virtually indispensable, for one of the important products of a comparative linguistic analysis is just this: the identification of the semantically relevant cues and of the sources of interference between native language and target language habits. Often, such analyses point directly to test items we need to construct; this topic has been well discussed by Lado (1961). We are fortunate in having excellent, pedagogically oriented linguistic analyses, such as those of Mueller and Mayer (1958), Politzer (1960), and Valdman (1961) for French; Politzer and Staubach (1961), Bowen and Stockwell (1960), Cárdenas (1961), and O'Connor, Haden, and Durand (1962) for Spanish; and Kufner (1962), Marchand (1961), and Moulton (1962) for German.

The second part of the Pimsleur Listening Comprehension Test measures comprehension of meaningful utterances. The student hears something said in the foreign language and must choose, from among four sentences on his answer sheet, the one which would make the best rejoinder to what was said. Three of the choices make little or no sense, while one is a logical response to what was said. Here are some sample items of this type:

> (VOICE: Avez-vous acheté des fleurs?)
> Oui, mais elles étaient très chères.
> Oui, j'ai acheté une belle voiture.
> Non, je ne pleure pas.
> Non, elle s'appelait Rose.

> (VOICE: Donne-moi un autre bonbon.)
> As-tu soif?
> Non, tu en as assez mangé.
> Il faut le laver.
> Voici une porte.

As with the MLA test, complete data are not yet available on the reliability and validity of this test. An experimental edition has been administered in a number of high schools, and these data will be presented when the tests are published in their final form.

It will be instructive, I think, to take an imaginary tour in a test constructor's workshop and to accompany him in some of the steps he takes to refine a test. The test of listening comprehension we have just seen will serve as a typical case. In a certain item, the student hears a voice ask, *Quel temps fait-il ici au mois de juillet?*, and he chooses from among four responses. The first, *Aujourd'hui,* is simply an irrelevant answer. The second, *Assez chaud,* is the correct response. The third, *Cinq heures et demie,* will be chosen by students who think *temps* mean "time" in the stimulus sentence. The fourth, *Oui, mais il est parti,* plays upon the subject word *il*. This item is from the first version of Form D of the test. This form was given to three high school classes in Columbus, Ohio, toward the end of their second year of French. It was taken by seventy-seven students in all. Each of the forty-three items in that form was then analyzed. To use the item you have just seen as an example, it was first examined for degree of difficulty. The question here is: How many of the seventy-seven students got it right? The answer is that forty-five of them, or 58 percent, got it right. Thus far, this is a good sign. It seems the item is at about the correct level of difficulty for these students. But a further question remains: *Which* students got it right? Of course, we want the good students to get it right, but if the item were in some way badly constructed, it might actually turn out that the poorer students got it right, while the better students chose some other misleading response. One technique used to analyze the items from this standpoint is to look at the choices made by the upper and lower quarters of the students. The assumption is made that if a student's total score was in the top 25 percent on this test, he is probably good at listening comprehension, and that if he got a score in the lower 25 percent, he is probably bad at it. We wish the good students to get our item correct substantially more frequently than the poor ones do. In the case of this particular item, nineteen out of the twenty-four good students got it right, while only seven of the twenty-four poor ones got it right. The item seems to be doing a good job of discriminating good from poor "compre-henders." One final step involves looking at the wrong choices to see that all three "distractors" are drawing some student responses; if only one is drawing responses, then it may be too tricky an item, tending to "catch" students rather than test them. In this, too, our item has come through, and it passes without revision into the next experimental edition of the test.

Now let us look at the item which appeared just next to that one in the same test form.

(VOICE: C'est un bel enfant.)
    Il ressemble à sa mère.
    Non, il n'est pas sage.
    Elle chante bien.
    Il est à la maison.

The analysis showed this item to have reasonably adequate power to discriminate, since twenty-two out of twenty-four good students got it right, versus only fifteen out of twenty-four poor ones. The trouble with it is that 82 percent of the seventy-seven students got it right. It is too easy an item for the second year. It may serve very well at the first-year level, but we may have to change the second response to eliminate *sage*, a fairly rare word in first-year courses. The item was relegated to Form B, a first-year form.

Later on in Form D, we come to this item:

(VOICE: Attention! Ce n'est pas encore mûr.)

    Je ne le regarderai pas.

    Je n'y toucherai pas.

    Je ferai très attention.

    Je ne le mangerai pas.

This item is a real disaster. Only four students out of seventy-seven, or 5 percent, got it right. Moreover, only one good student got it right, versus three poor ones. As we look at the item, we see why this occurred. (Of course hindsight makes us very clever.) The word *mûr* is no doubt too difficult, an unknown word for most of the students. Furthermore, all four choices might be considered correct to some extent; the one we marked right, the fourth response, is only slightly more appropriate than the others. No attempt was made to salvage this item; it was dropped into the wastebasket.

In similar fashion, every item in all the tests—some 200 for the four forms of the Pimsleur Listening Comprehension Test alone—was analyzed, using data from a sample of classes. The tests have all been revised in this manner, and now the improved versions have been given to larger samples, representing classes at different levels and in different locations. The same rigorous examination will take place again, and only those items which pass inspection in all respects will be included in the final published version.

This is the process known as item analysis. It is not the property of any particular test expert but is applied to all tests that are constructed by testing specialists. It is the conscientious application of these techniques which imparts to a test its internal or statistical validity. And it is the knowledge that such analyses have been performed and reperformed that gives the user confidence in the tests he chooses to employ. It is not to be expected that teachers will go through this elaborate process for every quiz they give. This, in fact, is what distinguishes a standardized test: every component has been scrutinized in this fashion. Yet something of the same thinking surely would raise the quality of teacher tests as well.

REFERENCES

Agard, F. B., and H. B. Dunkel. *An investigation of second-language learning.* Boston: Ginn and Company, 1948.

Bovée, A. The relationship between audio and visual thought comprehension in French. *French Review,* 1948, **21,** 120–123.

Bowen, Donald J., and Robert P. Stockwell. *Patterns of Spanish pronunciation.* Chicago: The University of Chicago Press, 1960.

Brooks, Nelson. *Cooperative French Listening Comprehension Test.* Princeton, N.J.: Educational Testing Service, Cooperative Test Division, 1955.

Cárdenas, Daniel N. *Applied linguistics—Spanish.* (Ed. S. Belasco). Boston: D. C. Heath and Company, 1961.

Carroll, John B. *Notes on the measurement of achievement in foreign language.* 1954. (Mimeographed.)

Cole, R. D., and J. B. Tharp. *Modern foreign languages and their teaching.* New York: Appleton-Century-Crofts, Inc., 1937.

College Entrance Examination Board. *Foreign languages.* Princeton, N.J.: Educational Testing Service, 1963.

Kufner, Herbert L. *The grammatical structure of English and German.* Chicago: The University of Chicago Press, 1962.

Lado, Robert L. The linguistic science and language tests. *Language Learning,* 1950, **3,** 75–82.

Lado, Robert L. *Language testing.* London: Longmans, Green & Co., Ltd., 1961.

Marchand, James W. *Applied linguistics—German.* (Ed. S. Belasco) Boston: D. C. Heath and Company, 1961.

MLA Cooperative Foreign Language Tests. Princeton, N.J.: Educational Testing Service, 1964.

MLA Foreign Language Proficiency Tests for Teachers and Advanced Students. Princeton, N.J.: Educational Testing Service, 1962.

Moulton, William G. *The sounds of English and German.* Chicago: The University of Chicago Press, 1962.

Mueller, T., and E. Mayer. *La structure de la langue française.* Gainesville, Fla.: University of Florida, 1958.

Myers, C. T., and R. S. Melton. *A study of the relationship between scores on the MLA Foreign Language Proficiency Tests for Teachers and Advanced Students and ratings of teacher competence.* Princeton, N.J.: Educational Testing Service, 1964.

O'Connor, Patricia, E. Haden, and F. Durand. *Oral drill in Spanish.* Boston: Houghton Mifflin Company, 1962.

Pimsleur, Paul. *Pimsleur French Proficiency Tests—Test 1: Listening Comprehension.* (Experimental ed.) New York: Harcourt, Brace & World, Inc., 1964.

Politzer, Robert L. *Teaching French: An introduction to applied linguistics.* New York: Blaisdell Publishing Company, 1960.

Politzer, Robert L., and Charles N. Staubach. *Teaching Spanish: A linguistic orientation.* Boston: Ginn and Company, 1961.

Rulon, P. J. *Report on contract test constructed for ASTD, ASF.* Contract No. W–19–073 AST (SC–1)–26: Report on scales for measuring ability to speak German and Russian, Term 5. Cambridge, Mass.: Harvard University, 1943.

Sandri, L., and W. V. Kaulfers. An aural comprehension scale in Italian. *Italica,* 1946, **23,** 338–351.

Valdman, Albert. *Applied linguistics—French: A guide for teachers.* (Ed. S. Belasco) Boston: D. C. Heath and Company, 1961.

III.   Speaking Skill

In his book *Language Testing,* Robert Lado (1961) had this to say about speaking tests:

> The ability to speak a foreign language is without doubt the most highly prized language skill, and rightly so, because he who can speak a language well can also understand it and can learn to read it with relative ease. . . . Also, the ability to speak a language will greatly expedite and facilitate learning to write it. Yet testing the ability to speak a foreign language is perhaps the least developed and the least practiced in the language testing field.

This statement is true or at least *was* true until very recent years, when serious attacks have at last been made upon the problem of testing the speaking skill.

Little need be said, at the present juncture in foreign language teaching, about why it is necessary to test the speaking skill. Indeed, a great deal depends on such tests. The difference between merely paying lip service to the oral objective and actually achieving it resides in making clear to the students that their grades will depend to a considerable extent upon their speaking performance.

In our effort as teachers to test this performance, we try of course to be as objective as possible. Yet we are impaled upon a paradox. The effort to test the speaking skill objectively is fated always to fall short of complete success, for we are dependent upon the judgment of a listener, and he, however well trained he may be, is a subjective and not an objective scoring machine. Yet, all attempts to render these judgments objective are useful and instructive: they force us to define more carefully what we mean when we say someone can "speak French" or "speak Spanish."

In an article published in 1961 (Pimsleur, 1961), I reviewed the field of oral testing as follows:

> It is a simple matter to review past efforts in this area. As of 1953, Furness, reviewing aural-oral tests in Spanish (*MLJ*), reports that no test of either aural or oral proficiency had given serious evidence of validity and reliability. The same can be said for French. This is not to say that there were not worthy attempts made, but the author of a test is obliged to present evidence

on validity and reliability in order to be convincing, and this had not been done in the case of any audio-lingual tests. In aural testing this situation has been altered somewhat in recent years; as for oral testing, little has been done. . . . No speaking test now exists which meets the criteria of validity, reliability, ease of administration, and objectivity of scoring.

Since these comments were written, three tests of speaking proficiency have appeared which meet the criteria mentioned. They are my own French Speaking Proficiency Test (Pimsleur, 1964), the Speaking Test of the MLA Cooperative Foreign Language Test (1964), and the Speaking Test of the MLA Foreign Language Proficiency Tests for Teachers and Advanced Students (1962).

Let us examine first the French Speaking Proficiency Test (FSPT), both because of its seniority and because a review of its genesis, including the parts which have since been discarded, will be generally instructive. As has been said, it is difficult to arrive at objective evaluation of speaking ability. It was, in fact, as a sort of game or *gageure,* that I undertook, in 1958 and 1959, to construct a test which would try the limits to which objective scoring of the speaking skill could be brought. The problem was to break down the speaking skill into a number of testable components, without fragmenting it so much that the components no longer added up to the whole skill. Then, for each component, a scoring method was needed which would maximize the agreement among different judges. Furthermore, the whole test had to be extremely economical in time, to keep to an absolute minimum the time needed to score each student's responses.

For purposes of testing, French-speaking ability was broken down into five parts. Part 1 of the test measures knowledge of concrete vocabulary. The student sees in his booklet pictures of common objects. He must name each of the objects in French. He is given forty-five seconds, and his score is the number of objects he can name in that time. This part and Part 2, which is similar, differ from a conventional vocabulary test, first of all, in that the student must recall and say the names of things almost instantly as he is under time pressure; second, in that the stimulus is a picture rather than an English word; and, third, in that he has a problem of pronunciation but not of orthography. To avoid confusing the task, the gender of the word need not be said correctly (or an article given at all, for that matter), and the student is so informed in the instructions.

The shortcoming of this section is in the time factor it imposes. It places a premium on unusually quick thinking, rather than solely on knowledge of vocabulary. For this reason, Part 1 is slightly different in the most recent edition of the test. Now, the numbers are read (in

French) by the tape voice, and the student is given a four-second interval in which to name each picture. The time is equalized in this way for all the students.

The concrete words tested in Part 1 represent only one kind of words, those that can be pictured. What about abstract words, such as *busy, empty,* or *happy?* For these a different test was devised: Part 2, "Abstract Words." In this part, the student sees in his booklet a pair of pictures. The first shows a smiling boy, and the caption says *Le garçon est heureux.* The second shows the same boy crying, and the caption says, *Le garçon est* ———. The student must supply a word which correctly completes the caption. In the example, the word might be *malheureux, triste,* or *désolé.* By means of such pairs of pictures, abstract oppositions like *full-empty, night-day, more-less,* and *good-bad* are elicited. A time limit of one minute is allowed for this part. The score is the number right; there are sixteen items.

Despite a certain ingenuity, this part has two flaws. It gives an advantage to the clever student who can figure out what is expected in each item; it thereby tests IQ as well as French, which is not the object at all. Moreover, it requires relatively a long time, one full minute, to do only sixteen items. Since time is of the essence (let us remember the problem of scoring each recording), this technique is uneconomical. This part of the test has been eliminated in the present edition, and the assumption made that if a student does well on Part 1, "Concrete Nouns," then he probably knows his abstract vocabulary also. Thus, a high correlation between two tasks may be exploited in constructing a test, when one of the tasks lends itself more readily to measurement than the other.

The next section is Part 3, "Pronunciation." The student finds in his test booklet a list of twenty sentences. He is given time to practice them and then records his reading of them. (Features being tested are represented by items in italics.)

1. Il est *fou.*
2. Il est *beau.*
3. Nous sommes dans *la* sa*lle.*
4. J'ai vu le bé*bé* cet *été.*
5. Qu'est-ce qu'il a b*u?*
6. Regardez le *feu.*
7. J'en ai n*euf.*
8. Il m*e le* dit.
9. Ce train est l*ent.*
10. Qu'est-ce qu'ils f*ont?*

11. Servez le p*a*in.
12. Paris est gr*a*nd.
13. Il est‿à la maison de son‿oncle.
14. Quelle jolie *h*armonie!
15. Où est *Jean*? / Où est *Jeanne*?
16. Le vin est *bon*. / La viande est *bonne*.
17. Mon frère est ma*rin*. / Il est dans la ma*rine*.
18. J'ai vu la *fille*. / Elle est en *ville*.
19. Quel p*ays*! / Il y a du sol*eil*!
20. C'est un *jeu*. / Je *joue*.

In these twenty items, many of the important elements of French pronunciation are represented. In the interests of objective scoring, each sentence contains only one element which the scorer must listen to and judge. The first twelve items contain twelve different vowel sounds; the sound in question is usually in the last syllable, so that it will receive the tonic accent. Item 13 tests liaison. Item 14 tests the silent *h*. Items 15 through 20 contain oppositions (*Jean/Jeanne, bon/bonne, marin/marine, fille/ville, pays/soleil, jeu/joue*) which are among the more difficult ones for American students to maintain.

Here, scoring becomes a problem, for the scorer must judge the adequacy of the student's pronunciation in each item. Subjectivity necessarily enters the picture, and a scoring system must be found to keep it to a minimum. After examining other possible measuring scales, from a 2-point scale (right or wrong) to a 5-point scale (poor, fair, good, very good, excellent), it was decided that a 3-point scale would be the best compromise. The scale was numbered 2, 1, and 0, and a description given each score:

2 = like a native
1 = not native but adequate
0 = inadequate

This scale does not require very fine judgments on the part of the scorer, while still permitting a sufficient range of scores. The scorers are instructed to practice on at least ten recordings, so as to stabilize their judgments, before beginning actual scoring. This simple 2, 1, 0 system is also used in Parts 4 and 5 of the test. Some evidence concerning the degree of agreement among judges using this system will be presented below.

The original version of Part 3 is the one just described. Subsequent analyses of the individual items have permitted improvement of the test by the elimination of items on which most students get perfect scores (e.g., item 14), and the addition of items containing sounds of proved difficulty. The sentences have also been revised so as to contain two examples of the sound in question, one in stressed and the other in unstressed position. The revised pronunciation test is as follows:

1. Ils‿étaient‿ici.
2. C'est un bel *enf*ant.
3. Faites un p*eu* de f*eu*.
4. C'est un m*ot* nouv*eau*.
5. La *vieille* fait son trav*ail*.
6. Il trav*ai*lle dans un mag*a*sin.
7. L'*eau* est ch*au*de.
8. Nous *i*rons à Pa*r*is.
9. L'avez-v*ous* v*u*?
10. V*ous* êtes f*ou*.
11. Vous‿avez trois‿oncles.
12. J'ai pris un b*ain* ce mat*in*.
13. As-t*u* ta pl*u*me?
14. Vous êtes *a*llé à l'op*é*ra.
15. La *r*obe est *r*ouge.
16. *Où* est le lou*p*?
17. Je *joue* au *jeu*.
18. All*ez*! All*ez*!
19. Nous le s*ui*vons dans la n*ui*t.
20. Venez dem*ain* mat*in*.
21. Le m*u*r est n*u*.
22. M*a*ngez-*en*!
23. Il est h*eureux*.
24. C'est l*ui* qui fait la c*ui*sine.
25. Vous buv*ez* de th*é*.

Part 4 of the test measures syntax, the ability to use correct constructions in speaking. It was the most difficult section to construct, and as we shall see, the results, even after long efforts, were not entirely satisfactory.

The problem in testing oral syntax is this: How do you get the student to use the construction you have in mind? At first, it was thought pictures could be used to elicit the desired utterances. It is not difficult to draw reaction-producing pictures, like that of a boy washing his hands, to which we ask: *Que fait le garçon?* But even the clearest pictures tend to elicit a variety of utterances, rather than only the one we want. We run the danger that the bright students will find it easier than the others to figure out what we want them to say; then we have fallen into the error of testing IQ instead of French. Still more important, it turns out in practice to be difficult (in fact, well-nigh impossible) to devise pictures for all, or even most, of the varied grammatical points we are interested in testing. We can perhaps test the construction *je donne le paquet à mon professeur* by a picture (though nothing is to prevent some students from saying *au monsieur, à mon père, à l'homme,* etc.), but how do we test *je le lui donne?* We can, of course, instruct the students to use pronouns instead of nouns, but by such expedients we get further and further from the realistic conversational situation we would like to simulate and closer and closer to the old-fashioned use of grammatical terminology.

Hence, in the first version of this test, a more direct approach was used. The student heard sentences in English and was required to convey them in French immediately. In order to familiarize him with the technique, he was given some practice in it. Then he heard the following sentences in English and was to convey each at once in French. We note that each item involves particular syntactic problems and that these problems are roughly graded in order of difficulty. (The vocabulary intentionally presents little difficulty, so as to focus attention on the syntactic problems.)

1. Roger has friends.
   Roger a des amis. (avoir; partitive)

2. He doesn't like his friends.
   Il n'aime pas ses amis. (regular verb; possessive)

3. Louise is Roger's little sister.
   Louise est la petite sœur de Roger. (word order; adjective)

4. They go to the same school.
   Ils vont à la même école. (irregular verb; word order)

5. He gives her a few books.
   Il lui donne quelques livres. (indirect object; quelques)

6. They saw three friends yesterday.
   Ils ont vu trois amis hier. (present perfect)

7. The friends said something to them.
   Les amis leur ont dit quelque chose. (object; tense)

8. But Roger hadn't seen them.
   Mais Roger ne les avait pas vus. (object: pluperfect)

9. They won't speak to him tomorrow.
   Ils ne lui parleront pas demain. (future; negative)

10. Would you like to know Roger?
    Aimeriez-vous connaître Roger? (conditional; interrogative)

This part is scored on the 2, 1, 0 scale, where

2 = completely correct
1 = partially correct
0 = incorrect or missing

The major criticism of Part 4 lies in the use of English. It smacks of the translation tasks we have tried so hard in recent years to avoid. But is this really translation? We notice that the student must convey an idea in French, rather than translate specific words. The sentences were selected in such a way that they merely provide an input of information to be transmitted in French by the student. A word-for-word translation will not be the job, as an examination of the sentences will show.

Nevertheless, this point is sufficiently open to debate that it was decided to leave out the whole section and to reserve the testing of syntax for other, less polemic tests. Accordingly, the new version does not contain such a section.

The last part of the test measures fluency: the student's readiness to give forth a response in French in a conversational situation. To accomplish this objective, such a situation is created. The student is informed in advance what the conversation will be like. He is told: "We are going to hold a simple, everyday kind of conversation. I want you to imagine that we are both American students who have gone to Paris. We meet there, quite by accident, on the street. We say hello; then I ask you when you got to Paris, and you answer. I ask you where you live, and you tell me you live with a French family or in a hotel. Then I ask you what you're doing this evening, and you say you're going to the theater. I ask you what time the theater begins and if you can have dinner with me before going there. You accept, and we agree to meet at Maxim's restaurant at six o'clock."

The student records this conversation in French, with the tape taking one role and he himself the other.

This part is again scored on the 2, 1, 0 scale, where

2 = responded promptly and well
1 = responded promptly and poorly, or hesitantly but well
0 = responded hesitantly and poorly, or no response

To recapitulate: the present version of the test consists of three parts, which measure vocabulary, pronunciation, and fluency.

We must now examine the reliability and validity of the FSPT. The evidence on reliability will be of more than usual interest because of the difficulties inherent in constructing a test of speaking ability. We want to know about the test's interjudge reliability, by which we mean we want to know how well the scores of different judges agree. If Miss Jones scored Johnny's recording, would she give him exactly the same grade as if Mr. Brown scored it? If not, by how much might they differ?

Two kinds of evidence were gathered on the issue of interjudge reliability. In one type of situation, a variety of judges all scored the same few students. In the other, two judges both scored a large number of students.

To obtain the first kind of evidence, three cases were selected at random from among several hundred test recordings. Each of these three was corrected by five different judges—not always the same five (in all, seven different judges were represented). All judges were native speakers of French who were given a preliminary ten-minute training period in how to score the test. The results are presented in Table II. The mean total score was calculated for each subject, and the deviation of each of the five cases from this mean. These deviations were then made into a single distribution, whose standard deviation was calculated. (The correlational factor introduced by the fact that some of the judges made more than one judgment was simply ignored.) In this way, an estimate of the standard error, which turned out to be 3.5, was obtained.

The standard error of measurement is an estimate of the limits within which we can have confidence that the "true" score lies. In the case of a familiar score, like an IQ, we know that an IQ of 122 does not mean that the person's IQ is exactly 122 but rather that it is somewhere in that neighborhood. When informed that the standard error of an IQ is 5 points, we can say with some confidence (about a 68 percent chance of being right) that the person's IQ lies between 117 and 127 (plus or minus 1 standard error). We can say with even greater confidence (95 percent) that his true IQ lies between 112 and 132 (plus or minus 2 standard errors).

In the case of our test, a standard error of 3.5 means that a student's score of, let us say, 84 should be regarded as lying between 80.5 and 87.5 (plus or minus 1 standard error), or, for greater assurance, between 77 and 91 (plus or minus 2 standard errors).

The size of this standard error, 3.5, is very satisfactory. It compares favorably with that of many widely used tests and is particularly impressive when measuring an ability so difficult to judge objectively as the ability to speak French. It gives us confidence in the extent of interjudge agreement.

Further confidence may be gained from a different set of data. The test was administered to thirty-four students whose recordings were then corrected by two different judges. After an initial session in which they agreed on scoring procedure, the judges independently corrected the recordings. Their two sets of scores correlated to the extent of .93, a remarkably high correlation. If we look at these data in another way, the students were placed in rank order, from the highest to the lowest score, as assigned by each of the judges. The rank-order correlation was .91. Even if we grant that not all judges will agree this well, these correlations still show that the goal of objective scoring can be achieved.

Reliability concerns the accuracy of the test as a measuring instrument. We now turn to the question of validity, which concerns whether the test really measures the thing it claims to measure.

There are many kinds of validity. That is, there are many ways of asking whether this test really measures French-speaking proficiency. One may merely inspect it to satisfy oneself that the tasks and items have apparently been well chosen (face validity). One may compare results on this test with results on other tests of the same ability (congruent validity).

TABLE II   *Interjudge Reliability of French Speaking Proficiency Test*

SCORES GIVEN TO STUDENT A BY FIVE DIFFERENT JUDGES:

	PART 1	PART 2	PART 3	PART 4	PART 5	TOTAL SCORE
Judge 1	16	8	32	8	11	75
Judge 2	17	9	34	9	12	81
Judge 3	17	9	35	10	13	83
Judge 4	20	7	38	12	11	89
Judge 5	17	8	36	8	13	82
					Mean	82.0

SCORES GIVEN TO STUDENT B BY FIVE DIFFERENT JUDGES:

	PART 1	PART 2	PART 3	PART 4	PART 5	TOTAL SCORE
Judge 1	15	8	26	8	10	67
Judge 2	15	10	27	10	11	73
Judge 3	14	8	27	11	10	70
Judge 4	13	8	30	11	10	72
Judge 5	15	8	27	9	6	65
					Mean	69.4

SCORES GIVEN TO STUDENT C BY FIVE DIFFERENT JUDGES:

	PART 1	PART 2	PART 3	PART 4	PART 5	TOTAL SCORE
Judge 1	15	7	22	10	2	56
Judge 2	15	7	28	7	6	63
Judge 3	14	7	23	8	5	57
Judge 6	15	7	23	7	5	57
Judge 7	15	7	24	9	6	61
					Mean	58.8

Standard error = 3.48

One may examine the test's success in predicting how well a person can speak, as measured by some outside criterion, such as the opinion of a French teacher (predictive or concurrent validity).

This test rests largely on face validity and can fairly do so because it does not claim to measure anything more than what is measured in the subsections of the test. It does not attempt, like many psychological tests, to infer something about a person's inner workings. It merely structures some French-speaking tasks as a measure of the ability to speak French. The user must decide for himself to what extent he agrees that the items and tasks contained in the test really are relevant.

Evidence may be cited on the concurrent or predictive validity of the test. In a sample of thirty-three students at the University of California, Los Angeles, there was a correlation of .60 between their scores on the FSPT and the grades assigned for their oral work in the language laboratory, the latter being based on many observations during the semester. The two sets of scores are independent, since different scorers are involved. This correlation is satisfying, particularly in view of the unreliability to which teacher grades (in this case, grades assigned by a laboratory instructor) are subject. If allowance is made for this by assuming a reliability of .80 for the laboratory grades and one of .90 for the FSPT, then the correlation between the two, corrected for attenuation, rises to .71.

Practicability, that is, ease of administration and scoring, is a consideration in regard to any test. In the case of a speaking test, it is more than usually crucial because of the need for special equipment and the impossibility of using the usual rapid scoring methods. The FSPT takes about fifteen minutes to administer. It can be administered to individuals or to groups but requires the school to have certain equipment. It must be played on a tape recorder which feeds into the earphones of each examinee. Each examinee must be seated before his own recording machine; hence the size of the group which can take the test at one time is limited by the school's laboratory setup. The test yields a four-minute recording for each student, which must be corrected by using the scoring sheet. With a little practice, the scorer can judge the recording as it is playing, without having to stop it or repeat.

There have recently appeared two sets of tests of great importance for the language teaching profession. Both sets have resulted from joint efforts of the Modern Language Association and the Educational Testing Service; the funds for both projects were supplied by the U.S. Office of Education under Title VI of the NDEA. One set is designed for measuring student achievement, and the other for measuring the proficiency of teachers and advanced students. The two differ in some respects, but as concerns the testing of speaking, they are quite similar in design though not, of course, in content. We shall examine the student test or, to use its full name, the Speaking Test of the MLA Cooperative Foreign Language Tests. This test, like the others of both series, has appeared in five languages: French, German, Italian, Russian, and Spanish. It has appeared at two levels of difficulty, with alternate forms at each level. The format for all being the same, let us look at Form LA of the Speaking Test for the Spanish language.

In Part 1, "Mimicry," the student repeats short sentences after the native voice; the sentences contain various problems of pronunciation and intonation. Here, taken from one of the pretest forms, are the sentences comprising this part of the test.

1–2.	¿Tiene usted un pe*rr*o?	1.	r	2.	Intonation
3–4.	No, tengo *tres* gatos.	3.	tr	4.	Intonation
5–6.	¿Dónde *d*uermen?	5.	ð	6.	Intonation
7.	Duermen conmigo en la *c*ama.	7.	k		
8–9.	¡Pero su cama es tan pequeñ*a*!	8.	a	9.	Intonation
10.	No impo*r*ta.	10.	rt		
11–12.	¿Toman leche los gato*s*?	11.	o	12.	Intonation
13.	¡No, se*ñ*or! Toman café.	13.	ñ		
14.	Pues, son animales cu*r*iosos.	14.	r		
15.	Si, ¡es *v*erdad!	15.	b		

The students' repetitions of these sentences are, of course, recorded for later scoring. In each sentence, one segmental feature, shown in the middle column, is scored right or wrong; in addition, several sentences are scored for intonation, again, right or wrong.

The basic question about this part is whether mimicry is a good testing device. It offers a way to see how well the student produces certain segmental and prosodic features of speech. It tests whether he can produce them at all, even under the best of circumstances, when someone has just given him a correct model to work from. It does not test whether he will produce them himself when he has no model to work from; this is tested in the next section.

In Part B, the student reads aloud. Here is a paragraph he is asked to read:

Un sargento habla a un grupo de veinte soldados que no trabajan bien.
—¡Oigan Uds.! Tengo una tarea muy fácil y agradable para el hombre más perezoso. Levante la mano el más perezoso! Diecinueve soldados levantan la mano, pero uno no se mueve. Pregunta el sargento a éste: —¿Por qué no ha levantado la mano Ud.? Responde el soldado: —No tengo la energía.

To show the manner of scoring, here is the same paragraph, with certain features italicized:

Un sargento habla a un *grupo de* veinte soldados que no *trabajan bien.* —¡*Oigan Uds.*! Tengo una tarea muy fácil y agradable para el hombre más perezoso. Levante la mano el más perezoso? Diecinueve *soldados* levantan la mano, pe*r*o uno no se mueve. Pregunta el sargento a éste: —¿Po*r qué* no ha levantado la mano Ud.? Responde el soldado: —No tengo la energía.

Each of the italicized features is scored right or wrong. In addition, the student is given a global rating for the overall quality of his reading, including such features as word grouping, rhythm, and intonation. He is given a score from 0 to 5, in which 0 means "not attempted," 1 means "scarcely intelligible," and 5 means "close approximation of native characteristics; consistently good in all respects."

The next part of the test is called "Picture Questions." The student's booklet contains four pictures. He is asked a question about each picture and is given eight seconds to answer it. His answers are scored either 3, 2, 1, or 0, 3 being for a "natural and meaningful response," 2 for a "meaningful response with minor errors in pronunciation," and so on.

The last part is called "Picture Descriptions." Here, the student talks about what he sees in his booklet. For example, he sees a sequence of pictures which tell a story and is given two minutes in which to describe what seems to be happening. His performance on these tasks is rated in several ways. His use of vocabulary is given a score of 0 to 5, ranging from 0, "not attempted" or "unacceptable," to 5, "excellent; consistent use of appropriate words." His pronunciation is rated from "no approximation of native standards" to "close approximation of native standards." The structures he used are rated from "complete lack of ability to deal with structural patterns" to "wide range of patterns, with no errors." Finally, his fluency is rated from "exceedingly halting or meaningless jumble" to "complete, meaningful sentences, with no sign of strain or stumbling."

The reliability and validity of this test cannot be discussed at present because this information has not yet appeared, but if we can generalize from the teacher tests to the student tests—and we probably can, since they are quite similar in design—then we can assume the reliability and validity figures for the latter will be quite satisfactory. As for practicality, this Speaking Test, like the one we discussed earlier, is typically administered in a language laboratory to as many students as can make recordings simultaneously. The test takes ten minutes to administer; since each student records all ten minutes of it, it takes about that long to score each one.

In conclusion, it can be said that the problem of objective testing of speaking ability has largely been overcome in recent years, principally by the tests discussed here. The problem that remains is to win acceptance for such tests in the schools. Because they hold student speaking performance up to impartial scrutiny, the tests may be viewed with suspicion by teachers. Yet this poses a dilemma, for students, in the main, put forth effort only in directions where it pays off in the form of grades. Testing of speaking achievement is therefore an absolutely essential ingredient in any program which truly wishes to teach the speaking skill. This is not to say the tests need necessarily be standardized ones; teacher-made tests may well suffice, though a combination of frequent teacher-made tests and occasional standardized ones is probably desirable. What is incontestable is that speaking ability must be tested regularly. The tests we have discussed encourage the teacher to test the speaking skill and offer avenues for him to follow in doing so.

REFERENCES

Buros, O. (Ed.) *Mental measurements yearbook.* (6th ed.) (1966.)

Carroll, John B. *Notes on the measurement of achievement in foreign language.* 1954. (Mimeographed.)

Frith, J. R. Selection for language training by a trial course. *Georgetown University monograph series in languages and linguistics,* No. 4, 1953.

Henmon, V. *Prognosis tests in the modern foreign languages.* New York: The Macmillan Company, 1929.

Kaulfers, W. V. Wartime developments in modern-language achievement testing. *Modern Language Journal,* 1944, **28,** 136–150.

Lado, Robert L. *Language testing.* London: Longmans, Green & Co., Ltd., 1961.

MLA Cooperative Foreign Language Tests. Princeton, N.J.: Educational Testing Service, 1964.

MLA Foreign Language Proficiency Tests for Teachers and Advanced Students. Princeton, N.J.: Educational Testing Service, 1962.

Pimsleur, Paul. French Speaking Proficiency Test. *French Review,* 1961, **34,** 5.

Pimsleur, Paul. New tests for a new era. *Audio-visual Instruction,* pp. 634–636, 1962.

Pimsleur, Paul. *Pimsleur French Proficiency Tests—Test 2: Speaking Proficiency.* (Experimental ed.) New York: Harcourt, Brace & World, Inc., 1964.

Stabb, M. S. An experiment in oral testing. *Modern Language Journal,* 1955, **39,** 232–236.

Starr, W. MLA Foreign Language Proficiency Tests for Teachers and

Advanced Students. *Proceedings of the Modern Language Association,* 1962, **77**, 4.

IV. Reading Comprehension

Our task in this section is to examine the most widely used tests of the reading skill. Let us begin at once with an older one, which will serve, by contrast, to point up the advances made in objective testing in recent years.

The Cooperative Spanish Test (J. Greenberg, et al.)—not the MLA Cooperative Test, which will be examined below—bears the copyright date 1938. It was designed to measure the aspects of achievement then considered important. These were reading, vocabulary, and grammar; a subtest was devoted to each. The very names of the subtests ring somewhat quaintly now. How did our profession tolerate having achievement measured in this fashion? The words *reading, vocabulary,* and *grammar* make an odd juxtaposition, a little like grouping the words *jump, cat,* and *dog.* The first, reading, is a skill; the student is expected to learn to read. But is he expected to "vocab" or to "gram"? Reading is something one does for its own sake; vocabulary and grammar are means to other objectives, such as speaking, writing, or, indeed, reading.

Be that as it may, let us look at a few items from the Reading Subtest of Elementary Form O. Reading is supposedly measured here, by forty questions of this type:

1. Juan salió a plantar algunas flores. Estará en
    1–1. el comedor.
    1–2. el jardín.
    1–3. el salón.
    1–4. la cocina.
    1–5. la biblioteca . . . . 1 (   ).

2. Esa dama es mi tía, porque es
    2–1. la madre de mi esposa.
    2–2. la hija de mis amigos.
    2–3. la hermana de mi padre.
    2–4. una desconocida.
    2–5. más joven que yo . . . . . . 2 (   ).

A brief examination shows that the items measure virtually one thing only, vocabulary. Each item hinges on the student's knowledge of one or a few words. In item 1, the word *plantar* in the stem attaches to *el jardín* in the answer. Such other features as the use of the preterite tense in

Juan salió or of the future of supposition in *Estará* are totally irrelevant insofar as what counts in getting the answer right. All that counts is to match *plantar flores* with *jardín*. Similarly, in item 2, the answer is simply a definition of the word *tía*. This subtest, though called "Reading," really measures the same thing as another subtest, called "Vocabulary."

Subtest 2, "Vocabulary," looks entirely anachronistic to us now, for it gives a Spanish word, for example, *azul,* and then five English choices:

1.   island
2.   insurance
3.   blue
4.   anvil
5.   amber

It is a reflection of our professional progress that such a test now looks as creaky to us as a suit of medieval armor. I have pointed the finger at the Cooperative Tests only that we may clearly see this progress. It must be said in their defense that they were, for a very long time, the only foreign language tests in public use which were built in conformity with recognized standards of test construction.

We shift now to the new **MLA Cooperative Foreign Language Tests,** published in 1964. And with this shift we encompass all the changes wrought in language teaching by World War II, the postwar period, and, more recently, the NDEA. Let us look at the new Reading Test, published after an interval of twenty-six years by the same organization that published the Cooperative Tests. Part A consists of items like these:

2.   No puedo hallar el reloj y no tengo tiempo para (   ).
    a.   perderlo
    b.   destruirlo
    c.   echarlo
    d.   buscarlo

3.   Al oír del accidente de su buen amigo,
    Paco se puso (   ).
    a.   alegre
    b.   fatigado
    c.   hambriento
    d.   desconsolado

At first glance, they look very much like the items which made up the Reading Subtest of the old Cooperative Tests. But items of this type make up only half the new test: there are twenty-five such items and twenty-five of a quite different sort. We see that some of the items shown above are more dependent upon the student's comprehension of an entire idea than upon his knowledge of a single word: item 2, for instance. Others, like item 3, depend mainly on one word, but even this can be defended on the ground that the new test, unlike the old one, contains no other section in which the student's vocabulary is measured.

If one can debate whether Part A really tests reading ability, no such quarrel is possible with Part B. Here is a sample of three items built around one reading paragraph.

La madre y los hermanos de Amalia la llaman "la dormilona." Casi todos los días de la semana la chica se levanta muy tarde y a menudo llega a sus clases media hora después que sus compañeras. En cambio, en los fines de semana cuando sus padres no tienen que levantarse tan temprano, Amalia se levanta muy tempranito. Esta costumbre le molesta mucho a su mamá en particular, y por eso ella le dice a Amalia que la familia tendrá que obtener un nuevo tipo de calendario — uno sin el sábado y el domingo.

44. A Amalia la han nombrado "dormilona" porque
  f.   se levanta temprano todos los sábados y domingos.
  g.   se acuesta tarde cada noche de la semana.
  h.   se despierta media hora después que sus amigas.
  j.   se levanta tarde durante la semana.

45. Refiriéndose al calendario sin el sábado y el domingo, la madre de Amalia le habla en
  a.   broma.
  b.   balde.
  c.   serio.
  d.   vano.

46. Los padres de Amalia tienen que levantarse temprano
  f.   el sábado y el domingo.
  g.   cada día menos el sábado y el domingo.
  h.   cuando su hija no se despierta.
  j.   todos los días.

This part clearly measures reading comprehension. The only objection, a minor one, that might be made is whether it is necessary to have the students read a story 100 words long in order to then ask them three questions. As we shall see in a moment, it is possible to economize testing time by carefully trimming the passage length.

The MLA Reading Test contains fifty items in all and takes thirty-five minutes of working time.

It is not possible to report reliability and validity figures for these tests, as they are still being processed as of this writing. They are scheduled to be published in the near future.

Turning to Test 3: Reading Comprehension of the Pimsleur French Proficiency Tests (1964), we find they use only one type of item. Here is a sample group of items:

"Une étoile ici? Pas possible," disait Jacques. "Comment peut-il y avoir une étoile dans une ville? Et au dixième étage d'un immeuble?"
"Pourtant, cet objet a bien l'air d'une étoile," répondait Louis. "N'es-tu pas de mon avis?"

39. On a l'impression que Jacques et Louis sont des
    a. hommes.
    b. professeurs.
    c. grandes personnes.
    d. garçons.

40. Les étoiles se trouvent généralement
    a. sur la mer.
    b. dans le ciel.
    c. dans la cuisine.
    d. par terre.

41. Cette scène se passe
    a. à la campagne.
    b. sur la plage.
    c. dans un appartement.
    d. dans un restaurant.

42. Une étoile ici? Jacques ne peut pas y
    a. croire.
    b. ressembler.
    c. regarder.
    d. écouter.

43. On pourrait remplacer le dernier mot, *avis,* par le mot
    a. oncle
    b. école.
    c. village.
    d. opinion.

We note that five items have been written around one reading passage. The items are of different types, and not all will survive the tryout process. Item 39 asks for a simple inference based on the tone of the passage. In one first-year high school class to which these items were administered, 52 percent of the students got this right; its difficulty is about as it should be for this level. Item 40 is, in effect, a vocabulary question; the student must understand both *étoiles* and *ciel* and must also understand the verb *se trouvent*. Only 37 percent of the students got this one right, which probably indicates that one or more of the key words were not familiar to them. Since both *étoile* and *ciel* are among the first 500 words on the *Français élémentaire* list (Gougenheim et al., 1956), I felt it was appropriate to include them, but if this item does not fare better than this when tried out with another, larger sample, it will have to be eliminated. Item 41 asks for comprehension of the reference to *un immeuble*, another word in the top 500. It was answered by 41 percent of this class. If this percentage goes up somewhat on a larger sample, the item stays in; if it goes down a bit, it is out; if it stays about the same, I shall worry. Item 42 makes good sense in French: it seems to have good validity. But the trouble is that the students do not know this much French (only 33 percent got it right); no matter how valid the item may be, it will have to go if it does not show the proper respect for statistics. The last item, 43, is strictly on vocabulary. It is at about the right level of difficulty (56 percent got it right), and it discriminates well between good and poor students. Nonetheless, I do not feel a reading test should have very many straight vocabulary items, items which test only the dictionary definition of a word and so could be answered without reading the passage at all. Vocabulary items should test the meanings of words as they are used in a particular context. In all, then, it will be fortunate if three good items are left out of these five after all the analyses have been completed.

Let me cite another example, to show further how a test item takes shape.

FIRST VERSION:

> Le soleil se couche et chacun des animaux se demande, sans oser élever la voix pour ne pas inquiéter les autres: "Où a-t-elle pu aller; elle avait dit qu'elle serait rentrée à 9 heures . . . pour le dîner!"

32. L'on comprend que cette histoire est destinée aux
   a. amateurs.
   b. animaux.
   c. enfants.
   d. étudiants.

33. En ce moment
   a. il est 9 heures.
   b. le soleil brille.
   c. le jour vient de se lever.
   d. c'est la fin de la journée.

34. Ils parlent tous
    a. trop fort.
    b. très fort.
    c. très bas.
    d. trop bas.

35. Les animaux
    a. élèvent la voix.
    b. sont inquiets.
    c. se parlent un peu.
    d. rentrent pour le dîner.

SECOND VERSION:

Le soleil se couche et chacun des animaux se demande, sans élever la voix pour ne pas inquiéter les autres: "Où a-t-elle pu aller; elle avait dit qu'elle serait rentrée à 9 heures pour le dîner!"

32. L'on comprend que cette histoire est pour les
    a. amateurs.
    b. animaux.
    c. enfants.
    d. étudiants.

33. En ce moment
    a. il est 9 heures.
    b. le soleil brille.
    c. le jour vient de se lever.
    d. c'est la fin de la journée.

34. Ces animaux
    a. parlent très fort.
    b. parlent trop fort.
    c. ne parlent pas fort.
    d. ne parlent que fort.

35. Les animaux
    a. élèvent la voix.
    b. s'inquiètent.
    c. parlent beaucoup.
    d. rentrent pour le dîner.

Reading the passage in its first version, we find at least two words which are probably too difficult for first-year students: *oser* and *inquiéter*. A check of several leading textbooks confirms this. The problem of *oser* is easy to solve; it can be left out, and the sentence still makes good sense:

it merely reads *sans élever la voix* instead of *sans oser élever la voix*. As for *inquiéter,* it should also come out, but it occurs to us to exploit it for an item instead. After all, students often come upon words they do not understand in their reading, and they must have the ability to sense how the unknown word relates to the rest of the words; this often gives the clue to "getting" its meaning by the context, without searching in the dictionary. This is how item 35 has come into being.

Looking at the items in turn, first at item 32, what are we to do if told that it must either be made easier or discarded? How are we to do this? The choice words are all very simple, and the idea of the stem is an easy one, except for the phrase *destinée aux.* Since this particular phrase is not essential to the item, let us change it to *pour les;* this is the way it appears in the revised version. Item 33 proved, in the first tryout, to be of about the right level of difficulty, and it discriminated well between good and poor students; so it goes into the revised version unchanged. Item 34 had good discriminative power, but it was a little too hard; so we look around for a way to simplify it somewhat. The difficult words seem to be *tous* and *bas;* so in the revised version we rephrase the stem and all the choices, using simpler language. Item 35, by which we had hoped to test the student's ability to respond appropriately even to a word he did not know, proved much too difficult. Thinking this to be due, perhaps, to the phrasing of choice *b* and to the attractiveness of choice *c,* these features are changed in the revision. In all, then, most of the items need some rewriting after the first data analysis. Not more than three good items out of the four will remain in the version that is finally published.

The revised version has been tried out on about two hundred students in a number of high schools; these data are now being analyzed and will serve as a basis for further refinement. No figures on either reliability or validity can be reported as yet, but there is reason to believe they will both be good. Reliability will be achieved by including a sufficient number of items, probably thirty to forty of them, which will have been refined to weed out sources of random variation. The test should have good validity because of the way the items were devised. In part, they were adapted from elementary readers and so represent a sample of the material the students are supposed to have mastered by the end of the year, when they take this test. And in part they were devised by examining the vocabulary and the structures contained in elementary textbooks and then writing items to include this vocabulary and these structures. This, again, is material the students are supposed to be able to comprehend when they read it.

This paper, in a certain sense, has attempted to offer a Cook's tour of the atelier of a test author, to show some of the directions the class-room teacher should take in improving his own tests. The first, and probably most important, step is to curb one's desire to sit down and begin writing test questions. One must begin instead by spending quite a bit of time reminding oneself of the domain to be tested: the scope and type of knowledge the student is supposed to have ingurgitated. Then one must spend another session thinking of a sensible way to break this knowledge down for testing. After this one is ready to begin writing questions; and at that point, though one may be guided by scientific principles, one is in the realm of creation.

It does not matter how many pious things are said about the importance of speaking the foreign language or of reading it if tests are collections of fragmentary facts about grammar, vocabulary, and even pronunciation, returned to the teacher by the student in much the same form in which he received them but never put together into a fabric of habits we call a skill. Tests are the truest reflections of the teacher's pedagogical aims: he should beware of his tests, for they tell the truth about his objectives as a teacher.

References

Carroll, John B. *Notes on the measurement of achievement in foreign language.* 1954. (Mimeographed.)

Gougenheim, G. et al. *L'élaboration du français élémentaire.* Paris: Didier, 1956.

Greenberg, J. et al. *Cooperative (Spanish, French) Test.* Princeton, N.J.: Educational Testing Service, 1938.

Lado, Robert L. *Language testing.* London: Longmans, Green & Co., Ltd., 1961.

MLA Cooperative Foreign Language Tests. Princeton, N.J.: Educational Testing Service, 1964.

MLA Foreign Language Proficiency Tests for Teachers and Advanced Students. Princeton, N.J.: Educational Testing Service, 1962.

Pimsleur (French, Spanish) Proficiency Tests—Test 3: Reading Comprehension. (Experimental ed.) New York: Harcourt, Brace & World, Inc., 1964.

12

THE LANGUAGE LABORATORY: EQUIPMENT AND UTILIZATION

JOSEPH C. HUTCHINSON

Joseph C. Hutchinson (1920–   ) received degrees from Emory University and the University of North Carolina. He has directed language laboratories at North Carolina, Tulane University, and the United States Army Counter-intelligence Corps School in Baltimore. He has taught at the University of North Carolina, Tulane University, Emory University, Sweet Briar College, and Technological High School in Atlanta. He served for five years as a foreign language specialist in the U.S. Office of Education in the Title III program of the National Defense Education Act and is the author of several publications on the technology of language learning. Since 1964 he has been chief of the Research and Standards Division at the headquarters of the Department of Defense Language Institute in Washington.

After several years of work under the National Defense Education Act (NDEA), many will agree that there is no longer so much need to remain in a tentative or transitional situation with regard to recommendations about the "new" methods, materials, and media: we can be quite bold and sure about many principles which have been found successful. We can now state quite unequivocally that secondary schools should be well equipped with electronic classrooms, language laboratories, and tape recorders, which are basic and integral components of a foreign language program, and that the latter is in turn a basic and integral component of a curriculum of general education.

Both schools and colleges need to remind themselves that professional answers to educational problems do not always come in ready-made packages and that in the case of language laboratory facilities it is much more important to understand the basic principles involved, particularly for the new materials and methodology, so that useful criteria may be followed in judging whether a particular foreign language program is going in the desired direction. A team approach representing administrative, pedagogical, and technical elements is a prerequisite of successful planning in this field. The rationale for language laboratory facilities and sound advice on planning and utilization are well covered by Hayes (1963), Hocking (1964), and Hutchinson (1961).

The number of language laboratories in the secondary schools has grown dramatically since the late 1950s, from a few dozen to almost 10,000, which are of many types and sizes. College and university installations over the same period have increased from 250 to well over 1,000.

How effective has this innovation been? There is still some evidence, despite the tremendous improvements schools have recently made in the teaching of modern foreign languages with the aid of the language laboratory, that in some quarters the laboratory is being misused and its function misunderstood. This is not surprising: every new teaching aid goes through a period when some users persist in grasping it as the final solution to their teaching problems and in trying to use it for purposes for which it was never intended and in ways for which it is unsuited. Every new teaching tool undergoes a probationary period in which educators experiment with it to discover its potentialities, to define the objectives it can help them achieve, and to find the most productive methods of using it. For most schools and many colleges the language laboratory is still in this early period: we have barely scratched the surface of its potentiality.

Like any tool or instrument, the language laboratory is most useful in the hands of a craftsman who knows how to use it skillfully. As every good teacher of a modern foreign language knows, the effective use of the language laboratory is a composite of the effectiveness of at least five elements: (1) the teacher, (2) the teaching materials, (3) the testing and grading programs, (4) the student practice session, and (5) the equipment. Each of these elements must meet certain criteria if the language laboratory is to produce the results expected of it.

THE TEACHER

The teacher must be interested in getting the most out of the equipment and materials, and he must have some skill in the effective use of these aids in helping students develop the skills of listening comprehension and speaking.

A good teacher can make up for deficiencies in equipment and materials, just as an uninterested and unskilled teacher can negate whatever value students might obtain from even the finest equipment and materials. But teachers today are caught between the pressures of a transitional period, and however skillful and dedicated they may be, in practice they lag behind the recent developments in methodological theory and instructional technology. This is why good in-service preparation of the teacher is an indispensable part of any school's or college's plans for a language laboratory. One cannot expect to teach well with a language laboratory if he cannot teach well without it. A more positive expression of the idea would be that if one can teach well without laboratory equipment, he can teach even better with it. In addition, the language laboratory is neutral, for it can amplify and extend inferior as well as superior instruction.

But the teacher's qualifications cannot be considered in isolation from the circumstances around him. Careful planning by administrators and teachers together is an essential part of the introduction of language laboratory facilities into any school program. In the planning, the specific language program should surely have as much weight as administrative and budgetary considerations. In other words, the idea behind the language laboratory—the idea of *substance*—is more important by far than the facilities themselves, which are *form* only. In its broadest sense, the language laboratory concept means much more than any specific combination of electronic devices. It means the regular and frequent use of recorded materials specially prepared as an integral part of a program in which audiolingual instruction forms the basis for the progressive and continuous development of all the language skills. It is further understood that full coordination and synchronization of class and laboratory activities and materials are achieved, for language laboratory facilities are not worth the expense involved when used on a sporadic or an uncoordinated basis, as was apparently the case with some of the schools covered by the Keating Report (Keating, 1963).

Like other educational media, the language laboratory is a means to an end. But since language itself is also a medium, or system of symbols representing reality, we sometimes find it difficult to persuade budget planners of the importance of this medium twice removed from reality. Yet the essential function of the language laboratory is to serve as a practice instrument which will indeed help human beings bridge the important but deeply complex gaps of interpersonal and intercultural communication.

Close cooperation and understanding between administrative and teaching staffs are essential not only in the planning for language laboratories but also in their use. Administrative decisions can easily mean the difference between an effective and an ineffective program, especially when such decisions preempt pedagogical decisions and ignore the specific needs of teachers and students. Therefore, the readiness of the school and the teachers is a prime factor in the successful use of any kind of language laboratory facilities. The fear that machines will replace teachers is not really valid, for there is an increasing demand for good foreign language teachers. Most machine-oriented efforts are directed at supporting the teacher or, at worst, substituting in the absence of a qualified teacher.

TEACHING MATERIALS

Teaching materials which are designed to develop the listening and speaking skills efficiently and which also integrate class and laboratory work must be used. The challenge for the teacher is in choosing what is productive in learning and rejecting what is not. The present use of much of the old ineffective materials or even revised versions of them, which are still being employed in schools today, is an appalling situation. If they are put on tape (or even on video tape with a lively teacher), they are still old and ineffective. What is more, they give the language laboratory a bad name. It is interesting to note that in Europe there is currently a large surge of interest in language laboratories rather similar to that which occurred in the United States several years ago. Unfortunately, many of the same problems of misunderstanding are taking place, including the production of taped materials which not only are filled with unproductive inanities such as *on my face are two eyes* but also include unauthentic and distorted voicings of the materials. Actually teachers in the United States and in Europe now have a choice of several excellent series of materials that were designed for class *and* laboratory use. The problem of preparing good materials fast enough to meet the changing demands is aggravated by the additional time it takes (sometimes years) for many school systems to adopt the new materials. Unfortunately, many schools are still struggling through this schizophrenic nightmare.

To use the new materials, experience has already shown us, the teacher needs new skills and new insights. Many teachers learn during a summer institute how to teach the first semester or the first year of an elementary course, but for lack of complete understanding and further experience they are unable to extend these techniques into higher levels. Some teachers have not yet learned what to do beyond taking the students through the first steps of imitation and memorization of dialogue material; a larger number do not yet know how to make the transition to effective structure drills; and a still larger number do not know how to make the transition to the creative use of the spoken language, that is, to have the students recombine in new situations the dialogue and drill materials they have already mastered. Very few teachers, we realize, give their students enough practice in listening before they plunge them into imitation of models.

Strangely enough, some foreign language teachers who are teaching their native language believe that the laboratory is useful only for teachers who are not fluent; consequently some fine teachers have resisted using a language laboratory. They seem to forget that the laboratory is primarily for the *student,* not for the teacher. The student needs it to intensify, individualize, and internalize his practice of the spoken language as it has been modeled for him by a variety of native speakers—experience which no single teacher, no matter how proficient, can give him. By letting other voices take over the presentation of practice material, the teacher actually gains time for individualized creative teaching. The arithmetic of simultaneous individualized responses is overwhelming when compared with single responses. Each member of a class may produce twenty to thirty different sentences per minute. The conventional classroom can support only *one* oral communication at a time, one individual at a time. Even choral drill, as useful as it is, is not individualized until the students have been equipped with audioactive microphone-headphones.

TESTING AND GRADING

The testing and grading program must give due weight to achievement in listening and speaking. The use of the new Modern Language Association-Educational Testing Service Cooperative Tests should help solve many of the problems that result from use of traditional tests, which place at a disadvantage those students who have learned a language primarily through listening and speaking. The entire program of measuring the listening and speaking skills has been a major stumbling block in research on the effectiveness of the new materials and methods and of the language laboratory. Teachers should continue to use the effective device of giving daily laboratory grades.

STUDENT PRACTICE SESSIONS

The practice sessions must be frequent enough and long enough to enable the students to develop the skills of listening and speaking.

The successful language laboratory program provides the student with adequate practice sessions for developing his skills. Schools are gradually realizing the importance of regular and frequent practice and are adjusting their programs accordingly; and many schools, to minimize the problem of scheduling practice periods, have installed simplified language laboratory equipment in each foreign language classroom (electronic classroom), so that practice sessions can be held at any time during any class period.

Experienced teachers continue to report that students need more practice before they can internalize the basic structures and sounds of the foreign language. Not only does the student need to know what the correct sounds are (discrimination), but he also must be able to produce the sounds he intends to say (articulation). Even when students have achieved an acceptable pronunciation and understand the principles underlying grammatical structures, there still remains the goal of automaticity, which is one of the main objectives of pattern practice in the language laboratory.

Despite the efforts of many schools to make maximum use of their language laboratory equipment both during and outside class periods, the evidence still points to a grossly inadequate provision of machine-guided practice in most schools. More than half of the 1,000 secondary schools that were reported in a language laboratory study indicated that first-year foreign language students were given a total practice time of twenty to sixty minutes per week during sessions scheduled once or twice per week. This is far from the recommended average of twenty minutes of total practice time per student per day.

EQUIPMENT

The equipment must be good enough and flexible enough to permit efficient operation on a regular basis. Students practice individually with audio equipment, but the teacher must continue to relate to the student's performance while letting the tape carry on the presentation function. Tape does become impersonal and even ugly when the teacher allows it to take over completely. All machines require some human control at various stages and are never more intelligent than their masters. The need for student practice and for the human verification of response can both be fulfilled in electronic classrooms, where the teacher can also provide a balanced variety of learning activities. Language laboratory equipment was never intended to provide answers to all classroom problems, and unrealistic claims have been harmful and in some cases have caused a kind of language laboratory backlash in attitudes. Boredom is always latent in drill sessions and may set in at any time unless the teacher is constantly alert. Junior high school teachers quickly learn that teaching with tape does not mean that every minute will be filled with purposeful activity, for a one-minute void used to rewind a tape or adjust equipment may break the spell and set up distractions for sensitive youngsters full of energy. We can compare our adult impatience with similar audio situations in which every second seems like an eternity, such as waiting a whole minute for someone to come to the telephone. Language laboratory equipment which is not constantly serviced and maintained in good condition is sometimes worse than no equipment at all, for malfunctions disrupt and deteriorate a potentially good learning situation and may lead to distracting behavior. Mediocre audio quality can also be a prime cause of fatigue. It should be substantially clear that inefficient equipment or inefficient use of equipment is worse than a good classroom situation with no equipment at all.

The more we rely on recorded audio models for language learning, the more accurate the sound must be. The "state of the art" in audio quality is improving so that there is now no valid reason for schools to contend with mediocre quality of sound. The industry is willing to help, but it needs leadership—and sometimes a hard nudge—from schools, universities, and governmental and professional groups. At the Defense Language Institute we have been able to obtain reasonably priced equipment with audio quality tested by government engineer inspectors to meet our specifications, which are based on those proposed by Alfred S. Hayes in his *Technical Guide for the Selection, Purchase, Use, and Maintenance of Language Laboratory Facilities*, written for the Electronic Industries Association and the U.S. Department of Health, Education, and Welfare. These recommended specifications should be used as an absolute minimum by all educational institutions. Their teachers and students deserve this minimum protection and quality at the very least. Since there is still a lack of standardized methods of measurement for all components, it is recommended that unbiased, technically qualified assistance be secured to assure that the specifications have actually been met.

USE AND MISUSE OF THE LANGUAGE LABORATORY

Evidence that language laboratories and the audiolingual approach have not yet had an opportunity to prove themselves is presented in a report by

Joseph Axelrod and Donald N. Bigelow (1962), who with others in the fall of 1960 visited forty-six university language and area centers (these centers are highly specialized programs for teaching the "neglected" languages to persons who will be using them—college professors, for example, and representatives of government and industry). A similar report (Bigelow & Letgers) on fifty of these NDEA centers in 1964 shows that lack of effective use of language laboratories is still prevalent. Many of these centers have changed their programs and practices since the first ratings were made, but the status of the programs at that time is symptomatic of the transition period through which all foreign language programs have been passing and shows that there is a constant need for regular and well-planned in-service training programs for *all* levels and types of instructors (secondary school, college, university, native speakers, and nonnative speakers) in the use of language laboratory equipment and in the concepts underlying the new materials based on applied linguistics and psychology.

Both the Foreign Service Institute (Department of State) and the Defense Language Institute (Department of Defense), like many colleges and universities, have for many years experimented with various techniques and procedures for language training; and the use they make of language laboratory facilities is based on their own findings, not merely on the experience of others. The fact that both of these programs use these facilities as an integral part of their intensive language courses, even though their classes rarely have more than ten students and are always taught by native speakers, indicates that they consider regular and frequent practice indispensable for learning to speak a foreign language.

Some of the basic problems found in secondary schools are revealed in a 1962–1963 cooperative survey of foreign language instructional equipment in sixteen states (Gaarder & Hutchinson, 1964). Almost half (2,673 out of 6,423) of the foreign language teachers reported in the study had received no training in the use of audiovisual equipment during the four years preceding the survey. The training received varied from one hour in a workshop to an eight-week NDEA institute. Yet the pedagogical effectiveness of any language laboratory installation depends not on its mere use but on the way in which it is used. One can learn how to operate a tape recorder in one hour, but the functional and effective pedagogical use of a language laboratory requires many hours of thoughtful discussion and practice.

Only about 40 percent (1,490) of the total number of schools reporting (3,695) had some kind of language laboratory installation, 748 of these installations had half or less than half of the number of student positions required to accommodate a full class in one session, and 694 installations were of the passive-listening type (headphones only). Another self-defeating condition reported was an appalling number of classes of thirty students and even a surprising number containing as many as forty students.

Somehow, well-meaning administrators have inadvertently created a static and outdated concept that *one* language laboratory per secondary school should be the standard, regardless of size. The 1960 *Evaluative Criteria* of the National Association of Secondary School Principals includes this item: "Does the school have a language laboratory?" Initially this question was an official recognition of the existence of language laboratories in secondary schools. The answer to the question today might be paraphrased along the lines of the much-publicized Keating Report: "Yes, and it is used once a week on a haphazard unintegrated basis with any old kind of materials and methods." No one is very happy about the situation.

Misunderstandings about effective use of language laboratory equipment and gross misuse have been and still are annoying problems. The trial-and-error period used to be the rule of the day because of the lack of expert guidance, but this is no longer the case today, for a considerable amount of expert and experienced guidance is available in print from such sources as the U.S. Office of Education and state foreign language supervisors. In addition, consultant help is available through Title III of the NDEA, from state departments of education.

In spite of the flow of information and increased inservice training programs we still find experienced teachers who continue to hold foreign language class recitation activities in laboratory rooms which are equipped with booths, instead of taking the class back to a regular classroom after a half period in the laboratory so that regular class activities may proceed unhampered and another class can have access to the laboratory. Also, when we do have a separate laboratory room, why does it have to be so far from the foreign language classrooms that trips to it are discouraging for both teachers and students?

It should be abundantly clear that problems of this type, as well as those caused by lack of adequate service and maintenance of equipment, are doing harm, for it is difficult enough to teach effectively under favorable conditions with or without equipment. Unless equipment is planned and used so that it truly becomes an *aid* to the teacher, its potential unfortunately becomes a negative influence and we are worse off than if we did not have it.

Other areas of confusion concerning language laboratory activity include the question of class as preparation for laboratory or laboratory as preparation for class and the related question of whether new material should ever be introduced in the laboratory first. Although many people have strong opinions on these questions, there is actually no valid reason for a rigid attitude since answers to both depend on other factors. Some types and levels of programs and materials can be handled either way without loss of effectiveness. In addition, extensive familiarization listening practice in advance of speaking is usually quite beneficial.

Another issue concerns record-playback-compare activities. There have been obvious indications that these activities can be wasteful but not necessarily under all conditions. It is usually the playback delayed after several minutes that is wasteful. Playback within seconds is beginning to gain new interest among researchers. Naturally, discrimination and articulation training are also relevant factors, since there are considerable individual differences in the ability to evaluate oneself. Another useful technique is for the student to record only when he has practiced enough and feels that he is ready to test himself. After several successive recorded approximations he can signal the instructor and offer what he considers to be his best-recorded version for a brief critique over the intercommunication system. Then he can present the utterance "live" and receive immediate live confirmation from the instructor. The critique and confirmation can be accomplished within thirty seconds. An advantage of recorders in student booths which is sometimes overlooked is the fact that self-pacing is possible when each student controls his own program.

Generally speaking, teachers should not try to make their own laboratory materials except for a few special supplementary exercises or quizzes. Since not all types of classtype exercises are suitable for laboratory use, it is advisable to rehearse any new type with another teacher either through the laboratory intercommunication system or over a telephone. This test will usually show right away whether or not the material is appropriate in a purely audio situation. Tapes should not be longer than half of the length of the laboratory session and in no case longer than thirty minutes. Individual segments for imitation should not be longer than about seven syllables for students in the early stages, since studies of auditory memory span show a severe limitation on the number of verbal units that a foreign language learner can remember accurately (Lado, 1964b). As the student gains more control of the language, his memory span increases.

Another minor problem in recording word pairs or multiple voicing of short utterances is the tendency to change the intonation pattern. This can become a major problem if the pairs are used as "same-different" items on a test for Oriental learners of English, since the "same" sounds would be perceived and scored as "different" by speakers of tonal languages.

The format of recorded material for student imitation or response has often been stimulus-response-confirmation (S-R-C). This three-cycle drill has frequently been frustrating to students who earnestly want to make a second response which will be more correct, as no time is allowed before the following stimulus begins. The four-cycle drill (S-R-C-R) appears to be much more comfortable for most students, but the five-cycle drill (S-R-C-R-C) has the further advantage of having the student hear the acoustic image of the model before proceeding to the next program segment.

Finally, according to psycholinguists the most sophisticated and expensive electronic gear and superior teaching materials will be of no avail in helping a student perfect his pronunciation unless he really "cares" if it is correct or accurate.

LANGUAGE LABORATORY METHODS

We need to steer away from extremist approaches and examine with an open mind what appear to be the mainstream and promising directions for the future in language teaching. There are, of course, still with us some unsettled questions of various preferences and choices, more often based on empathy and taste than on reason and experience. There are some who, without ever having had the experience of teaching with a recording laboratory, speak out boldly about the dangers of students' recording their response and comparing it with the model. It is not a question of dialogue *or* pattern drills *or* free *or* controlled conversation, any more than it is a question of listen *or* respond *or* compare *or* monitor *or* confirm. Language is complex; language learning is complex. It takes a variety of organized activities to teach language successfully, for the art and science of teaching include the judicious selection, timing, measuring, and blending of the many ingredients involved.

A certain amount of confusion is still caused by terminological problems. For example, there really is no *language laboratory method*. Also, the term *language laboratory* includes the essentially synonymous term *electronic classroom*. The difference between the two is administrative rather than electronic or pedagogical. The laboratory was originally thought of as a room apart from the classroom, into which students were scheduled during a portion of the class period or in addition to the regular class period. The electronic classroom is a laboratory installed in the modern foreign language classroom itself. It makes possible some machine-guided practice during every class period without having to move the students to another room. Electronic classroom installations are usually simpler and more economical than laboratories, thus making it possible to equip as many as four to six classrooms for the price of one completely equipped laboratory and to serve correspondingly more numerous students. The electronic classroom is usually an audioactive system of interconnected headphones and microphones with emphasis on "classroom" activities.

There is also considerable confusion, even among foreign language teachers, about "conversational" courses, "audiovisual" courses, "audio-lingual" courses, or "direct method" courses, since labels of this type can be used by anyone. It was hoped that the term *audiolingual,* created and defined by Nelson Brooks, would be useful to distinguish the really new materials and procedures from other similar teaching concepts, but the term has been misused as much as the term *language laboratory.* It still needs to be pointed out that almost any kind of method or materials can be adapted for language laboratory use, but that does not mean that they will be effective. The use of records and other audio aids goes back to the beginning of the century, but the very nature and rationale of their use were quite different from what we now mean when we say "truly contemporary materials" (Léon, 1962). Perhaps these should be called the *structural* method or approach, since they are based on structural linguistics (also called descriptive linguistics, or even linguistic science, and including both theoretical and applied aspects of the field). A structural approach includes not only a systematic progression through a carefully selected variety of everyday situations but an integrated use of a graduated variety of basic structural pattern exercises. Other differences between this and other approaches are given in detail by Brooks (1964) and Lado (1964a). Suffice it to say that the methods of effective use of audio aids in language teaching as we know it today were developed along with the refinements of the structural approach so that the two are more compatible with each other than with other systems. Incidentally, even the term *pattern drill* is sometimes misused, as was observed recently in a class in which the instructor directed students to "conjugate the pattern."

Many colleges are finding that they need flexible laboratory facilities for both controlled group use and individual use of the library type. It should be remembered that supervised and monitored laboratory sessions do not necessarily constitute a "lockstep" procedure, for just as soldiers march in lockstep formation, they also "break step" when crossing a bridge. Yet they are still in formation. Self-pacing can be achieved in group laboratory sessions. In fact, laboratory facilities are too expensive to be allowed to stand idle. Some kind of scheduling is usually needed to assure that the facilities are used regularly on an economical basis.

Innovations for teaching can sometimes become a story of frustration and defeat unless appropriate changes in the instructional program are also made. To superimpose a language laboratory of any kind on an old curriculum, old schedule, old techniques, and old concepts of language and language learning would be a grave mistake, but it has happened. And not always because of "old" people! On the other hand, equipment should not dictate in pedagogical matters.

RECENT DEVELOPMENTS

In the search for newer simplified and more flexible types of equipment, several novel approaches have appeared. Each one seems to bring new advantages, but it also brings disadvantages. Schools need to be certain that they understand exactly what they are getting. For example, a "wireless" language laboratory removes the problem of fixed cables, but it also places limits on the number of simultaneous programs and eliminates the important two-way intercommunication feature. Of course, wires can be added to provide these features, but doing this negates the original wireless advantage. The same is true of the simplified nonelectronic acoustical feedback "microphone," which requires unusual procedures for the addition of the intercommunication feature. Any type of system has its own limitations, just as do booths, separate laboratory rooms, full-record facilities, etc. In addition, budgetary considerations are often the deciding factor. Yet language laboratory facilities should be planned to fit the individual institution's needs, just as a prescription is prepared for an individual patient. Thus far, it seems that the happy medium for the average secondary school is an electronic classroom type of arrangement for each foreign language classroom with headset-microphone at each desk (no booth) and with a full intercommunication system to the teacher, who has a small console on wheels which can be plugged in or out of the fixed but hidden wiring system and rolled aside or to another room when not in use.

More elaborate installations also have their place when the institution can afford them. Whether telephone dial networks or other kinds of remote-control systems or any other novel technical approach is made, the essential good quality of sound is always needed and should be insisted upon. This is also true of the slower speeds in tape recorders, the quality of which is improving.

There has always been a place for creative visual aids in language teaching, but audio still dominates because it has more to offer, is less expensive, and has a well-defined and successful methodology which has evolved from the theoretical stage to practical application. A few excellent sets of motion pictures, slides, and filmstrips have been produced for use in language teaching, but they are still relatively expensive. Even the most successful visual aids do not entirely do away with the need for translation or reinforcement of the actual meaning. They do reduce this need and add other useful elements, and there is no questioning the contribution of films in terms of experiencing authentic details of a foreign culture. They can also be most useful in previewing and reviewing dialogue situations and in teacher training. The choice of visual aids depends on the nature of the learning task, and there are some tasks to which pictorial matter can make little if any contribution. Perhaps the oldest and still most common use is that of pictures as cues for various exercises. Their use can be very productive in dialogue and pattern practice or in eliciting conversation on higher levels, but on a basic level it may easily degenerate into a recital of vocabulary items instead of productive speech patterns.

It is difficult to see how television in its present form can be changed from a lockstep medium to one providing truly individual instruction, since its very nature precludes such a transformation. We should, however, expect a real breakthrough in the use of visual aids whenever video tape reaches the same practical and inexpensive stage as did the audio tape recorder. A most convenient form of film projector for small-group or individual use is already available in 8-mm cartridge form. The endless loop for film presentation does not seem to pose the same pedagogical problems as it does for audio tape in language learning use. If more care were taken in the preparation of commercial language learning materials than on the many elaborate presentation modes, we should probably have even better learning results with a simpler package and would be relieved of the cumbersome weight and expense of too much paraphernalia.

It will be useful at this point to indicate a few interesting areas of research related to the technology of language learning. Working with a machine which is capable of performing a kind of acoustic tachistoscopic processing and which compresses or expands the time rate of normal recorded speech (to as low as 50 words per minute or as high as 475) while preserving all other speech features, researchers of the American Institute of Research have demonstrated that comprehension of speeded speech in one's own language is trainable. Further research in this area appears promising and may lead to the development of techniques which can train a foreign language student to proceed from slowed speech to accurate perception, comprehension, and articulation at normal speed (Orr & Friedman, 1964).

Other attempts in Europe to condition articulation by changing the character of the acoustic sidetone feedback are accomplished by electronic filters and appear to hold some promise, but the actual definition of the specific speech features and training techniques have not evolved in spite of the fact that experiments have been going on for several years. My personal observation of this phenomenon is that the shaping of the signal tends to shape the timbre of the subject's voice in the direction of the predetermined average level of speakers of that language. There is no doubt that there is much more to this combination which will bear watching, especially should further research lead to the development of a truly remedial aid in shaping pronunciation (Van Teslaar, 1963).

Research comparing phonetic characteristics of English, Spanish, German, and French by applying four special research techniques to thirty-five phonetic differences among these languages can be applied to the study of what really makes a foreign accent, that is, the phonetic features that make the difference between one language and another (Delattre, 1963). Lado (1964b) considers memory span a factor in language learning and a dimension in the measurement of proficiency in a foreign language. Lambert (1963) used speed of response as a measure of individual variations in bilingual skill and found that it correlated highly with the students' active vocabulary. These and other research efforts (Golden-Eisler, 1964) relating to time and tempo in language learning and testing should be fertile fields for further research which would apply these parameters, along with others, to the construction of learning and testing materials to be used in the language laboratory.

A LOOK TO THE FUTURE

After my own experience in working with the foreign language program of Title III of NDEA for five years (Hutchinson, 1961; Hutchinson, 1963; Hutchinson, 1964), I now feel keenly aware of the kinds of changes that can take place in half a decade in education. Therefore, I am bold enough to venture a few predictions on what the situation will be like five years from now:

1. Simplified electronic classrooms will be more useful than ever for daily guided practice and correction of students. Such facilities will be available in most foreign language classrooms in most secondary schools. Audio programs may in some cases be piped in through various kinds of centralized remote-control systems, but the teacher must continue to have full control over the movement of the program, including random access to its elements, and not just start and stop a given audio lesson.

2. Secondary schools of medium and large size will be equipped

with language laboratory rooms containing student booths and recorders (probably with individual remote control) for individualized independent study with the more successful versions of current programmed instruction efforts. Large groups can be accommodated in such a facility; yet each student will work at his own pace.

3.   As an integral part of basic-level programmed language self-instruction, there will be small-group (three to five students) display sessions or speech clinics with an instructor for fifteen to thirty minutes once or twice a week (Valdman, 1964). It is almost impossible to dispense with the responsive, live human touch entirely. Verbal output just does not seem to be able to flourish with machines as it does with other living creatures. It will also be a long time before a machine can confirm the accuracy of oral response. A live supervisory element also seems necessary to keep slower students from bogging down in a rut or dawdling.

4.   Simplified audio tape machines with one or two controls which provide a choice of several learning modes of sophisticated tape handling on an automatic measuring basis, as well as immediate and repetitive retrieval playback of any program segment or student response of any given (variable) length, all without the need for conventional rewinding of tape, will be available from industry. Such devices will be used either with programmed self-instructional materials (with some permissible branching) or with current audiolingual dialogue and pattern-drill tapes with or without built-in pauses or repetitions. Some of these features are already available on a limited basis, but a real breakthrough is imminent for a device which does all these things in split-second, "apple-pie" order and with consistent accuracy. It is amazing to experience what a difference it makes in a record-compare cycle when the model and response are retrieved and compared while their acoustic images are still ringing in one's ears. We all know that the auditory memory span for these acoustic images is extremely short and fleeting. These devices will be available as lightweight portable units or as student positions in standard language laboratory systems in which timing and sequencing may be controlled for a whole group or released to the individual for self-pacing. The past ten to fifteen years have seen very little basic change in language laboratory equipment, but the next five years will show major improvements in quality and sophistication.

5.   Student record-playback-compare learning activities will be accepted again as productive and used on a more sophisticated basis, especially with improved audio discrimination-training materials and techniques.

6.   New kinds of audio learning materials and techniques with special acoustic adjustments, such as speeded or slowed speech without dis-

tortion or electronically filtered sidetone to provide certain compensations for individual differences, will become available.

7. Small projectors and video tape machines will be used more and more to present authentic contemporary intercultural material for large-group and individualized reviewing and previewing. Among the new materials will be filmed demonstrations of contrastive paralanguage and kinesic behavior patterns in context, such as gestures commonly used in the foreign cultures.

8. We should not expect any unusual breakthrough of the science-fiction type in which sleep learning, "instant" language, "total immersion," and other glib approaches claim to yield a better product on a crash or cash basis. Yet we can expect to learn a great deal more from research in psycholinguistics about the nature of language and language learning, and students will be able to reach more efficiently levels of proficiency not heretofore achievable under school conditions.

9. Telephone-type audio learning systems will appear on more university campuses, and the possibilities of simplified mass oral testing through centralized telephone facilities will be realized.

10. Satellite communications will revolutionize the availability of fresh audio and video materials from the major continents of the world. Educational repositories for such materials will also make selective availability similar to that of library books and periodicals a reality.

CONCLUSION

Through research in colleges and universities and through practice and trial in the schools, the usefulness of the language laboratory concept has been validated over and over again—and is constantly being validated currently—in situations in which both teachers and administrators recognize the potentialities of the laboratory concept and plan together to find the best ways of integrating the new methods into the total foreign language curriculum. If in some places the language laboratory is still considered a fad or a status symbol, lack of careful and cooperative planning by administrators and teachers is probably to blame.

For at least fifteen years the materials, methods, and procedures needed for effective use of the language laboratory have been evolving. There is still a great need for better-trained teachers and for enough facilities to give first- and second-year language students the practice time they need. For more advanced courses much progress also has been made in the development of materials and procedures, but before the nation-wide situation can be called anywhere near satisfactory, we shall have to expend much more time and effort.

All during the period when most secondary schools have struggled to adapt to changes and to meet the demands placed upon them, college and university professors have played an uneven role: they have shown themselves both enlightened and uninformed; some have been trailblazers while others have put up obstacles to change. The famous American know-how that produced the technology of the language laboratory is unfortunately not present in all school systems or colleges to receive the laboratory equipment when it arrives. Teachers must be taught how to use the new equipment and the new materials; but many states, though they have approved purchase of equipment and materials with the aid of Federal funds provided under Title III of the NDEA, have been less eager to use funds available under the same program to provide in-service programs for the teachers.

Despite the problems and the handicaps, however, schools and colleges both in this country and abroad have made tremendous strides toward the fully effective use of equipment and materials in foreign language classrooms. We already know that the language laboratory (or electronic classroom) can be effective; what remains to be seen is how long it will take for our schools and colleges not only to acquire adequate laboratory facilities but to learn how to use them effectively.

REFERENCES

Axelrod, Joseph, and Donald N. Bigelow. *Resources for language and area studies.* Washington, D.C.: American Council on Education, 1962.

Bigelow, Donald N., and Lyman H. Letgers. *NDEA language and area centers: A report on the first five years.* U.S. Office of Education Bulletin 41, 1964.

Brooks, Nelson. *Language and language learning: Theory and practice.* (2d ed.) New York: Harcourt, Brace & World, Inc., 1964.

Delattre, Pierre. Research techniques for phonetic comparison of languages. *International Review of Applied Linguistics in Language Teaching,* 1963, **1**, 85–97.

Gaarder, A. Bruce, and Joseph C. Hutchinson: *A pilot survey of foreign language teaching equipment in 16 states.* U.S. Office of Education, 1964. (Processed.)

Goldman-Eisler, Frieda. Discussion and further comments. In Eric H. Lenneberg (Ed.), *New directions in the study of language.* Cambridge, Mass.: The M.I.T. Press, 1964.

Hayes, Alfred S. *Technical guide for the selection, purchase, use, and maintenance of language laboratory facilities.* U.S. Office of Education Bulletin 37, 1963.

Hocking, Elton. *Language laboratory and language learning.* Department of Audiovisual Instruction, Monograph No. 2. Washington, D.C.: National Education Association, 1964.

Hutchinson, Joseph C. *Modern foreign languages in high school: The language laboratory.* U.S. Office of Education Bulletin 23, 1961.

Hutchinson, Joseph C. The technology of modern language learning. *Curricular change in the foreign languages.* Princeton, N.J.: College Entrance Examination Board, 1963.

Hutchinson, Joseph C. *The language laboratory: How effective is it?* U.S. Office of Education, 1964.

Keating, Raymond F. *A study of the effectiveness of the language laboratory.* New York: Institute of Administrative Research, Teachers College, Columbia University, 1963.

Lado, Robert L. *Language teaching: A scientific approach.* New York: McGraw-Hill Book Company, 1964. (a)

Lado, Robert L. Memory span as a factor in second language learning. *International conference: Modern foreign language teaching. Papers and reports of groups and committees. Preprints,* Part 1. Berlin: Paedagogische Arbeitsstelle und Sekretariat, Paedagogisches Zentrum, 1964. (b)

Lambert, Wallace E. Psychological approaches to second-language learning and bilingualism. *Curricular change in the foreign languages.* Princeton, N.J.: College Entrance Examination Board, 1963.

Léon, Pierre. *Le laboratoire de langues et correction phonétique.* Paris: Didier, 1962.

Orr, David B., and Herbert L. Friedman. *Research on speeded speech as an educational medium.* Washington, D.C.: American Institute for Research, 1964. (Processed.)

Valdman, Albert. Toward self-instruction in foreign language learning. *International Review of Applied Linguistics in Language Teaching,* 1964, **2**, 1–36.

Van Teslaar, A. P. Les domaines de la linguistique appliquée (I). *International Review of Applied Linguistics in Language Teaching,* 1963, **1**, 50–72.

13

MODERN FOREIGN LANGUAGE TEACHING BY TELEVISION

S. PIT CORDER

S. Pit Corder (1918–) was graduated from Oxford University before World War II. He taught French in England before joining the British Council, under whose auspices he taught English in Austria, Turkey, and Colombia. After further graduate studies in applied linguistics he taught that subject at the University of Leeds, where he also ran an experimental educational television studio. He has published books and articles on television language teaching and himself taught English by television on a national network. He is at present head of the Department of Applied Linguistics in the University of Edinburgh.

Many readers will have met educational television in some form or other; some will have formed some notions of how it may help them in the educational system they are involved in; many may have reservations about its usefulness; some may be downright suspicious of it. But the chances are that their experience of educational television is limited to the approach current in their own educational system and that they may not be aware of the ways it has been used elsewhere.

What I propose to do, therefore, is to make some observations about educational television in general and some descriptive statements about television language teaching as it has been done in various places and in differing educational situations, then discuss some immediate possibilities of development, consider some of the theoretical problems associated with television language teaching, and, lastly, take a peep into the future.

EDUCATIONAL TELEVISION

Educational television has been with some of us for about ten years, in some places for a much shorter time than that, and in many parts of the world it has not yet arrived, although I do not believe that this is a situation which will exist much longer. Already we are able to discern certain patterns in its development, and we can see how it has begun to take on a particular aspect in each country which enables it to play a useful role in the educational system. This is a process which is likely to go on at an ever-increasing pace.

Nevertheless, in spite of the time educational television has been with us and of all that we have learned thus far, I would say that it is still in its comparative infancy, that its methodology and its techniques are still primitive. Until now the major part of research into educational television has been devoted to proving that it can teach as well as conventional methods. Educational television is still on the defensive. In one educational TV operation I know, the educational authority has taken great pains to inform every parent that no child in the school system ever receives more than one television lesson a day, and yet this is an educational authority which, because of sudden influxes of population, has only been able to maintain an educational service at all because it has resorted to television to do so.

It is significant that practically no research has yet been devoted to the important problem of the future, of discovering how best to teach by television: which techniques or teaching methods give the best results. It has been sufficient to show television can teach as well as conventional methods; the danger is that we shall now sit back and rest on our laurels.

Now that there are signs that educational television is beginning to fall into the hands of educators and that educators are beginning to realize that television has techniques which need learning, there are hopes that progress may start on developing teaching techniques which are specific to television. Educational television still has to win over a majority of the teachers in the classroom and a majority of school authorities. Until this has happened, we can only expect that progress will be slow.

What point have we in fact reached? What can TV do in education? First of all, it can provide live teaching where there are no schools. I do not mean that there are places where schools do not exist, though this is also true: I mean that there are all over the world learners and would-be learners who have no access to formal teaching, because they are too far away or too busy, or too poor, or immobile, or sick; in other words, learners for whom the problems of attendance at formally instituted classes are too great. These people are normally adults.

Second, television can provide instruction where there are schools, perhaps, but where there are not teachers enough for all subjects. The result of such a situation is that the curriculum is poor; educational television has brought a great enrichment of the school teaching program, not the least in the area of modern foreign languages.

On the other hand, there may be enough teachers, but they may be inadequately trained. Here TV can take over all or part of the responsibility; it can give help and guidance and can cooperate with the available teachers. This is the sort of situation in which TV has often done a useful job of teacher training by stealth. I have seen several situations in which the teacher has learned a language alongside her pupils.

But there may be trained teachers available and in sufficient numbers. Where does TV fit in then? There are many things a qualified teacher simply cannot do at all in the classroom, however well trained or equipped he may be. Indeed the better trained he is, the more he will realize how much he cannot do in the classroom that he would wish. Or there are things which he can only do inadequately, or with difficulty, or at great expense of effort, time, or money. These are things which TV can often do better, quicker, and more efficiently.

Briefly, the role of educational TV is to teach where there are no schools, to teach where there are not enough teachers, to help teach where the teachers are inadequately trained, and to use teaching techniques and materials which even trained teachers cannot economically or practically use in the classroom themselves.

Technically, TV is a vehicle and nothing more; it carries vision and sound from one place to another, and since recording can also be done, it carries vision and sound from one time to another. All electromechanical aids are themselves inert. This does not mean that they are neutral when applied to teaching, but it does mean that the oft-repeated phrase "TV can never replace the teacher" is meaningless. Whether the TV teacher will one day replace the classroom teacher is quite a different matter.

Now, TV can be, and often is, used in a classroom or a lecture hall to show more clearly what the lecturer is doing and talking about. In such a case, of course, it can scarcely be said to carry vision or even sound any distance in space or time. On the other hand, a program you see today could have been recorded five years ago and in another country. In this respect, as a vehicle, it differs little from film, except in the technical aspects of how it is produced and in the financial aspects of how much each costs to do particular jobs. Wherever cameras and microphones can be set up, teaching programs can originate. And this is the important point for the language teacher: TV can set formal teaching free from the constricting walls of the classroom. This fact alone will one day transform language teaching.

Surprising as it may seem, TV instruction in its earliest days did all it could to re-create the classroom in the TV studio: teacher, blackboard, textbook, and even, believe it or not, pupils! What the supposed television student received was not teaching but a spectacle, like a play or a documentary program on classroom techniques. He was not himself a learner at all but merely an eavesdropper or a spectator. This sort of program might be instructive to teachers in training, but it was irrelevant for the pupil.

What I meant earlier by saying that we are still in a primitive stage in educational television methodology was precisely that we have scarcely yet allowed TV to influence how we teach, even less what we teach. We still tend to use TV simply as a technical means of transferring our familiar and comfortable conventional classroom teaching from one place to another and from one time to another.

What can TV offer us? Since TV may partly or wholly teach thousands or tens of thousands of learners at a time, it offers us the opportunity of concentrating our resources, of bringing these learners the best of everything, particularly teachers, when we have found them. But let us not imagine that the face that appears on the screen is that of the teacher. The "teacher" on the screen, if such a person appears at all, is only one of a group of people who are all involved in the teaching operation. TV is a team job: the actors, the cameramen, the director, the scriptwriter, are all teachers in some measure. But then even classroom teaching is more of a team operation than most teachers are aware of or willing even to admit. What about the textbook writer; is he not a teacher, too? What about the man who designed the wall pictures, or the filmstrip, or the film? What about the man who prepared the tape or the voices who spoke the recording? Are these not all teachers, too? The difference is that TV cannot be done without this sort of cooperative effort.

TV can offer us more time to prepare our teaching. TV teachers and directors, of course, always complain that they are short of time, and they are right. They know that they could do better if they had more of it. But compared with the classroom teacher, they are well-off. What classroom teacher can spend perhaps two or three hours actually rehearsing each lesson?

TV can offer us greater resources in terms of staff, aids, and equipment than any school can offer a classroom teacher. It can do this because it has more money. I know that educational television directors always complain about lack of funds, but if you gave a classroom teacher the money and facilities a television teacher normally enjoys, he would not know what to do with them—nor do all TV teachers.

What is the apparent result of these facts? Because more time, effort, and money go into a program, *other things being equal,* the teaching will be more efficient. The learner will learn more in the same amount of time, or he will learn better in the same amount of time, or he will need less time to learn the same amount. In other words, television teaching should lead to a greater intensity and a greater efficiency, other things being equal. But other things are, indeed, rarely equal, and that is why we have the problem of television teaching at all.

The reader may feel that I have painted a rosy picture of educational television thus far, that I have made it look as if television had advantages over classroom teaching all along the line. This is far from the case, and I should especially emphasize that it is not so in the case of language teaching by television.

Television teaching suffers from one very serious defect: it is a vehicle of *one-way communication*—teacher to learner. In this respect it resembles programmed learning without the built-in reinforcement. Now, in teaching certain subjects this is obviously very much less of a disadvantage than it is in language teaching. Language is essentially a type of behavior indulged in by two or more people; that is, it is social behavior. We can, of course, *show* such behavior on the TV screen; we can show people talking to each other. But one element in language teaching, the productive practice element in which teacher and pupils enter into dialogue with each other, is absent on TV. The essential element of learning to adjust verbal behavior to a constantly changing situation is absent. Imagine trying to teach your ordinary class through a microphone with a soundproof glass panel between yourself and the pupils. Such a situation might well disturb or inconvenience a teacher of, say, geography or biology, but would perhaps, if he were a good teacher, not wholly impair his efficiency. Could the same be said of the language teacher? Any competent language teacher who is used to using modern situational teaching methods would be dismayed—I would go further and say ought to be dismayed—by such a prospect. And yet this is the plight of the TV teacher; furthermore, he cannot even see his pupils—he does not even know them.

The absence of this immediate two-way communication between pupil and teacher is indeed an appalling obstacle to the full exploitation of television in language teaching. And yet, I would add parenthetically, you will constantly read of television directors who especially single out language teaching as one of the things which television really can do.

There are, of course, other disadvantages. TV is thought to be expensive; we have just seen that, but we have to ask: "Is it really expensive in terms of cash per head of learner?" If we do this, we shall find that when we are teaching enough pupils by television, it is absurdly cheap. We can here enunciate an axiom: the fullest proper use of TV in education involves a radical reorganization of the distribution of educational funds. This is particularly true as far as language teaching is concerned, since, as we shall see, the fullest exploitation of TV for this purpose probably costs more than any other sort of instructional television.

TV teaching requires training and experience over and above that possessed by the ordinary teacher. Anyone proposing to teach by TV should know more about TV studio techniques than can be learned simply by sitting in front of a camera. He should receive formal and practical instruction in such things as camera work, lighting, designing, script writing, direction, and production. These are all part of *teaching*, and just as it has been said that war is too serious to leave to the generals, we may say that educational television is too serious to leave to the TV producer and the high school and college student, as is too often the case. I see no hope of rapid advance in educational TV in general until TV teachers understand from their own experience what TV can and cannot do for them.

I have spoken thus far about TV in education in general, although it will have been clear, I hope, that all I have said applies with equal force to the teaching of languages by television, to which I shall now specifically turn.

MODERN FOREIGN LANGUAGE TEACHING BY TV

In the specialized field of foreign language teaching by television we can usefully distinguish three main types of language teaching operation. These are what I shall call the *whole-job operation,* the *major-job operation,* and the *minor-job operation.* I shall say something about each of these in turn.

WHOLE-JOB OPERATION   In the whole-job operation all the teaching is done by TV, and there is no other teacher or formal teaching. Situations of this kind are most frequently found where language teaching programs are put out for the general viewing public, either as a public service by a commercial TV organization or as part of an organized adult education operation on an officially operated TV network. It is rare that such a teaching program is aimed at schools. Note that when I speak of the whole job, I mean that all the teaching that is done is done by TV. I do not wish at this stage to imply that by such programs TV does, or indeed can do, all the teaching that needs to be done.

The characteristics of this type of teaching program are three. First, the program can follow its own syllabus; it does not have to integrate itself into any scheme or textbook used by any other teachers. The consequences of this are two: the program does not need to be produced locally but can be made in another country by native speakers using authentic local settings and material, and this often enjoys strong financial advantages. The second characteristic is that the program does not have to adopt any particular technique of teaching, selection of material, or grading of this material and is consequently free to use entirely new and unorthodox methods if they are considered to be likely to give the best results. I shall revert to this topic at a later stage. Third, such whole-job teaching programs may set out to teach all the linguistic skills from the beginning or may be directed to learners who already have achieved a certain ability. On the other hand, the programs may limit themselves to the teaching of a restricted range of skills; for example, they may offer only practice in hearing the language, or they may be aimed only at advanced learners, or prospective tourists, or businessmen. Such courses are nowadays normally accompanied by a rather complete students' textbook which can be bought by viewers and, more recently, by audio aids on record and tape.

The drawbacks, of course, of this sort of teaching operation are fairly obvious: first of all, the virtually complete lack of any practical channels for feedback of any sort from the learner to the teacher; and, second, the possibly extreme irregularity of viewing by the learner. Very few reliable figures are available from any source, but generally speaking noncaptive audiences appear to be, for the most part, very irregular in their viewing of TV lessons. The effects of this are that a very much greater amount of redundancy must be built into any serious teaching program series than in the case of programs for the captive audience in schools, where attendance (though perhaps not attention) can be compelled.

The writer of programmed learning courses will know the difficulties of producing a program which consists of regular and logical steps so graded that no learner can get lost on the way. Let him try to devise a program for a set of learners who he knows will skip a random two out of every three frames and still succeed in keeping his learners with him!

As far as the lack of feedback in whole-job teaching is concerned, it means first of all that productive practice, which is an essential element of any language learning, is left almost entirely to the learner himself; he must practice voluntarily, and no doubt at least some of those few who are regular viewers can be relied upon to do so, but they must monitor their own practice. Unless copious follow-up material is not only available but actually purchased by the learner, it is difficult to believe that any large number of learners can benefit much at the present time from this type of teaching. Its value is probably largely motivational. If, however, the course has only limited aims, such as the refurbishing of receptive skills, then some useful learning may take place.

The second effect of lack of feedback is that the TV teacher has no means of knowing what has been well learned, what badly learned, or if any of his pupils have learned anything at all, if indeed he has any serious pupils. This highly discouraging situation may account for the high fees very often paid to TV performers.

It is in this field that much of the work in TV language teaching has been done in Europe. One of the earliest such courses was "This Is English," produced by Swedish Television. In this course the linguistic syllabus used was the familiar classroom one, and at this point in TV language teaching it is not surprising that this was the case. The presentation of the material was also conventionally derived from classroom methodology. On the other hand, an attempt was made to exploit as fully as possible specifically TV techniques, such as insert and the split screen. Whether this was always done for genuinely pedagogic reasons or as a motivational factor can be debated. At all events, this program has enjoyed a wide popularity and has been shown on all the important Western European networks. Since the pioneering days of "This Is English," some people have been concerned in discovering a language teaching methodology more appropriate to TV. As an example, we may take the series "Walter and Connie," produced by the British Broadcasting Corporation (BBC). It is a course of thirty-nine lessons (first series) for teaching English to adult beginners of European cultural background. It presents the language material in dramatic scenes but also gives explanations of the linguistic points in the vernacular. There is no teacher figure in the program. The linguistic syllabus again follows very closely the traditional classroom order, however, and this leads to what might be regarded as wildly exotic situations and, for instance, most unusual intonation patterns in a beginner's course. These features are entirely predictable in any course which tries to marry real-life situational teaching with a syllabus designed for the classroom.

Hence the interest in another BBC course, "Parliamo Italiano," a limited-aim course of thirty lessons. The object here is to give linguistic-cultural help to the tourist. The linguistic syllabus can here be more closely defined, and the terminal behavior specified. The situations chosen are those of high frequency for tourists: shopping, asking the way, garage language, etc. Thus the material presented, when and if learned, has a high surrender value and produces high motivation for the learner. This could not so easily be said of "Walter and Connie," which, like conventional classroom teaching, has low surrender value and is forced therefore to depend to a considerable degree on motivating factors, namely, comedy, which are largely irrelevant to teaching.

The techniques used in "Parliamo Italiano" are some of the most advanced yet tried and promise well for the future: the virtual elimination of the invisible barrier between reality and make-believe possible only on TV, where the actors turn teacher in the middle of a scene or where the teacher, if there is one, becomes a participant in a real-life episode. Very similar techniques were used in Associated Rediffusion's "Try out Your French" (1962), and the current BBC Foreign Language program, "Komm Mit" (1965), employs the same method. The advantages of this are obvious: explanation and practice can take place at the point of the original utterance with all the situational stimuli present to fill it with meaning.

MAJOR-JOB OPERATION Under this heading I include all those teaching programs which are directed to audiences having ordinary classroom teachers but whose teachers are inadequately trained. They may, of course, be qualified teachers of other subjects than language, and their knowledge of the language taught may be deficient to the point of being little more than that of their pupils. On the other hand, they may be native speakers of the language who are untrained as teachers. The latter situation is more promising for reasons which will emerge. Neither of these two types of untrained teacher is competent to teach the language without very considerable help. Even with a good textbook and adequate audio and visual aids, they are probably not capable of doing more than a poor job. For them the TV language teaching program is not just a help or a prop: it is a lifeline. It undertakes the responsibility of preparing the linguistic syllabus, that is, the whole business of selecting and grading the linguistic materials to be taught and of devising the situations in which it shall be presented. Furthermore, it undertakes the central role of actually presenting these materials. It leaves, perforce, to the classroom teacher the job of organizing the learner's productive practice. But it will not leave to the classroom teacher the responsibility for devising practice methods, for the TV teacher will also specify how practice shall be conducted, and he will most often provide the material in the form of audio aids and texts.

Nevertheless, although all the major linguistic and methodological decisions are taken by the TV teacher, he must still rely upon an untrained classroom teacher to control the practice element. Not only this, but he must rely on him to enter into a dialogue with the learner, creating situations which will allow the latter to use the language socially. The native speaker of the language, though untrained as a teacher, of course, is capable of doing this, and here one might expect TV teaching's most successful application. On the other hand, where the classroom teacher has little or no knowledge of the language, learning will remain at a holophrastic level: that is, the pupils will learn to repeat, perhaps perfectly, what they have heard on TV but will not learn to generalize; they will learn to speak and understand whole sentences but not sentence patterns.

The major-job type of TV language teaching is, of course, normally directed toward those schools which do not have trained language teachers, and this, in most educational systems, means primary schools and beginner learners.

Here I would refer you to the findings reported by Prof. E. S. Randall in a paper presented to the International Conference on Modern Foreign Language Teaching, held in Berlin in 1964, based upon the investigations carried out under the Modern Language Project, Boston, and particularly to his conclusions that progress is effective only if the classroom teacher is interested and conducts careful follow-up practice.

The major-job type of TV language teaching is largely an American use of the medium (Reid, 1961). Europe has not yet developed the local educational TV station serving a small school area, but a start is being made in Great Britain with the setting up in 1965 of two such services, and other countries having a similar decentralized educational system will surely follow shortly. The pattern is likely to be normal in many countries in Africa.

Since this type of TV teaching will be the most familiar to the reader, nothing more need be said about it than has been already. The difference between the techniques used in this type of TV language teaching, largely conventional classroom ones minimally adapted to TV, and those just described as used in the whole-job teaching program, however, are the result of one simple factor: a gross difference in the amount of money available to the producer and teacher in the two operations. This is reflected in the technical TV resources used, the number and expertise of the personnel, and the quality and authority of the linguistic element in the course. When you have money, you can contemplate the use of trained native actors, the creation of more or less elaborate sets, and hence the production of convincing dramatic presentations of language. It is true that sporadic and valiant attempts to do this without the prerequisite resources have been made. The results have not always been very happy.

It is my belief that this is the direction in which major-job TV language teaching must go and, as the development of "Parlons Français" has shown, when more adequate funds became available, is the direction which appears natural.

It is of interest in this connection to take a look at what may be a unique series of programs, "English for Everyone," now being prepared at the Center for Educational Television Overseas in London, England, whose work is the production of educational television programs on tape and film and in script form for use in educational TV stations in developing countries, especially in the Commonwealth. This program is an ingenious combination of an animated cartoon film, which is employed for the presentation of the linguistic material, with a script and supporting material, to be used by the local teacher and producer. We have thus a situation in which the material exploits the capacities of TV, maintains a local flavor and adaptability, and enjoys the authority of the expert in language, television, and visual support material not normally available to the small local educational TV station.

It may well turn out that a similar sort of operation may prove to be the way out of what is, in my opinion, the present impasse in which small local educational TV systems find themselves. The lack of money, local technical TV facilities, and production skills, combined with restricted teaching skills and linguistic knowledge, at present prevent development locally of better TV teaching techniques. And yet it is both inevitable and desirable that these systems maintain a local flavor and contact with schools: in sum, meet specific local needs. The present method of improving these programs has often been to use recorded material made in more favorably placed situations; hence the widespread use of "Parlons Français" throughout the United States and Europe. An alternative solution, not yet tried out to my knowledge, is to centralize the production of visual material on film, tape, caption, etc., using native-speaking actors and the best TV techniques. This material can then be *incorporated* into a locally produced and perhaps scripted program presented by local teachers, using only those sequences which fit the syllabus they are in the process of preparing. By this means advantage can be taken of the things that TV can especially offer, situational contexts, authoritative use of language, and native pronunciation; at the same time the program can be geared to the needs of the local school system.

MINOR-JOB OPERATION   What I have called the minor-job program is the type of teaching course directed toward learners who are in the hands of a competent, trained teacher, whose command of the language is likely to be very good, in fact, the sort of teacher who, before TV arrived, taught his class as adequately as ordinary classroom techniques then permitted. What can TV do for this sort of teacher and his pupils? It can help the teacher by doing something for him which he would like to be able to do in the classroom but cannot; for example, by showing native speakers talking to each other in their home environment or by taking his pupils on a conducted tour of the Louvre, or it can do something else, perhaps more quickly or more efficiently than he can do.

In general, one can characterize the minor-job type of course as enrichment, either cultural or motivational. TV can present demonstrations of language used in realistic or actual situations. It can bring the native speaker, talking directly in his own language, to the learner. These are all very limited but directly linguistic teaching functions, though they may have, as secondary aims, a motivational effect upon the learner toward learning. This may be, for example, the first contact with a native speaker which the learner has, and he may be delighted to find that he can understand him.

Alternatively, the program may be aimed at presenting information about the culture, history, or social life of the speakers of the language; in this case, the direct linguistic teaching takes a secondary place, and the program is not, strictly speaking, any longer a language teaching program. The minor type of teaching job tends to be directed toward more advanced captive learners in secondary schools. The ability to follow a more or less natural dialogue spoken by native speakers even when some degree of linguistic control has been exercised and the ability to follow documentary or descriptive cultural programs in the language imply advanced knowledge.

In the absence of local educational TV stations in Europe, any school service which exists has been undertaken by national TV networks. This has meant that the amount of money available has normally been greater than for the majority of TV language teaching programs in the United States, resulting in a glossier product in a technical sense. An additional feature which has also given an advantage to the European TV teacher is the *proximity* of the country whose language is being taught and the facilities which exist for reciprocal technical services under Eurovision (European TV network). This has meant that a documentary-style approach in these programs is feasible. The demonstration of life and language of the French marketplace is shot on location with actors mixing naturally with the ordinary market folk. Language here is fully contextual. Or the teacher is taken on a personally conducted tour of the Comédie Française by the director himself, or the learner is introduced to life in a German hospital by two nurses.

I need hardly point out that these three main types of television language teaching—the whole-job, the major-job, and the minor-job—cannot be regarded as entirely separate but rather as points on a continuum. There are intermediate types, and although certain techniques and methods seem more appropriate to one than another, considerable overlap and mixing are found.

So much for the descriptive part of what I have to say. I now turn to the future and to the more speculative and theoretical aspects of TV language teaching.

THE FUTURE

My first suggestion is not a particularly striking one. It is that we should consider the possibility of making a combined use of the new technical means we have for language teaching. By this I mean the combined use of television and language laboratory, or television and audiovisual course, and possibly, though here I confess I am more doubtful, the combined use of television and programmed instruction. Or why not a combination of three techniques? I can, for instance, see a great deal to be said for piping an audiovisual course via television to pupils in a language laboratory. Audiovisual courses in language laboratories are already a commonplace, and their combination with TV has certain attractions: the classroom teacher is wholly free from electrical and mechanical preoccupations; a much larger range of audiovisual material can be available from a central television service; and live presentation or film can be alternated with still-picture sequences where desired. A certain amount of useful productive practice can go on in the absence of a teacher. From the television programming side, the advantages are that ready-made, tried, and tested material can be broadcast in the absence of a TV production team. In these circumstances, TV reverts to its primary function as a distributor of sound and vision.

Now for a more theoretical and speculative look at television language teaching in the future. I said at the beginning that I considered educational television to be still in a primitive stage methodologically. Many TV educationists who are of the same opinion look forward to a time in the future when TV will actually have begun to have a serious impact on education. This can scarcely be said to be the case at present, even in America. For, by "serious impact," we can only mean that television will no longer be used to do perhaps marginally better what we have long been accustomed to doing in the classroom but will, on the contrary, have brought about a change in *how* we teach and, indeed, eventually in *what* we teach. This is what should really be the meaning of education by television. We must expect that schools as we know them will suffer a radical change. It may well be that children will receive some part, perhaps a considerable part, of their instruction at home. There is no telling now what form the impact of television may eventually have, or how far the changes it brings will go. What is certain is that we ought to be thinking about it now, planning, researching, and experimenting. I said just now that television in education will bring about changes in how we teach and also in what we teach. In the matter of language teaching, of course, there can be no important change in what we teach—language is still a form of social behavior, television or no television—but it may bring about a radical change in *how* we teach it.

The challenge, then, that TV presents to the language teacher is to devise a method of teaching which can do the whole job without the aid of a classroom teacher, and here by the whole job I mean teach all the language skills from the beginning. It will only do this by exploiting what TV can do better than any classroom teaching situation and in such a way that the manifest disadvantages under which it labors, especially that of one-way communication and lack of feedback, shall be more than compensated for.

This challenge is by no means an illusory one. We have already seen that where competent, trained language teachers are available, TV has played, until now at least, only a marginal and probably readily dispensable role. But there are many places at the present moment where trained teachers are not available, and in many places there seems to be little prospect of an increasing supply of trained teachers in the future. Indeed, it has to some extent been the prospect of diminishing numbers of qualified teachers that has acted as a stimulus to the development and exploitation of the newer technical means of teaching, television among them. In language teaching, furthermore, the now widespread policy of starting foreign language teaching earlier in the school career has had the same effect. At the same time, we are experiencing an increased demand for second language teaching in the newly developing countries.

This is the challenge. We shall have to try and meet it, but thus far all methods of teaching language by TV have been little more than modified classroom methods. All have been based upon a linguistic syllabus, and many upon a syllabus devised specifically for classroom use.

By *linguistic syllabus,* I mean a syllabus based on the linguistic description of the language to be taught and, of course, more recently on linguistic comparisons between foreign language and mother tongue. Furthermore, this syllabus has been arrived at as a result of generations of language teaching in the classroom and research and study directed to that end. It is a linguistic syllabus, then, and also a syllabus devised for a specific teaching situation, in which teacher and pupil confront each other in direct communication surrounded by all the familiar properties of the classroom—chalkboard, chalk, wall pictures, desks, chairs, and textbooks. Furthermore it is a syllabus predicated upon the possibility of massive monitored productive practice.

It is not unreasonable, therefore, to reflect that in a new teaching situation, in which teaching originates in a TV studio and is received on a small screen perhaps in the learner's own home but certainly in a room specially designed for TV viewing, a new approach might be required. It is not unreasonable that this approach might be more consciously behavioral, since behavior is what we are teaching, and perhaps less linguistic and academic, but largely because TV is likely to be favorable to such an approach.

To achieve a better use of TV we must exploit what TV can do best, that is, use it *contextually;* by this I mean show language behavior in natural situations. After all, language is not language unless it is used meaningfully. It is only a complex set of patterns of sound. These have no meaning initially for the learner until they are uttered in a situation to which they can be related. If there is one thing that TV can do above all others, it is to present real life or a simulation of it. The viewer cannot readily tell the difference. Our starting point for a TV method therefore should be language presented in a context. We must start, as it were, from the other end. Instead of beginning with individual sounds and gradually building them up into more and more complex patterns and only lastly teaching the meaningful use of these by description or translation, we must start from situations, selected with all the care and skill hitherto devoted to the selection of the linguistic items, and then show the language which grows out of them or, if you wish, belongs in them (Corder,

1960). We may note, in passing, that the infant learns his mother tongue in this way, by what we may call situational or behavioral means.

Now there is nothing theoretically new or revolutionary about this notion; it rests on sound linguistic and behavioral theory. Indeed, more and more in our classroom work we are approaching language teaching from the behavioral end.

In fact, some sort of a compromise between a linguistic and a behavioral course has already been achieved in the classroom. Anyone who has to teach immigrants (as have, for example, the Americans or the Australians) will know this. A linguistically oriented course is "no use" in a practical sense for quite a long time; it has, in the language of the insurance people, a *low surrender* value. You cannot get by with only one number, one mood, one tense, and one or two persons.

A compromise between the linguistic and the behavioral approaches is, however, an uneasy one, since it leads to the constant introduction of ungraded material. We shall, no doubt, have to live with this situation for a long time, and, indeed, a complete abandonment of the linguistic approach in the classroom as we know it is unthinkable, but its abandonment on TV is, I submit, logical.

As I have suggested already, some of the best recent work on TV has achieved some sort of compromise between linguistic and behavioral approaches. I use the word *compromise* here because there is always an inherent conflict between the two approaches. In the purely linguistically oriented course, the language is closely controlled at all times according to the categories of linguistic description.

In our everyday behavior, on the other hand, our language is not restricted in any ordinary linguistic way. For example, we can ask a question (which is a behavioral category) in imperative, declarative, or interrogative mood. We can also issue an order or make a statement in all three moods. There is no 1 to 1 relationship between the linguistic category and the behavioral category. And yet our linguistic method of teaching encourages this belief.

Let me take just one example of what I mean from German. There is, in German, a linguistic item *bitte,* very often translated "please" (usually wrongly so). Now this item is one, or possibly two, linguistic items: it is, however, very clearly a larger number of quite different behavioral items. We say *bitte* when we hand something to someone; we say *bitte* when we want someone to repeat what they have just said; we say *bitte* when we accept an offer; we say *bitte* when someone thanks us; we say *bitte* when we ask someone to do something; and, finally, we say *bitte* when someone asks our permission to do something.

What is holding us up in making a start with this approach is not a theoretical difficulty but a question of factual knowledge. We do not yet know enough about the psychology of verbal behavior, nor do we know enough about the specific form that the behavior takes in particular situations. In other words we cannot yet predict what people will say in any particular situation (except perhaps in a few common public situations). Until we know a great deal more about these things, we shall have to adopt a pragmatic approach, as has been done so often under the pressure of demand. We shall have to find out by trial and error what works and what does not.

If we carry out such a plan systematically and conscientiously, the fact that TV provides only one-way communication and hence lacks immediate response to the teacher should matter less. It will always remain true that we shall not be able to control the learner's productive practice or provide him with a live situation in which he can practice the language socially, but the fact that he will learn holophrastically (which, you will recall, was the result of lack of feedback in the case of a linguistically oriented course), far from being a grave disadvantage, is the situation which we are actually seeking to produce in the first instance. In a behaviorally oriented course we really do want the learner to learn complete responses. Whether these are sentences or words is quite irrelevant.

Dare I say that this is a major element in the learning of our mother tongue? Indeed, I take it that the renewed interest in the way a child learns his mother tongue is a sign of a growing awareness that there are other ways of teaching language than those based upon a linguistic analysis.

Our task, as I see it now, is to press on with experiment and research; experiment in a more radical behavioral type of teaching program, on the one hand, and research into the psychology of language and the study of language in situation, on the other. What we shall discover may benefit not only TV language teaching but foreign language teaching generally.

REFERENCES

Corder, S. Pit. *English language teaching and television.* London: Longmans, Green & Co., Ltd., 1960.

Reid, Richard J. *An exploratory survey of foreign language teaching by television in the United States.* Modern Language Association of America Report, 1961.

14

FLES: ACHIEVEMENT
AND PROBLEMS

H. H. STERN

*H. H. Stern (1913–   ), was born in Germany and received the
major portion of his higher education at King's College and the
Institute of Education in the University of London. He taught languages in an English grammar school and was for the past fifteen
years in charge of educational psychology and methodology of foreign
language teaching at the University of Hull, England, with interruptions for periods as research officer at the UNESCO Institute for
Education, Hamburg, and as editor of the* International Review of
Education. *He was recently appointed reader in the Language Center,
University of Essex, and is currently chairman of the Modern Language Association of Great Britain. His publications include* Foreign
Languages in Primary Education *and* Modern Languages in the
Universities: A Guide.

Foreign language teaching in elementary schools (FLES) is an
American term, but the trend of development it names—the
teaching of a foreign language to children from a low age
upward in the general schools of an educational system—has
parallels in many countries. The present paper is based on
(1) personal knowledge of the British equivalent of FLES, the
teaching of foreign languages in primary schools which cater
for children between the ages of five and eleven or twelve;

and (2) acquaintance with similar movements in several countries in Europe and other parts of the world.

Like many other language teaching reforms, FLES is the result of widespread dissatisfaction with conventional language teaching. Such teaching in most countries usually begins and ends within the framework of the secondary school. The criticism of this practice implied in FLES programs—a criticism that its advocates frequently voice—is directed against the amount of language teaching, the time element in language instruction, the objectives pursued by language teachers, the methods and materials employed by them, and, of course, the results of traditional teaching of foreign languages. Briefly, FLES argues that there is altogether too little language teaching, that the little there is comes too late, and that it misses what Havighurst (1953) has called the "teachable moment." It also reacts against the deeply rooted emphasis on the written language and the grammar-translation approach, which is still widely practiced by teachers in secondary schools.

FLES today represents a significant body of experience on all these points, and the present chapter attempts to evaluate its achievements and to indicate some current problems.

RECENT TRENDS

It is not necessary to describe here the development of FLES from its early beginnings. Its history is sufficiently documented, for example, for the United States by Andersson (1953) and Birkmaier (1960) and for many countries, including the United States, in a recent international study (Stern, 1963). All that needs to be said here is that FLES in the modern sense really started after World War II, mainly in the fifties. American FLES has thus by now a history of at least fifteen years. Reports usually describe the phenomenal spread of the movement, but it is not a story of unmitigated success; rather it is a mixture of successes, problems, and failures. Yet, in spite of the difficulties, FLES has not flagged; on the contrary, it is gaining in strength all over the world.

American FLES has pioneered language teaching for younger children. Although the idea as such is not new and has not originated with the FLES movement, as a deliberate educational policy and as part of. primary education it is a phenomenon of the postwar world, and the American movement has given it a decisive impulse.

In European countries the start in a foreign language in the second decade of life, mainly at the beginning of the secondary stage of schooling, is widely established and so much taken for granted that without the interest aroused by American FLES one would hardly have thought of seeking a solution to the language learning problem in an early start in the primary phase of education. But by the mid-fifties the question began to be examined in the light of American experience, and experiments were initiated here and there, for example, in France and Sweden around 1956. In the Soviet Union, Ginsberg's well-known investigation on teaching languages in Leningrad nursery schools began in 1957.[1] The beginnings of current work in Britain, which will be described below, date back to the same period.

Activities of the FLES type were also of interest to UNESCO, largely, no doubt, as a result of Professor T. Andersson's advocacy of FLES at the seminar on foreign language teaching held at Nuwara Eliya, Ceylon, in 1953 (*The Teaching of Modern Languages,* 1955) ; and in its 1961–1962 program UNESCO charged one of its associated institutions, the Unesco Institute for Education in Hamburg, to convene (with financial help from UNESCO) a meeting of experts "to plan a long-term program of investigations into the psychological and pedagogical aspects of the problem of teaching foreign languages in the primary stage."

At the time of the Hamburg meeting (1962) it was clear that FLES was spreading. But just as it had had its ups and downs in America, in other countries, too, it was not plain sailing either. Linguists in particular gave it a mixed reception. For some people it was the answer to the language problem in the modern world; skeptics, however, stressed the difficulties and questioned the arguments that were customarily advanced by the advocates of FLES. UNESCO and the Unesco Institute for Education took the view that FLES had come to a point at which dispassionate inquiry was needed; the Hamburg meeting was accordingly not conceived as an international send-off for FLES but as an occasion to question and examine its premises, to study the facts, and, if possible, to recommend research and future developments.

The Hamburg inquiries revealed some interesting trends: (1) Early language learning in primary schools is an established practice in a large number of school systems. (2) Far from being an educational luxury or even a matter of educational choice it is in some parts of the world and, in certain circumstances, anywhere, an absolute necessity. (3) While FLES-type experiments and practices are widespread, the differences in educational, linguistic, and historical contexts produce differences in emphasis. (4) In spite of these divergences, which it is important to bear in mind in comparing FLES programs in different countries, much common ground exists in the approach to methods and materials. (5) Finally, the broad general conclusion which was reached after a critical examina-

[1] For details and references, see Stern (1963).

tion was that FLES cannot be dismissed as a momentary fashion. It was recognized as a movement of significance in language teaching and of importance, too, for the development of primary education. The existence of difficulties and problems was not overlooked; these were treated as matters for investigation, experiments, and research, and a detailed list of research proposals was included in the Hamburg Report (Carroll, 1963).

In the years which have passed since the Hamburg Conference experimentation has continued. In 1964 another international meeting, held in Berlin, offered a further opportunity to review recent developments in several countries.[2] The chief conclusion of this renewed international confrontation was that the developments and trends which were noted at the Hamburg Conference in 1962 "have continued, increased in scope and indeed accelerated with marked improvements in methods, materials, and teaching aids" (*International Conference: Modern Foreign Language Teaching,* 1964).

CURRENT DEVELOPMENTS

Much experience has by now been gathered, and several experiments, some of which were already described in the Hamburg Report, have since been completed, and the results published. One such study is the Swedish experiment to teach English to young children by means of simple audiovisual lessons in classes whose teachers had no qualifications and in many cases no knowledge of English (Gorosch & Axelsson, 1964). Another is the Kassel experiment (Martens, 1964), in which English was started in grade 3 in some classes in a limited number of elementary schools in the city of Kassel, Germany. Reports of viable FLES-type programs have recently also come from France (Cohen, 1964), Britain (Kellermann, 1964), and the United States (Eriksson, Forest, & Mulhauser, 1964).

ENGLISH EXPERIMENT, 1963–1969   At the same time new experiments have been started. Noteworthy among these is the Pilot Scheme for the Teaching of French in Primary Schools, which was initiated in England by the Ministry of Education, recently reorganized under the name of Department of Education and Science (Great Britain, Ministry of Education, 1964).

As a result of many criticisms of language teaching in Britain, British

---

[2] For a brief report on this meeting, see Roeming (1964). The full collection of papers and reports produced for and during this gathering is being published in several volumes by the chief organizers of the conference, the Paedagogische Arbeitsstelle and Sekretariat, Paedagogisches Zentrum, Berlin.

educators became interested in FLES in the period after World War II. The teaching of languages in primary schools was first given limited official approval in a Ministry of Education pamphlet on the teaching of modern languages published in 1956 (Great Britain, Ministry of Education, 1956), but as late as 1959 an official publication expressed itself with extreme caution on attempts to introduce languages into the curriculum of the primary school.

A change occurred in about 1960 or 1961. Much interest was aroused by a substantial teaching experiment carried out in Leeds from 1961 onward. This was sponsored by the Leeds Education Authority in cooperation with the Nuffield Foundation. The details of this experiment were recently described in the small book, already mentioned (Kellermann, 1964), which was written by the teacher in this investigation. The public interest in the venture was widespread. While a good deal of experimentation in primary schools in other parts of the country was going on about the same time, it was undoubtedly the Leeds experiment, together with the awareness of FLES experiments abroad and a considerable interest in them, which brought about a change of attitude among linguists and educators in Britain. Until then the value of an approach to language teaching at the primary stage was considered of marginal interest or was dismissed as irrelevant. After the Leeds experiment, FLES began to be taken seriously, and the interest has continued to spread.

The stamp of official approval on a national scale came in December, 1962, when the Minister of Education announced in the House of Commons plans to investigate more widely the possibilities of teaching languages in primary schools; and in March, 1963, the national Pilot Scheme for the Teaching of French in Primary Schools was announced. The principal aim of this project is to study in a realistic way the practicability of introducing French into the primary curriculum in a wide variety of schools. It is a remarkable educational venture offering a new approach to curriculum change in Britain, quite apart from its possible contribution to language teaching.

There is today much criticism of superficial and ephemeral FLES programs. Those who voice such criticisms will be particularly interested in these features of the British pilot scheme: its scope and duration, the teacher training program, and the preparation of teaching materials.

In response to the Ministry's invitation sent to all local education authorities (school boards) to take part in this scheme, some seventy-three authorities (roughly half of the total number) put forward proposals of local projects, and from these applications the Ministry selected thirteen localities, with a view to gaining experience of language teaching in different types of school milieus, urban and rural, northern and southern, depressed and affluent, etc. It meant that a total of 6,000 children aged eight or so all over England and Wales in September, 1964, began to learn French in some 120 primary schools. The experiment will continue until July, 1969, when the first entrants, who began learning French in 1964, will be thirteen and will have had two years of secondary schooling. The scheme is therefore designed to provide experience not only in the early start at the primary stage but in methods of continuation at the secondary stage. All children who enter the experimental schools in the course of these five years will in turn learn French and advance to secondary schools where they will also be able to continue at least up to the age of thirteen. No decision has yet been taken on further language study after this five-year program.

The teachers in the experimental scheme are all trained and experienced primary school class teachers, not foreign language specialists. While interested enough to volunteer for the project, most of them started with only a school knowledge of French; but a condition of their participation in the scheme was that they must be prepared to accept prolonged and intensive training in French, and much of this in their leisure time. The training program began in 1963. In all the localities the teachers went to French evening classes twice a week for about seven or eight months, generally in technical colleges with language laboratories. These courses were intended purely to improve the teachers' proficiency in French and were not specifically directed toward the teaching material they were to use in the primary schools, except that the main emphasis was laid on oral command. The teachers then attended for nearly three months a full-time course at one of two centers in France, the Institut Britannique in Paris or the Centre de Linguistique Appliquée at Besançon. A third center for such full-time intensive study was recently opened in England at the Holborn College of Law, Languages, and Commerce in London. After this intensive period of study, the teachers took a ten-day course in England on the methodology of teaching languages to young children, and upon their return to their own localities they continued language classes in local colleges. A similar sequence of training will be available for subsequent groups of teachers, because, as each year, until 1969, fresh eight-year-olds in the areas of the experiment enter the 120 primary schools, the number of classes learning French will increase, and consequently the number of teachers must keep step.

Teaching materials for the experiment are not prescribed, and schools are free to introduce what they consider most suitable, but in order to put adequate course material at the disposal of teachers the Department of Education and Science is cooperating in its scheme with an institution recently set up by the Nuffield Foundation, the Nuffield

Foundation Foreign Languages Teaching Materials Project. This project, with its center at Leeds, is a more permanent outcome of the Nuffield Foundation's enterprise in Leeds and forms part of the Foundation's general interest in language teaching and other curriculum subjects. In the short time of the existence of this project an information center has been set up at the Leeds headquarters where teachers can study internationally available course materials. The project has further issued a number of valuable publications on language teaching (e.g., Lazaro, 1963; Moore & Antrobus, 1964; Nuffield Foundation, 1965; Rowlands, 1964). One of its main tasks, however, is to prepare a French course for the pilot scheme. This course is, in fact, in use in 100 out of the 120 participating schools. Russian, German, and Spanish sections of the Nuffield project have also been set up. These are charged with producing beginners' courses in these languages for children starting a second foreign language at the age of eleven.

In the production of the course material the project is breaking new ground. Here, too, as in the teaching program, continuity and systematic progression are aimed at. The preparation of the courses is treated as a team effort. The members of the French course include a linguist, who is the organizer of the entire project; a primary teacher, specially released from his work to help in the course preparation; a French native speaker; and an artist. With slight variations the other language sections of the Nuffield project are similarly organized in teams. An important role in the team effort is played by the teachers who test the material. The lessons are first pretested in a small number of schools not in the scheme. As a result of this preliminary tryout the first draft is produced. In this form the material is sent to the schools in the scheme which have opted to use the Nuffield material. On the basis of their experience, which is collected by questionnaires, a second revision is prepared and tried out on the next generation of children in the experimental schools. The results of this further testing are embodied in the final version of the teaching material, which is then made more widely available. Some features of the Nuffield teaching material will be outlined below.

In addition to the thirteen areas which take part in the experimental scheme, a number of areas which have expressed interest have been invited to become "associated" with the scheme. In these areas the school boards make their own arrangements for the language training of the teachers, and they play no part in the early stages of the testing of the Nuffield material; but they are offered the opportunity to receive the teaching material after it has passed through its stages of testing and revision, and they generally share in the results of the experience of the scheme and also contribute their own findings.

NEW TEACHING MATERIALS The ingenuity, skill, and care that have gone into the preparation of some of the latest language teaching materials for younger children, particularly in French, constitute perhaps the most notable advance of the last few years. One example, too well known in the United States and other countries to require description here, is the television and film course "Parlons Français," which was originated in 1959 by the Modern Language Project of the Massachusetts Council for Public Schools, Boston (Randall, 1964b). Another example of a recent course is "Bonjour Line," an audiovisual course for children between eight and eleven years of age, produced by the Centre de Recherche et d'Étude pour la Diffusion du Français (CREDIF) and published in 1963. It is based on *français fondamental*[3] and, like the senior version of the CREDIF course, "Voix et Images de France," the "Bonjour Line" presents materials on filmstrips with corresponding dramatized dialogues on tape. For the purpose of the course the authors have checked the vocabulary and grammar of *français fondamental* against recorded children's conversations. These have shown that the child's language in certain respects is like that of adults on which *français fondamental* is based but is different in others. Nouns, for example, differ markedly in the child's language: common nouns (such as *table, chair, bread, coat*, etc.) occur in children's conversation with a higher degree of frequency than in that of adults; their choice of topics (games, animals, schools, fairy tales) is also different. On the other hand, children use the same grammatical function words as adults, and 80 percent of their verbs are those of *français fondamental*. The children's syntax is marked by redundancies, repetition, and what by adult standards would be regarded as wrong usage. In devising the course for children a compromise was reached between the language prompted by these observations and development toward correct adult speech. But, for example, redundancy and repetition were regarded as elements which characterize children's speech and happily also have their uses in teaching French as a foreign language.

In terms of phonology, grammar, and vocabulary, there is a planned progression, but the whole course can hardly be described as programmed. Each lesson contains a considerable amount of material. Lesson units are divided into two parts: the first is a dramatized situation or story, e.g., "Breakfast," "The Snowman," "The Fair," "In the Forest," etc.; in the second part, called "Jeux des Questions," which always opens with the words that have given the course its name, "Bonjour Line!" a professorial figure questions a puppet representing an obedient little girl who knows

---

[3] "Basic" French whose grammar and vocabulary were established on the basis of frequency in sample everyday conversational tests especially recorded for the study.

all the answers. The text is spoken in a dramatized way but in a slightly detached manner, hinting at characters rather than completely impersonating them. The chief figures are three children, aged eleven, eight, and five, their mother, father, friends, and a narrator.

The teaching procedure for this material suggested by the authors is as follows: first, the filmstrip is shown, and the recording played; this procedure is then repeated but interrupted by questions which are asked in the children's native language. At a later stage this questioning could be done in French. The object is to ensure that everything is understood. The teacher is urged not to translate but merely to forestall major misunderstandings. The third step is repetition, in chorus and individually, of each utterance while the filmstrip is shown and the tape recorder halted at appropriate intervals. The sequence of listening, repeating, and listening is continued until the teacher feels reassured that the whole class as a group and students individually can repeat the sequence with understanding and a good pronunciation. A more advanced exercise is to play the filmstrip silently and to let students provide the appropriate words for each situation. The next part is "Jeux des Questions." The children listen to Line's answers to the teacher's questions and then learn to reply in the same manner. Other possibilities of follow-up are suggested: the children perform the roles of the various characters in the story, or taking the utterances and exchanges as models they modify them and apply them to their own situation. There are also some revision lessons and practice exercises with pictures. To the children the language work is presented entirely in terms of pictures, games, and mime, never in terms of word lists, word-for-word translation, or grammatical analysis.

Although this course offers a structural progression, this is so much embedded in a situational context that the children need hardly be aware of the structures which they are taught; all they have to do is to pay attention to the meaning or, in other words, to the function of the patterns in the situation. This approach to language learning in the primary school is at present widespread and popular. It is welcomed as a whiff of fresh air and a break from the traditional formal study of the language, which in the not so distant past was the lot of all children whatever their age and readiness for language study.

A somewhat different set of principles underlies the course which the Nuffield team is preparing. The members of this team are aware of the trend which we have just described, but they believe that while the presentation of interesting situations has an immediate appeal, a situational approach is likely to get bogged down in linguistic difficulties, especially when the teaching is in the hands of relatively inexperienced teachers. Therefore the Nuffield course is based on a slow, carefully programmed progression in terms of structures without sacrificing altogether an appeal to children's interests. The course makes use of attractive flannelgraph pictures; it presents songs, rhymes, and games, and each lesson has a "situation" with a dramatized story interest as well as information on France. But linguistic features dominate and appear undisguised in question-and-answer patterns related to classroom objects or the flannelgraph pictures which form part of the course, and after most lessons the teacher has at his disposal recorded pattern-practice exercises. The course unashamedly sets out to discover how far the kind of techniques commonly employed in programmed instruction and in language laboratories can be applied to the teaching of languages at this stage. It is believed by the authors that a conscious grasp of basic patterns will lay a surer foundation for a flexible and satisfying use of the language than starting the language by learning the use of utterances in relatively complex situations.

FLES PROBLEMS

FLES, then, is alive and making progress. Yet its prospects are by no means assured. It has its share of problems, difficulties, and failures. From a number of countries come reports of uncoordinated, ill-conceived, and unsuccessful schemes of language teaching to younger children which, far from being an improvement on traditional practice, have created new problems. In 1961 Alkonis and Brophy, who had surveyed FLES practices in the United States, wrote: "If the sixty-two school systems that we visited are representative, we are forced to conclude that the state of FLES in the United States needs a lot of improvement. . . . Before further encouragement is given to an increase in the number of FLES programs or to any kind of quantitative expansion there is a clear need . . . for a qualitative improvement of FLES." Likewise Dunkel and Pillet (1962, p. 145), on the basis of their five-year case study of language teaching in one elementary school, came to the conclusion that "FLES is due for many more years of growing pains." And more recently Professor Hocking (1964, p. 4) demanded that foreign language teachers should use their influence ". . . to discourage programs which do not provide these essential qualities: trained and superior teachers, continuity into high school, and assurance by the school board that the program will not be ended after a year or two." Similarly a British survey of the spread of language teaching in primary schools noted in 1963 "the wide range of results obtained, from the very good to the largely ineffective" (Lazaro, 1963). In this report 89 out of 150 classes assessed were considered substandard.

The causes of failure appear to be multiple: poor teaching, often the result of inadequate preparation of teachers for the task; lack of supervision and expert advice; absence of agreed objectives or a planned program; uncertainties of teaching methods; shortage of adequate teaching materials; failure to secure continuity; lack of understanding among administrators for the problems of language teaching; and, perhaps the most important of all, false and excessive expectations, naïve hopes, and often unrecognized mistaken assumptions.

The future of FLES, then, will largely depend on whether it can overcome its weaknesses, solve its major problems, and clear up certain confusions. In the following sections of this paper the attempt will be made to clarify a few of the issues involved and to draw attention to some of the major problems.

THE OPTIMUM-AGE ARGUMENT

Since the early fifties FLES programs have very largely been founded on the grounds that the early years of schooling are the best years for starting a foreign language and that to miss them would be to miss the most favorable moment of foreign language acquisition. The arguments for this view were partly commonsense observations and partly interpretations of scientific findings. It is often pointed out by teachers that adolescents are too self-conscious for language learning and that children are so much better at imitating, that they are "born mimics," that they pick up languages easily, and that they have a better memory. The psychological and neurological evidence which has tended to lend support to these widely held opinions of children's capacities for second language learning was frequently cited in support of the FLES claims, for example, in the writings of Andersson (1953; 1960). In 1956 the Modern Language Association of America invited a small number of persons experienced in language teaching to younger children together with a number of scholars, eminent in disciplines related to this problem, to discuss "Childhood and Second Language Learning" (Modern Language Association of America, 1956). The fields represented included neurophysiology (Wilder Penfield and Lamar Roberts), bilingualism (Uriel Weinreich and Werner Leopold), and child development (Frances Ilg). The consensus of this distinguished gathering on the optimum age for beginning to learn a second language was expressed in the following terms:

> The optimum age for *beginning* the continuous learning of a second language seems to fall within the span of ages 4 through 8, with superior performance to be anticipated at ages 8, 9, 10. In this early period the brain seems to have the greatest plasticity and specialized capacity needed for acquiring speech.

In a statement on developmental trends in language behavior, submitted to this symposium, Arnold Gesell and Frances Ilg gave further support to this view:

> The present trend toward providing opportunities for second-language learning in the early grades indicates a clearer recognition of the patterns and sequences of child development. The young child enjoys language experience. He is ready to learn, to listen, to communicate by word of mouth, in playful and dramatic situations. With favorable motivation he is emotionally amenable to a second and even a third language.

These views and other similar ones expressed with great conviction, wherever FLES programs were discussed, planned, or started, have done much to smooth the way for FLES. They were, however, not an unmixed blessing. While writers, such as Andersson, for example, expressed their conclusion with scientific caution when they said, "We are now ready to propose *tentatively* [italics mine] the optimum age . . . " (Andersson, 1960), these reservations have often been forgotten, and the notion of the optimum stage has led to excessive expectations and a naïve belief in the language learning capacities of young children of school age. One may suspect that these optimistic views have also contributed their share to inadequate planning and a lack of preparation. Such misguided hopes must inevitably have led to disappointment.

It must be pointed out that the current views on the optimum age were not founded on systematic observation of children learning foreign languages under classroom conditions but were extrapolations based on general knowledge of brain neurology and child development. A more cautious note was struck by Carroll (1960, p. 13), who in a review of research came to the conclusion that "except possibly with regard to the learning of pronunciation, there is considerable doubt that young children learn FL's any better and faster, given the same opportunities and amount of time." Also the Hamburg study came to the conclusion that it "is hardly even theoretically possible, to envisage *one* optimum period, nor is it in the interest of a sound language teaching policy in the primary school to overemphasize the merits of an early start" (Stern, 1963, p. 22). And more recently, in a psychological comparison of adults and children as second language learners, Ausubel (1964) boldly argued that "adults can acquire new languages more readily than can children." This view is, in fact, a return to an older viewpoint expressed many years ago by Thorndike (1928) on the basis of his comparison of adults and children as language learners.

There is now also a good deal of practical experience available from numerous teaching experiments. This does not lead to the conclusion that children "learn foreign languages with miraculous ease in school settings"

(Carroll, 1961). Wherever language teaching to young children has been truly successful, as for example, the teaching of English to French children at the Ecole Active Bilingue in Paris, it has been the outcome of careful planning and a program of teaching imaginatively and systematically carried into effect by skillful teachers over a period of years (Cohen, 1964). On the other hand, where there are no adequate preparation and planning and no suitable material and the teachers are incompetent, the child's supposed language learning capacity in no way seems to compensate for the deficiencies of the teaching condition. The conclusion we reach is that the current claim that the early years of schooling offer *optimal* conditions for language learning is open to question. The way it is commonly formulated implies that later learning in adolescent and adult life is not so good. Yet, there is no evidence for this. On the contrary, given similar conditions, it is likely, as Carroll and Ausubel have pointed out, that adolescents or adults can and in fact do learn languages successfully.

The claim of the optimal stage is also unhelpful to FLES for two reasons. First, in the desire to prove that the language learning capacities of children are greater than those of adolescents and adults, the unique contribution that FLES can make to the language development of children has not been sufficiently emphasized. This aspect will be considered in the next section of this paper. Second, by trying to make doubtful comparisons of younger language learners with older ones, one has tended to overlook something in good FLES programs which is a remarkable achievement: given adequate conditions, FLES has shown beyond doubt that it is possible to give an effective start in a foreign language to classroom groups of young children. Children respond to language teaching in a manner which is entirely comparable with their acceptance of the basic subjects of the primary curriculum. This result does not constitute the full case for a FLES program, but it establishes a solid basis for it. It has the additional advantage of not implying an unjustified attack upon, or comparison with, language learning at later stages. But the case for a FLES program must ultimately rest on evidence that (1) it is developmentally sound educational policy for the primary stage and (2) it makes a genuine contribution to the overall language teaching policy of a school system.

FLES AND CURRENT TRENDS IN PRIMARY EDUCATION

Given, then, that children can learn aspects of a foreign language as well as they learn to master other skills that customarily have their place in the primary curriculum, the following questions must be asked: What is the legitimate place of a foreign language in primary education, and what contribution can be expected from a foreign language at the stage of development of children in primary schools?

REEXAMINATION OF THE CURRICULUM In the Western world primary schools today are shaking off the last vestiges of nineteenth-century educational parsimony and nationalism. The older curriculum, which was dominated by a mechanical approach to the three R's, is regarded today as too thin a diet. The progressive education of the first half of the present century had already led to a liberalization of elementary schooling, but its tolerant and undemanding approach to the transmission of knowledge and the acquisition of skills had left the early stages of education with a relatively light load while the later, secondary phase of schooling had tended to become overcrowded by its sudden imposition of new disciplines, including foreign languages. Today a healthy reexamination of the distribution of curricular demands over the entire period of schooling is taking place, and the teachers of young children are responding with interest and enthusiasm to an expansion of the curriculum. Wherever FLES is planned, the forthcomingness of the teachers in the schools is indicative of this trend; it has been one of the main supports of the FLES movement everywhere. Rigid divisions between elementary (primary) and high (secondary) schools are seen more and more as obsolescent traditions. The distinctions between the two phases of education are being questioned: boundaries are more and more blurred, and a redistribution of activities is taking place.

It is widely held that some things are attempted too early, and others too late. In the light of Piagetian studies the traditional approach to knowledge is seen as demanding too much of children or demanding the wrong kind of learning. Thus a too early approach to numbers in terms of "mechanical arithmetic" may inhibit a true understanding of mathematics later. But given the right kind of material, children can be taught to think more effectively about space, quantity, or number relationships; they can learn more science and facts about the world. Foreign language learning is in line with this general redistribution. FLES experience has found children particularly amenable to meaningful sound discrimination, role playing, and simple linguistic behavior in social situations. On the other hand, grammatical abstractions are of little value. But story content and interesting situations do not inevitably lead to good learning; they may make too many demands and confuse. Therefore, as in the teaching of reading and arithmetic, enthusiasm on the part of the teacher and a belief in the child's learning capacity are no substitutes for appropriate materials and careful programming. Attractive pictures in a reader may motivate the young child to learn to read; they may also lead him to misinterpret or to guess. Similar problems recur in the foreign language in the use of visual materials.

Again, as in other parts of the primary curriculum, it is honest in FLES teaching not to rely exclusively on a playful induction into the language but to use repetition, pattern drill, and systematic practice. These, however, present their own problems in language teaching in general, but particularly so in the context of the primary school. Modern thought on primary education shows an awareness of the stimulus to the development of intelligence that the right kind of learning experiences can give. It is with this thought in mind that the primary schools reject more and more the emphasis on mechanical learning and on automatic drill which played such a dominant part in the elementary schools of a bygone age. In these circumstances it is unfortunate if linguists, in ignorance of these trends, recommend languages to the teacher of young children because of the child's supposed love of mechanical drill. Although languages require practice, such practice does not have to be unthinking and mechanical. At a time when primary education is emerging from an excess of drill in the basic subjects, it would be regrettable if the same approach made a reappearance in the guise of unthinking language drill. FLES is hardly defensible on educational grounds if it insults the growth of intelligence. Current reservations about unthinking imitation, mechanical drill, and automatic response in language learning (Rivers, 1964) apply to FLES as much as to any other phase of foreign language teaching and are in harmony with current thought on the mental growth of children.

THE BREAK WITH ETHNOCENTRISM In origin and character the elementary schools of the past had a parochial or nationalistic orientation. The chief emphasis was on the traditions of the community to which the children belonged. Also in reading and writing the attention was directed as a matter of course to a preoccupation with the native language. Consequently, children put through this intensive and prolonged monolingual training found themselves unconsciously reinforced in the child's naïve belief that the language of their milieu was the only valid medium of communication. Their teachers, trained in monolingual colleges of teacher education, lived in an equally restricted monolingual and monocultural setting. Consequently, in the present era of intensified cross-national communication, educational systems have become closed worlds encapsulating teachers and children alike and effectively separating them from other linguistic communities.

To break out of this intensive monolingual milieu later in life is a difficult task. Recent research on child development has convincingly shown that foundations of social attitudes, prejudices, and interests are laid in the primary years (Mussen, Conger, & Kagan, 1963). The monoglot experience of the first decade seems to create barriers which it is hard to remove at a later stage. It is in this sense that early foreign language learning offers optimal, indeed unique, opportunities. It is very difficult to establish a balanced outlook on foreign languages in later years if the whole early training has been rigidly monolingual.

If this interpretation is sound, one is led to the conclusion that the experience of languages besides the mother tongue as valid means of expression and communication should at no stage of the educational process be very remote from children. Or, in other words, foreign language activities should form a natural and integral part of a child's education throughout. If this were so, primary education would reflect more adequately linguistic and political realities of the modern world than does the current overvaluation of the mother tongue which is prevalent in most educational systems. Therefore the question should not be, as it is so often asked at present: What is the optimum age for starting a foreign language? It should be: *What can foreign languages and their culture contribute at every stage of the educational process?* In the long run, one may predict, there will be no hard-and-fast dateline at which a foreign language is started. Instead, as children grow, their schools, from the kindergarten stage upward, will bring them in contact with other countries and other languages through games, rhymes, songs, pictures, activities, information, books, and people (always at a level which is appropriate to the varying stages of development), and these activities will gradually merge into more systematic language learning and planned use of one or more than one foreign language.

FLES AND THE LANGUAGE ARTS   FLES has a special relationship to the teaching of the native language in elementary education. Because both are linguistic activities, there should be cross-fertilization and no interference or confusion. There are obvious similarities and much common ground, and the teaching of both should be founded on the same principles. But there are also differences which must not be overlooked: the learning of a language in the classroom cannot reproduce the conditions of first language acquisition. Both the common elements and the differences in conditions of learning must be taken into consideration when relating one to the other.

Some of the possibilities of cross-fertilization can be illustrated by the relationship between audiolingual and graphic aspects in the teaching of the native and the foreign languages. Thus some teachers of young children have already noted that social differences which tend to affect attainments in native language arts are far less important in learning a foreign language: here all children are alike; all start with the same disadvantage. The possibility of teaching a foreign language regardless of the previous background of verbal experience has suggested that some of the valuable audiovisual techniques of foreign language instruction might well be adapted to develop children's oral command in the native language and thus overcome a common sociolinguistic handicap which affects the child's educational progress. The systematic approach to a language by purely audiolingual and audiovisual means has also led some teachers to reexamine in a general way the preoccupation with reading and writing in native language instruction and the common neglect of listening and speaking as skills to be cultivated. A shift toward an emphasis on oral skills would be in line with current psychological knowledge on the development of language and thought.

In contrast with the teaching of native language arts, where the emphasis is so predominantly graphic, the foreign language is frequently introduced into primary education with a dogmatically antigraphic bias. But children who are already moderately literate in their own language find it hard to accept a foreign language without some support in reading and writing (Dunkel & Pillet, 1962, p. 46; Kellermann, 1964, p. 16; Martens, 1964, p. 14). The argument that they learned to speak their first language without reading ignores developmental differences between learning the native language in infancy and a second language under classroom conditions. Children are not incapable of understanding the limitations of writing as a representation of the spoken language; they can further be made aware of their own "handicap" as readers of one language trying to read another language. They can also understand the need for tackling the oral and graphic aspects separately and in stages. But they will find it hard to understand the emotional taboos on reading and writing, imposed by audiolingual fanatics: Why should reading and writing be virtues in the native language and vices in the foreign language? Here greater consistency must be aimed at. It is probably advisable to phase reading and writing, but the approach to such phasing should be experimental and not dogmatic. A good many fruitful suggestions on learning to read and write the foreign language might well be derived from the teaching of reading and writing the native language.

A common policy on language would attempt to achieve a rational approach to all language activities at all stages. FLES in fact must not be shut off from foreign language teaching at later stages or from other language activities in the elementary school. Because FLES is a latecomer to the curriculum of the grades, it is important that from the start, in this experimental phase, FLES should avoid repeating the mistakes of other school subjects which are now being painfully corrected. The trend here has been to bring the learning of children into line not only with child development but also with the basic principles of a discipline and desirable learning at later stages. This is clearly happening in mathematics. In language, there are beginnings in this direction, too (e.g., Fries, 1964), and it is important that FLES should seek the common basis for foreign and native language teaching which is ultimately provided by linguistics and the psychology of language development in children.

FLES AND A FOREIGN LANGUAGE POLICY

Most advocates of FLES have rightly pointed out the general and increasing importance of foreign languages in the world of today, stressing political, economic, commercial, and cultural advantages of more and better language teaching. This argument, however, points to the recognition of a planned foreign language policy *in general;* it does not *inevitably* lead to a demand for a FLES program. Ideally FLES should flow from an articulated foreign language policy of a society which has been arrived at on the basis of a careful analysis of the sociolinguistic situation and on the basis of discussions of such questions as these: Which languages are of greatest value to a community? How best should available language teaching resources be deployed? Which of these resources should be developed? Which are the best strategic points for the most effective approach? Far too many FLES programs have been started on a sudden impulse and on a wave of enthusiasm which has spent itself at the first signs of the inevitable problems of time, supply of teachers, materials, or finance.

The sociopolitical factors which have bearing on a FLES program are well known. Looked at internationally, the language situations differ in different communities, and this will affect the degree of urgency with which the need for FLES presents itself as well as the character of the program. A rough-and-ready classification of different types of situations was developed in connection with the Hamburg study (Stern, 1963). It distinguished five principal situations: (1) In countries and regions in which a multiplicity of languages and dialects occur, a second language as a lingua franca of education or society is a necessity at a very early stage in the educational process. (2) In countries such as Belgium, Switzerland, or Canada, with two or more official languages, the cohesion of the community may depend on a firmly rooted knowledge of a second language. (3) There are also a vast number of countries and regions with languages of very restricted distribution where the effective learning of one or two world languages is regarded as an indispensable means of contact with the outside world. (4) In countries such as the United States, Britain, France, the USSR, Spain, or the Latin American nations where the national language is a world language, it is characteristic of the present-day international situation that the speakers of these world languages do not consider themselves self-sufficient. (5) Lastly, there are a number of special situations which may occur anywhere in the world and in which language learning presents itself with a greater or lesser degree of urgency. Among these are the language problems arising through migration, the presence of linguistic minorities and the like (e.g., Puerto Ricans in New York, Pakistanis and Italians in Great Britain). Another is the special problem of Ireland, Israel, or Wales, where through a school system a national language is to be cultivated or revived.

A third illustration of a special situation is that of children in dependent schools of international communities and armed forces, scattered over the globe. For example, it was recently estimated that there were some 165,000 children of school age among the dependents of members of the American Armed Forces, of whom 115,000 were in Europe, Africa, and the Near East. All 115,000 children are offered the opportunity to learn the language of the country in which they live, and for grades 1 to 6 it is an integral part of the curriculum (Beerbaum, 1964). In this situation a FLES program is more than an obvious way of bringing American children into linguistic contact with host countries. It has political significance in that it demonstrates the intention of establishing good relations between United States citizens abroad and members of other nations. Such considerations may carry much more weight than the gain in terms of a semester or a year of instruction in comparison with a later start.

These broad classifications can be further refined by an analysis into more basic background variables which point to particular features of the language learning situation in different societies (Carroll, 1963). These include the degree of contact with a language, ranging from the use of the language spoken in the immediate environment to a language spoken a long distance away; the social status accorded to the language; its instrumental, cultural and political value; and, lastly, the opportunity to learn and use the language.

The alternatives to a FLES policy must also be examined as ways and means to improve foreign language learning in a society. These possibilities include (1) improvement of methods and materials of existing courses (rather than the creation of new ones); (2) expansion of language learning in further and adult education; (3) modernization of language teaching in universities and other institutions of higher education; (4) expansion of foreign language teaching in teacher training; and

(5) development of programmed instruction, audiovisual and audio-lingual courses, and technical aids, such as language laboratories. All these are justifiable points of attack, and some may produce a quicker result than a FLES program. But it may be said with some justification that FLES is the most thoroughgoing reform and therefore, perhaps, the most powerful. A FLES program which is not a purely ephemeral creation lays new early foundations of foreign language learning for a whole school system and entails reforms at all other levels. It inevitably leads to changes at the secondary stage. It produces a demand for more numerous teachers of languages and therefore affects the training of teachers and in turn leads to extended provision of modern languages in universities. FLES is thus most effective when it occurs as part of a program of reform at various levels. When it appears in isolation and without follow-up, it is not likely to produce a very marked improvement in standards and in the range of language learning. All school learning, if discontinued, leads to a deficit, and language learning is no exception.

A community weighing the merits and demerits of a FLES program must make an analysis in some such terms and ask itself in all sincerity what role it wishes to attribute to foreign languages in society and in its school system; it must also answer the question of whether it regards language learning as important enough to spend on it public money as well as teachers' and children's time and energy. It would seem that only when a positive conclusion has been reached with regard to these various questions is the community concerned ready to produce a FLES program of sufficient vitality and scope.

SOME PROBLEMS OF FLES PRACTICE

CHARACTERISTICS OF FLES PRACTICE   FLES, it was pointed out at the beginning of this paper, has been the outcome of a number of discontents. It has reacted not only against the late start in language learning but also against the conventional methods, the graphic and grammar-translation emphasis, of traditional language teaching. Considerable experience has been gathered on how to teach languages to younger children in elementary schools, and a widespread consensus of views on good practices exists. Without going into detail here the reader can be referred to a number of accounts of current methodology, e.g., in the books by Dunkel and Pillet (1962), Stern (1963), Eriksson et al. (1964), Gutschow (1964), and Cole (1965).

It is important at the present time to forestall the development of a narrow dogmatism in FLES practice. In spite of the broad lines of agreement on methodology, a number of problems and controversies exist.

In language teaching it is not uncommon to emphasize the merits of the new and the disadvantages of the old. But the critical attitudes to older approaches and the changes in content, materials, and methods often express no more than preferences for certain objectives or shifts of emphasis on a continuum. The current position and problems of FLES practice may be interpreted in terms of seven rating scales embodying some of the major choices.

On scale 1, FLES emphasis is clearly on the audiolingual side. The delay of reading and writing is widely accepted, and it is generally agreed that after the initial phase, interpreted differently from a fortnight to a year to two, a shift toward the graphic side should occur. Rather oddly, in many pronouncements on FLES the graphic emphasis of more advanced language study tends to be taken for granted. This may well mean that the audiolingual experience of the FLES part of instruction

Seven Language Teaching Rating Scales Applied to FLES

1. V*

Audiolingual   Graphic

2. V*

    Compound: Coordinate:
"read and translate"   "direct method"

3. V*

Grammar teaching   Structure drill

4. ?V*

    Formal: Functional:
structures and patterns   situations and topics

5. V*

Unconscious learning   Conscious learning

6. ?V*

Language uncontrolled   Language controlled:
                                                                                                  course programmed

7. V*

Country and culture   Language

V* = estimated position of FLES.

is so overlaid by conventional teaching at later stages that its ultimate effect may be negligible. To solve this problem we frequently hear today the demand for "continuity" or "better articulation," but the transition from the audiolingual to the graphic phase is not so much, as is widely believed today, a matter of method; it reveals rather the uncertainty of objectives. Without a reexamination of language teaching at *all* stages of a school program FLES cannot satisfactorily solve the problem of the respective roles of the oral and the graphic aspects of language learning or the problem of the transition from the first to the second. In the writer's view, FLES should become more tolerant of the wish to read and write the foreign language in the early stages in harmony with the positive outlook upon reading and writing in the teaching of the native tongue, but there should be less tolerance of the overemphasis on the graphic element which dominates language teaching at the secondary stage. Although continuity is desirable, it may well have to be achieved by a shift of emphasis toward audiolingual practices at the secondary stage.

On scale 2 the emphasis in FLES tends toward the direct method, but as in language teaching at other stages there is happily in this area no tendency to impose drastic and frustrating restrictions on the use of the native language as a medium of interpretation or explanation or, generally, as a support. It would indeed be a mistake to assume that children, just because they are young, have a kind of second sight or some special magic which would stop them from misusing or misunderstanding the language they are learning. A problem that remains is whether the brief contact with the foreign language provided by lessons is adequate or whether additional periods of functional use of the language, e.g., by the teaching of another subject through the medium of the foreign language, should be regarded as a necessary part or merely as a helpful addition under favorable circumstances.

On scale 3 the preference is for practice *of* the language rather than knowledge *about* the language. In this area FLES is clearly reacting against excessive presentation of formal grammar in traditional language teaching. It is, however, doubtful whether a complete absence of conceptualization in language learning, even for young children, is as helpful as is often dogmatically asserted. The interaction between practice and explanatory schemata for different age levels should be a matter for investigation rather than for prescriptive rule.

On scale 4 there is at present uncertainty of emphasis; possibly there is a preference for progression in terms of topics and situations rather than for a strictly linguistic progression. The experience of teachers of younger children tends toward situations as vehicles of language learning in preference to formal drills and the practice of patterns. But the last word has not been spoken on this issue; some recent courses, as was illustrated above, imply a preference either for a situational and topical approach (e.g., "Bonjour Line") or for a more formal emphasis (e.g., the Nuffield French course).

The position on scale 5 suggests that a good deal of faith is being placed in the capacity of children to absorb without conscious attention. It is likely that the capacity of children in this respect is overrated.

On scale 6 uncertainty of emphasis must be recorded for FLES. No clear policy has emerged. As the emphasis frequently tends toward interesting situations, it is found difficult to control in a precise way structures, lexis, or progression, and some attractive courses present difficulties for both teaching and learning, because the desire to offer pleasing material has often led to insufficient programming and a neglect of the control of the linguistic data offered.

On scale 7 the consensus is that the emphasis should be on the language side without neglecting cultural aspects. There are some instances in which the emphasis on life, culture, and country is so dominant that the program has virtually ceased to be a language course. As it will be pointed out again below, however, there is in this area a dearth of adequate background data on country and culture.

The choices which the practice of language teaching demands are largely choices of objectives. For the present, FLES is still inclined to make these choices as a reactive response, offering something new and better that it opposes to something which is rejected as old and bad. For the future of FLES it would be preferable if these decisions were increasingly made by reference to more objective criteria, such as the language needs of a community or the educational and psychological development of children. The results of experimentation should be taken into account; and the objectives with regard to levels of language, skills to be taught, information to be transmitted, and attitudes to be acquired should be defined as clearly as possible.

DIFFERENCES IN LANGUAGE ATTAINMENTS   Recent experiments in FLES have shown that students advance in the foreign language at different rates, just as they do in other subjects. There are great and widening differences in performance within each group. This is confirmed in the Chicago study (Dunkel & Pillet, 1962, p. 95), the Kassel study (Martens, 1964, p. 52), and the Leeds experiment (Kellermann, 1964, p. 52). The pattern of performance in primary schools in different parts of the world and on various assessments of pupils in foreign language instruction shows that approximately 20 percent are labeled excellent, 40 percent good, 25 percent fair, and 15 percent poor. This scatter confirms Carroll's view

(1963, p. 78) of measurable differences in linguistic ability even for young children.

Assuming that these differences exist, one urgent task of the future will be to devise methods to help slow language learners to achieve a modicum of success. If language teaching will take up a certain amount of school time each day, it is most important that pupils are not for years exposed to nothing but a daily dose of frustration and failure.

The easy way out—to allow them to abandon language study—would hardly offer a solution, as little as it can be suggested that pupils poor at reading and arithmetic should abandon their efforts. Studies of early language failure and of remedial measures should be priorities of research and experiment.

FIELD RESEARCH Apart from methodological research which is needed to improve practice, there is a strong awareness today of a lack of information on linguistic and cultural data on which to base FLES work (Stern, 1964). At present teachers and language course producers rely on their knowledge of the foreign language and the country, on their experience with children, and on their imagination to produce appropriate material. In recent years beginnings have been made to undertake systematic field studies which would provide data for teaching materials. In 1963 a small but significant research program was initiated in Paris on a basis of exchange between Britain and France jointly by CREDIF and the Nuffield Foundation Foreign Languages Teaching Materials Project. The proposal is to collect and analyze aspects of the language of children with a view to incorporating the results of such inquiries into French and English language courses (Handscombe, 1965). The first interim results of these studies are contained in two Nuffield reports (Hasan, 1964; Hasan, 1965). It is likely that work of this kind will transform language programs, for it introduces into a language course an element of authenticity or, to use a term from mental measurement, an element of *validity* which in the past hardly existed. Needless to say, the imaginative insight and creative impulse of the language course maker will continue to play an important part in the manner in which he uses the data that scientific research is beginning to put at his disposal.

TEACHERS AND TRAINING OF TEACHERS

FLES programs seem universally to suffer from a shortage of trained teachers qualified to teach languages. This poses two major problems: one, a short-term one, of how to establish an efficient program in spite of this shortage; and the other, a long-term one, of how to train teachers for this new task. The two problems are interrelated, because to overcome the shortage of teachers new ways of language teaching which will affect the kind of training teachers will require are being explored.

IMMEDIATE DEMANDS   Several approaches have been tried to meet the immediate demand for efficient instruction. They include television teaching, films, provision of tape and disc recordings, audiovisual courses, short in-service training, advisory help for teachers, printed guides, and a combination of several of these possibilities. The underlying question in deciding which of the measures to adopt has been in most cases whether better results can be attained by developing the teachers' skills in language teaching and letting them play a major role in the instruction or whether, in view of the teachers' lack of expertise, their active part in language teaching should be minimized. Several experiments to answer these questions have been carried out, especially in America, and experience of a nonexperimental kind is available from a number of countries.

The Swedish work by Gorosch and Axelsson (1964) was an experiment in audiovisual language instruction in which the teacher's role was minimal. Here it was found that certain aspects of elementary English can be taught with the help of a carefully devised course presented by filmstrip and tape record. There is no doubt that recent advances in language teaching materials have been considerable, and the possibility exists today of using audiovisual and audiolingual courses or other recorded material in such a way that they can offset the poor command of the language on the part of the teacher.

At the other extreme the demand is made from time to time that unless "trained and superior teachers" (Hocking, 1964) are available, the program should be abandoned. If this principle were universally adopted, much teaching of English as a foreign language in the countries of Asia and Africa, quite apart from many FLES schemes, would collapse.

Between the extremes of complete reliance on technical aids and the demands for highly qualified teachers is the middle ground of combining various levels of language expertise with various degrees of reliance on human and material aids. Several American studies have explored possible combinations of FLES television with classroom teaching. Summing up these findings, Randall (1964a) concludes that "evidence mounts up that only with the aid of teachers can television be an effective means of teaching FLES." "Parlons Français," which made use of television and films, was devised on the principle that although the film or the television lesson must teach, the classroom teacher has still an active role to perform in the follow-up of the work. In the present British pilot scheme and also in the Kassel study the teaching is primarily in the hands of the classroom teacher. The Kassel study relied very largely on the teacher's existing command of the language plus his skill as a primary teacher, but help was given through a study group which refreshed the teachers' knowledge of English and provided methodological aid and advice. The British pilot scheme relies on intensive short-term in-service training combined with a course guide and tape recordings.

On the negative side, there is evidence that where teachers are inexperienced as language teachers and have an insufficient command of a language, the results are likely to be disappointing when the teachers are left to themselves, even if they have a competently prepared course at their disposal.

The findings, then, lead to the conclusion that readily available course materials, whether presented on television, film, filmstrip, tape, or disc or in some other way, are of great merit and give language an authenticity it would otherwise not have. The material alone, however, is not the full answer to the short-term language teaching problem. Available courses are not programmed to such an extent that it would be possible to dispense with the skill of the teacher who uses them. Most of the teachers need preparation in methods of presentation and in techniques of follow-up. Courses are like musical instruments which can be well or badly played according to the skill and experience of the performer. The handling of a course can be greatly improved by training on the course material. The level of FLES programs staffed by nonexpert teachers can therefore be raised with the help of a supervisor or an adviser. If teachers do not work in isolation, if they can exchange ideas with each other and have regular access to an expert, their work is likely to be enhanced.

TEACHER TRAINING   The net outcome of the short-term experience is that however good the materials which are being developed, long-term improvement will depend largely on the teachers who use them. The necessary corollary of current experience is the provision in teachers colleges of language teaching and training in language teaching methods. If languages are to form an integral part of elementary or primary schools, then they must not be absent from the training of teachers. The foreign language program in teacher training must include preparation for FLES without necessarily confining the course to a narrow vocational objective. On the other hand, the program should not be a watered-down university course with a main emphasis on the history of literature and philology. It should center in an intensive study of the contemporary language with a stress on the spoken language. It should include background of the culture and country concerned, particularly its life and society today but also its literature, music, art, achievement, science, and technology, with emphasis on those aspects which have direct bearing on the lives of children and young people. The course must also concern itself with modern methodology of language teaching; teachers need some familiarity with existing courses and techniques and understanding of underlying psychological and linguistic principles. Finally student teachers should acquire a repertoire of games, songs, and activities which lend themselves to application in language work. As far as possible, opportunities should be offered for exchange of students or facilities for training in each other's countries and also exchanges of trainers of teachers.

The supply of teachers who are well equipped to teach languages in FLES programs is inevitably a slow development; it should not be made the condition of starting FLES. Recent experience has shown how much can be achieved by carefully guided teachers helped by expert advice, aids, and materials; but as a long-term policy a teacher training program must be regarded as an essential part of FLES.

THE FUTURE OF FLES

There is every indication that FLES is tackling the problems it has encountered. In doing so, it is no doubt changing. Even today it is no more quite the same as it was ten or fifteen years ago. Experience, experiments, and discussion have led to new approaches and shifts in viewpoints, which have been traced in this paper. But while these changes have occurred, FLES has more and more become accepted as a legitimate basis of foreign language teaching in a school system. Further changes must be expected, but even if allowance is made for these, it seems that FLES has come to stay.

It is not unlikely that in the coming decades FLES will become firmly established as a normal educational feature of many, if not most, school systems in the world. If this happened, what would be the consequences? It would mean that:

1. Foreign language activities would play some part in school life throughout the educational process from its early stages in the kindergarten to its final stages in high schools.

2. A language would normally be taught systematically within the first few years of compulsory schooling and would continue to be taught for periods of five to eight years or more.

3. One modern foreign language would be part of every child's school experience.

4. A second foreign language could be started two or three years after the first and brought to a high level of competence, and thus a

command of two foreign languages could be achieved by a considerable number of students.

5. Language teaching would greatly expand in higher education and the education of teachers, both in initial and in in-service courses of training.

6. A knowledge of one or two foreign languages would be regarded as a generally accepted part of normal literacy of the ordinary adult.

7. Foreign languages not normally taught in schools would be more widely learned by adults.

8. Lastly, the social, political, and cultural life of a society, including, for example, the use this society would make of mass media, would become more unselfconsciously multilingual and multicultural.

In the long run the success of FLES anywhere will depend on whether a community regards these consequences as worth achieving. Unless developments along these lines are regarded as a desirable outcome, the society concerned will hardly produce the necessary dynamism to make the required effort and to overcome the inevitable problems and difficulties.

REFERENCES

Alkonis, N. V., and M. A. Brophy. A survey of FLES practices. *Reports of survey and studies in the teaching of modern foreign languages.* New York: Modern Language Association of America, 1961. Pp. 213–217.

Andersson, T. *The teaching of foreign languages in the elementary school.* Boston: D. C. Heath and Company, 1953.

Andersson, T. The optimum age for beginning the study of modern languages. *International Review of Education,* 1960, **6,** 298–308.

Ausubel, D. P. Adults versus children in second-language learning: Psychological considerations. *Modern Language Journal,* 1964, **48,** 420–424.

Beerbaum, A. W. The foreign language program of the American dependents schools in Europe. *International conference: Modern foreign language teaching. Papers and reports of groups and committees.* Preprints, Part 1. Berlin: Paedagogische Arbeitsstelle und Sekretariat, Paedagogisches Zentrum, 1964.

Birkmaier, E. M. Modern languages in the elementary school curriculum. *Encyclopedia of educational research.* (3d ed.) New York: The Macmillan Company, 1960.

Carroll, John B. Foreign languages for children—what research says. *National Elementary Principal,* 1960, **39,** 12–15.

Carroll, John B. *Research on teaching foreign languages.* Publication of the Language Laboratory. Ann Arbor, Mich.: The University of Michigan Press, 1961.

Carroll, John B. Research problems concerning the teaching of foreign or second languages to younger children. *Foreign languages in primary education.* Chap. 20, 72–80, 1963 (see Stern, H. H., below).

Cohen, R. Practice with children in the *Ecole Active Bilingue* and organizational experiences. *International conference: Modern foreign language teaching. Papers and reports of groups and committees.* Preprints, Part 1. Berlin: Paedagogische Arbeitsstelle und Sekretariat, Paedagogisches Zentrum, 1964.

Cole, L. R. *Teaching French to juniors.* London: University Press, 1965.

Dunkel, H. B., and R. A. Pillet: *French in the elementary school: Five years' experience.* Chicago: The University of Chicago Press, 1962.

Eriksson, M., I. Forest, and R. Mulhauser. *Foreign languages in the elementary school.* Englewood Cliffs, N.J.: Prentice-Hall, Inc., 1964.

Fries, Charles C. *Linguistics and reading.* New York: Holt, Rinehart and Winston, Inc., 1964.

Gorosch, M., and C. A. Axelsson: *English without a book: A bilingual experiment in primary schools by audiovisual means.* Berlin and Bielefeld, West Germany: Cornelsen, 1964.

Great Britain, Ministry of Education. *Modern languages.* Ministry of Education Pamphlet 29. London: H. M. Stationary Office, 1956.

Great Britain, Ministry of Education. Notes by the Ministry of Education on the curriculum study group and the Ministry's pilot scheme for the teaching of French in primary schools. *Educational Research,* 1964, **6,** 83–85.

Gutschow, H. *Englisch an Volkschulen: Probleme und Arbeitsformen.* Berlin and Bielefeld, West Germany: Cornelsen, 1964.

Handscombe, R. J. Child language survey. *Times Educational Supplement,* March 12, 1965, p. 763.

Hasan, R. *The language of eight-year-old children.* Nuffield Foundation Foreign Languages Teaching Materials Project, Reports and Occasional Papers, No. 5. Leeds, England: 1964. (Mimeographed.)

Hasan, R. *Child language survey: Grammatical analysis code.* Nuffield Foundation Foreign Languages Teaching Materials Project, Reports and Occasional Papers, No. 6. Leeds, England: 1965. (Mimeographed.)

Havighurst, R. *Human development and education.* New York: Longmans, Green & Co., Inc., 1953.

Hocking, Elton. The decade ahead. *Modern Language Journal,* 1964, **48,** 3–6.

International conference: Modern foreign language teaching. Papers and reports of groups and committees. Preprints, Part 1. Berlin: Paedagogische Arbeitsstelle und Sekretariat, Paedagogisches Zentrum, 1964.

Kellermann, M. *Two experiments on language teaching in primary schools in Leeds.* London: Nuffield Foundation, 1964.

Lazaro, C. M. *Report on foreign language teaching in British primary schools: January–March, 1963.* Nuffield Foundation Foreign Languages Teaching Materials Project, Reports and Occasional Papers, No. 1. Leeds, England: 1963. (Mimeographed.)

Martens, R. *Englisch ab 3. Schuljahr: Ein Schulversuch in Kassel.* Berlin and Bielefeld, West Germany: Cornelsen, 1964.

Modern Language Association of America. *Childhood and second language learning: A conference report.* Foreign Language Bulletin 49, August, 1956. (Reprinted 1961.)

Moore, S., and A. L. Antrobus. *An introduction to the language laboratory.* Nuffield Foundation Foreign Languages Teaching Materials Project, Reports and Occasional Papers, No. 2. Leeds, England: 1964.

Mussen, P. H., J. J. Conger, and J. Kagan. *Child development and personality.* (2d ed.) New York: Harper & Row, Publishers, Incorporated, 1963.

Nuffield Foundation. *Audio-visual French courses for primary schools: An annotated bibliography.* Foreign Languages Teaching Materials Project. Leeds, England: E. J. Arnold, & Son, Ltd., 1965.

Randall, E. S. Research results in three large televised FLES programs. *International conference: Modern foreign language teaching. Papers and reports of groups and committees.* Preprints, Part 1. Berlin: Paedagogische Arbeitsstelle und Sekretariat, Paedagogisches Zentrum, 1964. (a)

Randall, E. S. The use of television in the FLES program. *International conference: Modern foreign language teaching. Papers and reports of groups and committees.* Preprints, Part 1. Berlin: Paedagogische Arbeitsstelle und Sekretariat, Paedagogisches Zentrum, 1964. (b)

Rivers, Wilga M. *The psychologist and the foreign language teacher.* Chicago: The University of Chicago Press, 1964.

Roeming, R. F. The Berlin international conference. *Modern Language Journal,* 1964, **48,** 438–440.

Rowlands, D. *The puppet theatre for use in language teaching.* Nuffield Foundation Foreign Languages Teaching Materials Project, Reports and Occasional Papers, No. 3. Leeds, England: 1964.

Stern, H. H. *Foreign languages in primary education: The teaching of foreign or second languages to younger children.* Report on an international meeting of experts, April 9–14, 1962. International Studies in Education. Hamburg: Unesco Institute for Education, 1963.

Stern, H. H. Curriculum research and the introduction of a foreign language into the primary school. *Educational Research,* 1964, **6,** 86–103.

Stern, H. H. *The teaching of modern languages.* A volume of studies deriving from the international seminar organized by the Secretariat of UNESCO at Nuwara Eliya, Ceylon, in August, 1953. Problems in Education series, vol. X. Paris: UNESCO, 1955.

Thorndike, Edward L. et al. *Adult learning.* New York: The Macmillan Company, 1928.

TECHNICAL SYMBOLS AND TERMS

TERMS

ACCENT   The prominence of one part of an utterance (word, syllable, vowel, etc.) over all parts. This prominence is usually achieved through a variety of means: higher pitch, greater length, and greater articulatory intensity (stress), as well as timing of the elements of an utterance relative to each other, which no doubt plays the major role. Accent may be phonemic, as in Spanish, where it differentiates *cantó* ("he sang") from *canto* ("I sing"), or demarcative, as in French, where it indicates the end of a phrase.

ALLOMORPH   Each of a class of sequences of phonemes that function as a single meaningful unit (morpheme). In English /wayf/ and /wayv/ are allomorphs of the morpheme *wife;* /wayv/ occurs before the plural morpheme, and /wayf/ elsewhere.

ALLOPHONE   Each of a class of sounds (phones) that function as a single distinctive sound unit (phoneme). The aspirated *p* of English *pat,* the unaspirated *p* of *spat,* and the weakly released *p* of *tap* are all allophones of the English phoneme /p/.

ALVEOLAR   A consonant sound produced by contact of the tip of the tongue and the gum ridge (alveolus). It is also referred to as apico-alveolar, that is, apex or tongue-tip alveolar.

ANOMIE   A feeling of nonparticipation, alienation, and dissatisfaction with two cultures or with two sets of values simultaneously.

ASPIRATION   A noise resulting from the egress of air which accompanies the production of stop consonants (*p, t, k*), e.g., English *pin.*

AUDIOLINGUAL APPROACH OR METHOD   An approach to language teaching that emphasizes the acquisition of listening comprehension and speaking and relies to a large extent on imitation and repetition of limited samples of the language.

BILINGUALISM   The demonstrated ability to engage in communication in two languages. Bilingualism does not presuppose complete and equal control of both languages, and it may take the form of the use of the two languages for different purposes and in different situations. Multilingualism refers to the ability to use more than two languages in this way.

BRANCHING   A type of programmed instruction technique in which the student's progress through the material is determined by the responses he made on preceding steps. In a branching program no two students necessarily pass through the same learning sequences.

CATEGORIZATION   The establishment of functional classes starting from physical or conceptual entities. Learning to distinguish the phonemes of a language from each other is an example of categorization.

CONFIRMATION   The provision of the correct response or the indication to the student that his response is appropriate.

CONSONANT   A phoneme that does not function as the center of a syllable. Consonants are realized as sounds characterized by movement and, often, by a constricted mouth cavity.

CONSONANT CLUSTER   A group of consonants that function as a single consonant, e.g., English *scrap,* in which *scr* functions as *c* does in *cap.*

Contrastive Analysis The comparison of equivalent portions of two languages for the purpose of isolating the probable problems that speakers of one language will have in acquiring the other.

Dental A consonant sound produced by contact or constriction between the tip of the tongue and the upper front teeth, e.g., French *t, d, n,* and *l.* It is also referred to as apicodental.

Derivation The affixation of morphological material to extend a root. Derivation, unlike inflection, may change the part-of-speech (form-class) affiliation of the resulting form; e.g., *beauty* (noun) plus *-ful* (derivational suffix) equals *beautiful* (adjective).

Diphthong A sequence of two vowels that function as a single vowel; i.e., the vowels constitute only one syllable. Diphthongs are rising when the second vowel is subordinate and falling when the first vowel is subordinate. Compare Spanish *lei* (rising) and *miedo* (falling).

Discrimination The ability to distinguish between two entities that are physically or functionally different.

Distribution The occurrence of phonemes relative to each other and to word boundaries. Distribution is an important aspect of the phonology of a language. For instance, it is of considerable importance to note that in English the vowels of *sit, set,* and *but,* among others, do not occur at the ends of words. A characteristic limitation of distribution in language is occurrence in the initial (beginning of a word), final, medial, or intervocalic (between two vowels) positions and in the immediate vicinity of an accented syllable.

Fles Foreign language in elementary school. The term refers to the special techniques, materials, and problems that are involved in teaching foreign languages to younger children within stringent limitations of contact time and with few trained teachers.

Frequency The occurrence of linguistic units in a given sample of the language or in the language as a whole. In teaching it is generally recognized that phonemes, grammatical patterns, or words which occur with high frequency should be presented before those which occur with low frequency.

Fricative A consonant sound characterized by a constricted mouth cavity and the presence of local turbulence at the point of constriction, e.g., English *f, s, z, ch, th,* etc.

FUNCTIONAL LOAD   In the total functioning of a language, a measure of the value of a linguistic unit based on the unit's ability to differentiate sentences.

GENERATIVE GRAMMAR   An attempt to state the structure of a language in terms of very explicit rules which generate all the grammatical sentences of that language and only those sentences. A generative grammar consists of three parts:

1.   Phrase-structure rules, which list the various elements that can constitute kernel sentences and which state the hierarchical relations among these elements.

2.   Transformation rules, which derive actually occurring sentences from underlying sentences by the deletion or permutation of elements or by the combination of two or more kernel sentences with resulting internal changes.

3.   Morphophonemic rules, which replace with phonetic features the abstract symbols that result from the application of phrase-structure and transformation rules.

GLIDE   A consonant that results from movement away or into a vowel articulation. Characteristically, a glide is produced by movement from or to the high vowels *i* and *u,* as in English *you, sea, win,* or *bow.* Glides combine with vowels to constitute diphthongs.

GLOTTAL STOP   A sound produced by the sudden opening, closing, or opening and closing of the vocal cords.

GRAPHEMICS   The part of the description of a language that deals with the relationship between grammatical units, phonological units, and the writing system. The minimal unit of a writing system is the grapheme.

INFLECTION   The expression of grammatical categories by the modification of units that are more or less equivalent to words. Such a modification may consist of the addition of grammatical material (affixation) at the end (suffixation), at the beginning (prefixation), or within (infixation) a word or of changes in the accentual pattern or form of the word, accompanied or unaccompanied by the addition of grammatical material (morphophonemic alternations).

INTERFERENCE   The inhibiting effect of native language habits on the acquisition of the target language. Interference is best interpreted as the negative transfer of native language habits. When such habits facilitate the acquisition of the target language, they constitute positive transfer.

INTONATION The system of pitch variation over sentence-length units which serves to express differences in meaning or to convey attitudes and emotions. Intonational differences are used particularly to contrast various types of interrogative sentences from each other and interrogative sentences from declarative sentences.

JUNCTURE Sound phenomena which occur at grammatical boundaries and serve to indicate the grammatical hierarchy of elements in a sentence. Junctures are of two types:

1. Internal or plus junctures, modifications in the pronunciation of vowels and consonants such as differentiate English *night rate* from *nitrate*.

2. Terminal junctures, pitch movements (as opposed to pitch levels which define intonational patterns) at the ends of phrases or sentences, accompanied by a slowing down in the rate of articulation of vowels and consonants. There are three terminal junctures in English: sustaining, which usually marks the end of a phrase or clause; rising, and falling.

LEXEME A morpheme with lexical meaning rather than grammatical function. Compare the lexeme *boy* and the grammatical morpheme "plural."

LEXICON OR LEXIS The stock of words and grammatical endings of a language.

LINEAR PROGRAMMING A type of programmed instruction technique in which all the students must follow the same series of learning steps. Students who do not acquire the specified (criterion) behavior at the end of a linear sequence must repeat the sequence.

LINGUA FRANCA A language which is the native language of neither of the persons involved in a communication situation, for example, English as used by a Chinese and a Russian diplomat. Lingua franca or Sabir was the name given to a trade language used by Western Mediterranean sailors and merchants in various trading contacts with the Levant.

METALANGUAGE A language used to describe or discuss language. Accurate and insightful linguistic analysis requires the elaboration of a complex and very explicit metalanguage.

MINIMAL PAIR A pair of linguistic forms contrasting by a single feature, e.g., English *pit* and *peat*, which are distinguished by the contrast between the vowels /i/ and /iy/, respectively.

MORPHOLOGY The description of the minimal grammatical units (morphemes) of a language and the patterns of the formation of words. The morpheme is the smallest element of a language that carries meaning. The English word *governments* contains three morphemes: the root *govern*, the derivational suffix *-ment*, and the inflectional suffix "plural." Morphemes may be realized by one or more allomorphs. The English plural morpheme is realized by three "regular" allomorphs: /ɨz/ as in *horses*, /-s/ as in *cats*, and /-z/ as in *dogs*.

MORPHOPHONEMICS The part of language structure concerned with the conversion of morphemes into phonemes. Morphophonemics may be handled by (1) devising a set of rules which convert abstract underlying units (morphophonemes) into phonemes or into still small units called distinctive features or (2) by listing variant phonemic shapes of morphemes (allomorphs).

NASALIZATION A pronunciation feature produced by the lowering of the soft palate (velum) and the formation of a passageway between the mouth and nose cavities. Vowels and consonants so produced are nasalized.

OBSTRUENT A consonant produced with complete closure or constriction of the mouth cavity. Obstruents consist of stops and fricatives and in many languages form voiced-voiceless pairs, such as English *p/b, t/d, f/v*, etc.

OPERANT A response, not conditioned by any stimuli, which, when omitted, allows the subject to act upon his environment. A pigeon who, when pecking at a key, triggers a mechanism that delivers pellets of food to him is operating on his environment; his pecking is an operant response. Programmed instruction involves rewarding (reinforcing) subjects who produce desired responses through carefully established operant-response chains.

PARALANGUAGE The sets of phenomena accompanying language and carrying information of an emotive, emphatic, or expressive nature. Paralanguage subsumes kinesics, voice qualifiers, coloration of the face, etc.

PATTERN PRACTICE A drill involving repetition of a grammatical construction with variation of the elements which may enter into the construction. In a pattern-practice drill the student's attention should be drawn away from the particular feature being taught. Drills of this type are designed to train the student to produce grammatical features accurately and automatically.

PHONEME   A class of sounds which contrasts with all other classes of sounds of the language. Phonemes are abstract units postulated by the linguist to account for the minimal grammatical units of a language (morphemes) in the simplest way. They are realized by one or more allophones which usually show phonetic similarities but which do not contrast with each other. Each language has its own network of contrastive relationships, and an individual phoneme can therefore have relevance only within the framework of a particular language. Although Spanish /p/ and French /p/ are almost identical from a phonetic point of view, they are different phonemes, for Spanish /p/ contrasts only with /b/ and /f/, whereas French /p/ contrasts with /b/, /f/, and /v/, to mention only one set of contrastive relationships.

PHONETICS   The physical description of the allophones of the phonemes of a language from the point of view of the organs involved in their articulation (articulatory phonetics) or of the characteristics of their sound wave (acoustic phonetics).

PHONOLOGY   The description of the contrastive relationships of the phonemes of a language (phonemics), their distribution (phonotactics), and the articulatory or acoustic features of their allophones (phonetics). Slant lines (/ /) refer to phonemic statements, and square brackets ([ ]) to phonetic statements.

PROSODY   The totality of the suprasegmental features of a language. Prosodic features consists of the psychological dimensions of pitch (voice melody), loudness, and tempo, which correspond, respectively, to the following physical parameters: frequency, measured in cycles per second (cps); intensity, measured in decibels (db); and temporal spacing, a function of time.

PSYCHOLINGUISTICS   The study of the psychological correlates of linguistic units.

REFERENTIAL MEANING   The basic or lexical meaning of a form, as opposed to the various meanings it assumes in the environment of other forms or in the context of particular situations (denotational meaning).

REGISTER The variation in language use determined by the situation; e.g., a professor uses different registers in lecturing to a large audience and in speaking to his children.

RETROFLEX A sound produced with the tip of the tongue retracted and pointed back, for instance, the *r* of English *red*.

ROOT The part of a complex form which carries the denotational meaning. Complex forms consist obligatorily of a root and optionally of derivational affixes followed by inflectional material. The English form *royalty* consists of the root *reg-* ("king") and the derivational suffixes *-al-* ("adjective forming") and *-ty-* ("noun forming"), to which may be added the inflectional suffix *-Z* ("plural").

SEGMENTAL A phoneme which occurs in a linear order relative to other phonemes. Segmental phonemes consist of vowels and consonants. Phonemes which occur simultaneously with segmental phonemes (accents, junctures, and pitch levels) are suprasegmental phonemes.

SEMANTIC Referring to meaning.

SHAPING In programmed instruction, the reinforcement of any response that approximates the desired terminal behavior and progression through successive approximations until the behavior has been obtained.

SIBILANT A fricative consonant produced with a particular type of local turbulence, e.g., *s* and *z*.

STEM A complex form consisting of a root plus one or more derivational affixes.

STOP A consonant sound produced with complete closure of the mouth cavity.

STRESS The prominence produced by greater force of articulation.

SYLLABLE A phonological unit that consists usually of a vowel as its nucleus and of one or more consonants as margins. The consonants may precede or follow the vocalic nucleus. Syllable-timed rhythm defines a type of accentual system, such as is found in the Romance languages, in which each syllable recurs at regular intervals. In contrast, English has an accent-timed rhythm: the units which recur at regular intervals are syllables bearing the accent, followed optionally by one or more unaccented syllables.

SYNTAGMATIC Referring to the order of linguistic elements relative to each other.

SYNTAX The part of the grammar of a language which describes the constitution of sentences and all other subordinate combinations of morphemes: clauses, phrases, words, etc.

TAGMEME A linguistic unit defined as a form class (noun, verb, adjective, etc.) occurring in a sentence position or slot. For instance, the English sentence *John walks* consists of the tagmemes noun-as-subject and verb-as-predicate.

TAP A consonant sound produced by the rapid contact of the tip of the tongue against a particular portion of the roof of the mouth. The Spanish *r* of *caro* is a dental tap.

TARGET LANGUAGE The language being learned as opposed to the student's native language.

TONE Pitch differences that occur over syllables and function as segmental phonemes do. In tone languages such as Chinese or many of the African languages tonal differences distinguish words or grammatical entities from each other.

TRILL A consonant sound produced by a series of rapid taps, e.g., the *rr* of Spanish *perro*.

UNASPIRATED STOP A stop produced without significant egress of air.

VOICED SOUND A sound produced with vibration of the vocal cords. A sound produced without this vibration is termed voiceless. The voiced-voiceless difference distinguishes such pairs of English consonants as *b/p*, *d/t*, and *v/f*.

VOWEL A sound that functions as the nucleus of a syllable. Vowels are characteristically steady-state sounds produced with a relatively open mouth cavity.

SYMBOLS

Symbols enclosed between slant lines (/ /) represent functional classes of sounds; their phonetic value is indicated by a key word. For phonemes which have variants that exhibit significant phonetic differences several key words are provided. Brackets ([ ]) indicate phonetic notation without reference to functional status. Frequently used alternative symbols are shown in parentheses.

	ENGLISH	FRENCH	SPANISH
CONSONANTS			
/p/	*p*in, s*p*in, ta*p*	*p*as	*p*aso
/b/	*b*in	*b*as	*b*asta
/t/	*t*in, s*t*ing, ca*t*	*t*as	*t*eja
/d/	*d*in	*d*ate	*d*eja
/k/	*k*in, s*k*in, ta*ck*	*c*as	*c*asa
/g/	*g*ain	*g*as	*g*asa
[d̆]	la*dd*er		
[t̆]	la*tt*er		
[b̵]			ha*b*er
[d̵]			la*d*o
[g̵]			la*g*o
/č/	*ch*in		mu*ch*o
/ǰ/ (g)	*g*in		
/f/	*f*in	*f*ace	*f*umo
/v/	*v*ain	*v*a	
/s/	*s*in	*ç*a	*s*ano
/z/	*z*inc	*z*ône [z]	de*s*de
/š/ (ʃ)	*sh*in	*ch*at	
/ž/ (ʒ)	vi*s*ion	*j*ars	
/θ/	*th*in		*c*ine
/ð/	*th*en		
/m/	*m*ain	*m*a	*m*udo
/n/	*n*o	*n*atte	*n*udo, de*n*tro, ci*n*co
/ñ/ (ɲ)		a*gn*eau	a*ñ*o
/ŋ/	thi*ng*		
/l/	*l*ime, mi*ll*	*l*à	*l*ana
/l̃/			*ll*amar
/y/ (j)	*y*et	*hi*er	*hi*erro
/w/	*w*et	*oi*seau	h*u*eso
/ẅ/ (ɥ)		h*ui*t	

	ENGLISH	FRENCH	SPANISH
CONSONANTS			
/x/			rojo
/h/	*h*im		
VOWELS			
/i/ (ɪ)	p*i*t	m*i*lle	p*i*so
/e/	p*e*t	(é) f*ée*	p*e*so
/ɛ/ (è)		f*ai*t	
/æ/	p*a*t		
/a/	p*o*t	m*a*l	p*a*so
/ɑ/ (â)		m*â*le	
/o/	h*o*le	(ó) f*au*x	p*o*so
/ɔ/	c*o*t	(ò) m*o*l	
/u/ (ʊ)	p*u*t	m*ou*le	p*u*so
/ü/ (y)		m*u*le	
/ø/ (œ́, ö)		m*eu*le	
/œ/ (œ̀)		p*eu*r	
/ə/	b*u*t	l*e*	
/ɨ/	hors*e*s		
/iy/ (i:)	s*ee*		
/ey/ (e:)	s*ay*		
/ay/	s*igh*		
/oy/	s*oy*		
/uw/ (u:)	b*oo*t		
/ow/	b*oa*t		
/aw/	b*ou*t		
/ẽ/ (ɛ̃)		f*in*	
/œ̃/		déf*un*t	
/ã/ (ɑ̃)		f*en*ds	
/õ/ (ɔ̃)		f*on*d	

NOTE: /:/ indicates a long vowel.

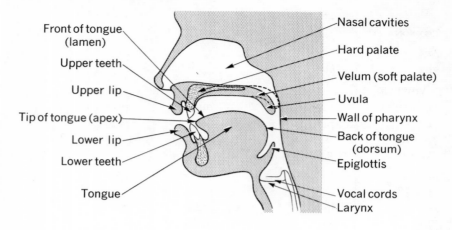

Front of tongue (lamen)

Upper teeth

Upper lip

Tip of tongue (apex)

Lower lip

Lower teeth

Tongue

Nasal cavities

Hard palate

Velum (soft palate)

Uvula

Wall of pharynx

Back of tongue (dorsum)

Epiglottis

Vocal cords

Larynx

Figure I   The organs of articulation

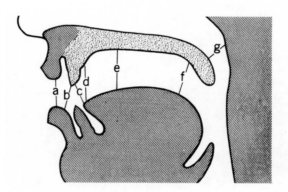

Figure II   Consonantal positions of articulation: (a) bilabial;   (b) labiodental;   (c) dental;   (d) alveolar;   (e) palatal;   (f) velar;   (g) nasal.

INDEX OF AUTHORS AND TITLES